COMING HOME

COMING HOME

A Woman's Story of Conversion to Judaism

LINDA M. SHIRES

Westview
PRESS

up

Copyright © 2003 by Westview Press, A Member of the Perseus Books Group

Westview Press books are available at special discounts for bulk purchases in the United States by corporations, institutions, and other organizations. For more information, please contact the Special Markets Department at the Perseus Books Group, 11 Cambridge Center, Cambridge, Mass. 02142, or call (617) 252–5298 or (800) 255–1514 or e-mail j.mccrary@perseusbooks.com.

Published in the United States of America by Westview Press, 5500 Central Avenue, Boulder, Colorado 80301–2877 and in the United Kingdom by Westview Press, 12 Hid's Copse Road, Cumnor Hill, Oxford OX2 9JJ.

Find us on the World Wide Web at www.westviewpress.com.

Library of Congress Cataloging-in-Publication Data

Shires, Linda M., 1950–
Coming home : a woman's story of conversion to Judaism / Linda M. Shires.
   p. cm.
   Includes bibliographical references and index.
   ISBN 0-8133-6596-1
   1. Shires, Linda M., 1950–   2. Jewish converts from Christianity—United States—Biography.
3. Women in Judaism.   4. Jewish way of life.   I. Title.

BM729.P7S55 2003
296.7'14'092—dc21

2003009901

The paper used in this publication meets the requirements of the American National Standard for Permanence of Paper for Printed Library Materials Z39.48–1984.

Typeface used in this text: Janson

10   9   8   7   6   5   4   3   2   1

CONTENTS

PREFACE   VII

1   FROM PASSING AS A JEW TO STANDING AT SINAI   I
Passage 1   Who Counts?
Thoughts on Bamidbar, Numbers 1:1–4:20   27

2   TIME, TIMELINESS, TIMELESSNESS   39
Passage 2   So God Turned Them
Thoughts on Beshalach, Exodus 13:17–17:16   67

3   GOD, WOMEN, AND GENDER   75
Passage 3   The Two Tamars
Thoughts on 2 Samuel 13 and on Vayeshev, Genesis 38   111

4   POLLUTION AND HOLINESS: THE BODY   125
Passage 4   The Akedah, the Binding of Isaac
Thoughts on Vayera, Genesis 22:1–24   153

5   FACE TO FACE: THE FATE OF THE OTHER   161
Passage 5   Their Faces Shall Be One Toward the Other
Thoughts on Terumah, Exodus 25:1–27:19   189

6   IN PIECES: FACING GERMANY   195
Passage 6   Coming Home Again
Thoughts on Yom Kippur   221

ACKNOWLEDGMENTS   227
GLOSSARY   229
NOTES   237
INDEX   255

PREFACE ✒

I consider my conversion to Judaism to be a secular turning point in my life, but I understand it chiefly as a religious rebirth, marked by immersion into the mikvah waters. At that moment I ceased being the person I was and assumed a new and Jewish identity.

This book itself turns, from inward to outward, from the self to others, from the past to the future, and from personal experience to history and politics. I do not believe that these emphases can be easily divorced in any chapter, but I am conscious that what started for me as primarily a joyous spiritual memoir rather quickly metamorphosed into a search for new bearings within Judaism. The long struggle to convert has left a legacy of significant wrestling, face to face, with the religion I joined.

The first two chapters remain highly personal reflections about my conversion experience and the relationship between aspects of my past and meaningful elements of Judaism. Subjective impressions and memories shape the narrative of these chapters. Chapter 3 betrays disquiet at my almost uncritical devotion, which was apparently necessary to get me to conversion day. But after eight weeks as a Conservative Jew, serious questioning returned, especially around the issues of social justice and the patriarchal nature of the religion. I knew that as a woman convert I had somehow to negotiate further the position of women within Judaism. Their representation in liturgy, Torah, and Talmud mattered to me; their halakhic (legal) status in current practice troubled me. I knew that as an American Jew I was concerned about the definition of Jewish community and its foundations, federations, and structures. I was not seeing in practice all that Judaism could be.

But that was only the beginning. I wanted a vibrant, living relationship among religious faith, ethics, and practices aimed toward a just society, so I knew that as a human being I needed to question the traditional statements on homosexuality, on disability, on women, and that I had to embrace a philosophy that features responsibility toward the other, any other, and all others.

Chapters 4 and 5, then, further explore important aspects of Judaism concerning sexuality, purity standards, and the holiness of all relationships: the relationship of body and spirit (fundamentally different in Judaism than in the Christian tradition out of which I came) and the philosophical and ethical principle of responsibility toward the other, which is intimately related to the possibility of a just society.

Chapter 6 is the second turn of the book. It continues the ethical, social, religious, and psychological inquiry but moves into history and the future. It discusses the Holocaust and Jewish-German relations today. It documents my first thoughtful encounter with Germany, with a historical period of unprecedented slaughter, and with the failure of the Western Enlightenment tradition to respond adequately at the time to the annihilation of six million Jews. As the wife of a Holocaust refugee, I journeyed to Germany to see for myself.

Handling any of these topics in a public forum such as a book, as a new convert and a woman, is a risky business. When the complexity and vastness of my topics, my lack of Jewish learning, and my convert status have felt like liabilities instead of challenges, I have reminded myself of the *Ethics of the Fathers, Pirkei Avot*, 2:21: "[Rabbi Tarfon] used to say: You are not required to complete the task [study of Torah], yet you are not free to withdraw from it."

Escalating violence in the Middle East and the terrorist events of 2001 and 2002 occurred after this book was drafted. In light of today's developing world politics, I might have altered my vision here, but I have chosen not to do so. Certain ideals can and should transcend historical moments; others are important as historical markers. A call for moral leadership and transformation within Judaism is more necessary than ever.

LINDA M. SHIRES
Princeton, New Jersey
18 Tevet 5763
23 December 2002

Chapter One

FROM PASSING AS A JEW TO STANDING AT SINAI

*Not with you alone do I seal this covenant and oath. I am
making it both with those here today before the Lord our God,
and also with those not here today.*

—DEUTERONOMY 29:13–14

*Converts are as hard [on] Israel as a leprous sore, as it is writ-
ten [Isaiah 14:1]: "And strangers shall join them and shall
cleave to the House of Jacob."*

—BABYLONIAN TALMUD, YEVAMOT 47B

Newark Airport, 1980, International Departures Lounge. A family of Jews clustered together, bound for London too. Father
and mother, three children. Going on to Israel? I didn't know.
Black hats, dark, long skirts, long-sleeved blouses, black stockings—
heavy clothes for summer. Strange people. They stood apart, talking qui-
etly among themselves. I watched them in spite of myself.

My boyfriend was seeing me off to England, where I was headed to
complete dissertation research and conduct interviews. All day I had
been quarreling with him. Finally, the perfect chance for cruel insult had
presented itself. "There are some of your people," I said derisively to
him. "Why don't you go hang out with *them* and leave me alone." They
were nothing to me but caricatures, cartoons, figures in a landscape to be
erased. Clothes without people, people without faces. A bunch of Jews.

It was a moment of intense hostility, of pure anti-Semitism, directed
toward a man whom it would hurt more than any other Jew I had known

1

or about whom I had cared. For he was more religious and more linked to European Jewry than any of my Jewish friends from high school or college. His family had fled the Holocaust; he had carved a life out of loss. My comment hit the mark. Irrationally, I wanted him to mean nothing to me as I left, so I made sure I meant less to him. My words were profoundly shocking and drove an emotional wedge between us. I got on the plane triumphantly.

My boyfriend was not Orthodox but Conservative. Nor was he devoutly observant. But I knew that he would identify nonetheless. To him they were not strangers or alien or odd or different. They were kin. Attracted to him and to his Jewishness, I preferred ignorance and separateness, which were easier.

But the attraction was as strong as the repulsion. That man became my husband. During the next years I lived with him and helped raise three of his Jewish children. We had our own son. Judaism was to be my bashert, my destiny. Eventually it became my religion and my chosen identity. I became a Conservative Jew-by-Choice, Emunah the daughter of Avraham and Sarah, on March 19, 1999, 2 Nisan, 5759.

For twenty years of our life together, I passed as a Jew whenever I pleased in my husband Uli's Jewish family, without knowing much about the religion or the traditions and without learning Hebrew. I never experienced this passing as detrimental. Rather, it allowed me to be Jewish when I wanted to be Jewish, and Christian when I wanted to be Christian. It allowed me to be in my current Jewish family but never leave my original Christian family. I did not have to cut ties or make new ones. My husband never asked me to do so. Moreover, I was able to share the cultural aspects of Judaism, which had attracted me since I first encountered them among my high school girlfriends. I actually enjoyed passing, though I didn't really give it much thought. Nor did I often suffer feelings of self-division on the issue of religion. Some of our friends always thought I was Jewish, and it never occurred to me to disabuse them; others recognized a level of ignorance mixed with hesitant curiosity in me that seemed to indicate I could not be Jewish.

After my husband's children Julie, Paul, and Daniel grew up and went on to college, we had our own son, Alexander, in 1990 and raised him from the start in Jewish traditions. We were High Holiday, Hanukkah, and Passover Jews, which means we were observant four times a year, except for the nights we lit memorial candles for my husband's parents. The family was Jewish in ethnicity, the children attended Hebrew school, and each boy celebrated his bar mitzvah. My husband had fled from Nazi Austria and Germany with his parents and relocated in Bolivia. Later his grandmother was able to join them. Some members of their family were exterminated in the Holocaust, and those who escaped to England or America lost all their belongings. In spite of my immersion in a Jewish family for twenty years, though, I had often sheltered myself from knowledge and feelings belonging to Judaism.

While my husband, a professor of English, was learned in the history of the Jews and passionate about modern Jewish matters, he longed for the deep knowledge of Torah that he remembered in his grandfather and father. He talked often with me about Jewish issues in the years we were engaged and in the early years of our marriage. But Judaism always remained somewhat alien to me. Though becoming a cultural pro-Semite, I was still a religious anti-Semite. My conversion to the religion took longer.

The ties I kept to my birth family and its religion and traditions were very strong. I was born into an upper-middle-class, Protestant, New England family as an only child. My family traced its ancestry on my father's side back to the Mayflower Pilgrim Stephen Hopkins, a religious Dissenter fleeing intolerance, and beyond that to the hardy Munroe clan of Inverness, Scotland. My father's mother's family had been listed in Boston's social register, which placed them in New England high society. On my mother's side, I could look back to hardworking sheep farmers in Sparta, Greece, and fishermen in Bergen, Norway. I felt divided, even split irrevocably, by my mixed heritage. Some might point to the vibrant mixture of a typical American hybrid family, but I experienced the mixtures of class, expectations, and religions as problematic, even divisive, in spite of the enormous mutual love and respect from each side of my family toward the other side. Given the fact that I was the only child, this division was also marked for me sexually. I was intimately drawn to the heritage of my mother but brought up in the very different heritage of my father.

My father set the tenor of my immediate family life. My mother converted from Greek Orthodoxy to my father's religion, and she adopted his customs and interests. My encounters with her traditions, which I found to be warm and loving, took place during visits to her parents and brother, who lived nearby. I should add, given what is to follow, that my father encouraged me to embrace those of varied races, religions, ages, classes, or ethnicities. He was an independent individualist and cast his nonprejudice in various ways, including in a marriage narrative. He explained to me several times when I was a teenager that he and my mother had agreed that I could marry whomever I wished.

Still, my upbringing was as a white, upper-middle-class, privileged daughter. I was presented to society in 1969 at the Debutante Assembly Ball in Providence, Rhode Island. I was brought up to revere family ties, traditions, status, history, and descent as much as I was raised to value education, service, and ethics. I found this emphasis as burdensome as it was privileging, though I could not have told you why at the time. But there was something rather scary about the fact that my father's grandfather, who had retired young as a wealthy man, had quickly died after he lost all his money in the stock market crash of 1929. His wife died soon after. The story of these deaths unnerved me in my youth, not because it marked the end of any family fortune, but because it spoke all too eloquently about identity, money, and pride in a certain prestige group. I wondered about their inner strength and faith. When their livelihoods and identities were crushed by loss, did they give up? This part of the family history was not told too often.

The fact that I experienced this split of two traditions and lived within it no doubt contributed to my ability to pass as a Jew, while remaining a Christian, for many years. The pressure of living in and personally juggling two traditions within my birth family was difficult. It had certainly been negotiated, but hardly resolved for me. It is against this background that I see my commitment to Judaism as, in part, a rapprochement with the difficulties and challenges of self-divisions and family divisions of various kinds.

Whatever I felt about my background and family ties, I was nevertheless a highly unlikely candidate for conversion to anything. There was little motivation. As I look back over my life, I can see how I was shaped by a religious upbringing, a strong sense of independence, and a somewhat vexed attitude toward my forced participation in groups like Children of the American Revolution, but I see little that would have pointed to a conversion to Judaism at the age of forty-eight. I see even less that points specifically to the Jewish religion, about which I continued to know nothing. But I was drawn to Jewish friends as well as to Christian ones.

My best friends at the all-female, private school I attended from ninth to twelfth grade were Jewish, and I frequently visited their homes. Their lives, families, cultural heritage, and rituals were different from mine and very attractive to me. I first learned about Jewish food, Hebrew school, and observance from Cheryl. Her mother served us knishes and latkes with sour cream and applesauce, and Cheryl wore the Star of David around her neck all the time and talked about Hebrew school with me. From my closest friend, Patricia, I learned a great deal too, and I am still grateful to her for sharing the teenage years with me. She encouraged me to value my own, female talents, to treasure a global cultural heritage of music and art, and to work with time differently, daily or even by the moment. Patricia, who was at home sick for a long part of one year, taught me to slow down and to savor every good relationship.

The most important relationships in my late twenties were with Jewish men. These men were incredibly giving and kind as well as exceptionally intelligent and multilingual, and they nurtured my talents and further widened my horizons. They were academics devoted to a life of the mind and to the treasures of the Western European culture and lifestyle. We analyzed texts together over bread and wine and cheese in Paris; we broke open figs on the hot walkways of Capri; we visited the Michelangelos and da Vincis in Florence and Rome; and we sat in the balconies of London opera houses several times a week. I was very conscious that they were Jewish, although we rarely, if ever, discussed it. But I associated them with a combination of intellectualism, cultural and textual analysis, love of languages, a savoring of nature and food, and a highly developed sensitivity toward other people. As I think through these associations, I realize that there is *nothing* exclusively "Jewish" about these men at all, then or now. They were not then observant, and I do not know whether they were widely read in Jewish texts, secular or religious. I know nothing about their lives as Jews, either the families from which they came or the families they produced. Yet they were distinctive in my life up to that point, and the worlds they opened to me reminded me of the expanding worlds of my Jewish girlfriends.

At the same time, I realized that my positive associations with Jews and my growing sense of what might be "Jewish" were not necessarily matched by the feelings of people around me. For example, some of my parents' friends held highly negative stereotypes of Jews and believed them to be pushy, greedy, tasteless, and arrogant. I didn't ignore these comments and was troubled by them: they did not seem to match my own experiences. I believe my men friends of these years also blended qualities of my maternal grandfather and my father that appealed to me deeply: generosity, service, ethics, and intellectual curiosity. If there is a pattern to be found in the early years about what led me to Judaism, as opposed to any other religion, my positive relationship with Jews and what they came to represent to me may have predisposed me in that direction.

I first decided to write this book during my conversion process. I had attended a panel at Princeton University where half a dozen feminist, Jewish women academics between the ages of fifty and seventy-five, all Jews by birth, reflected on the relationship of their Jewish identities to their scholarly work and their lives as academics. I found the panelists, with one exception, disappointingly unreflective. They told amusing, courageous, and telling anecdotes about how their lives had sometimes dovetailed with issues important to Judaism or feminism and sometimes not. Yet what troubled me was that these stories seemed filled with commonplace notions of Jews perpetuated by the dominant culture: the centrality of mother's chicken soup, the Yiddish-speaking neighborhood, the gaining of identity through loss as a task incumbent on all American Jews. Moreover, these elements, tropelike and repetitive even when challenged, took on a strange kind of equality. I became conscious that the Judaism of my conversion process was quite different. It was more impoverished in some ways, to be sure, but it also appeared to me richer in other ways. I began to see myself as separate and different from the panelists and also from the cultural Judaism that I had experienced and loved. I realized not only that my relationship to it was secondhand, but that I wanted more than it offered me.

Judging from the way the panelists spoke about Judaism, I had the impression that only one or perhaps two women were observant Jews, and that perhaps confused me most. I had close friends who were cultural and not observant Jews on principle, but observance seemed not an explicit issue at all to the members of the panel, except for the oldest member, who mentioned a minyan she went to in her early academic career.[1] Inexplicably to me, Torah was never mentioned. With almost every speaker, I was hearing about the relationship of an academic, secular, cultural Judaism to another academic field, whether history, Romance languages, English, or cultural studies, but the main religious texts of Judaism were omitted. There was no mention of Torah, Talmud, Targum, or the Shekhinah (the feminine indwelling principle of God); there was no mention of the ethical and legal precepts governing Jewish daily life (tzedakah, mitzvot, halakhah); there was no mention of the Jewish social agencies headed by women or the Jewish feminist teachers at the seminaries.

These women's lives were powerfully influenced by particular stages of American history, the 1960s to the 1990s, and of American feminism that were devoted to equal rights and minority rights. Their stories were important and emotional. Indeed, historians of contemporary Judaism may view this panel with fondness and even nostalgia, as did some of the Jews in the audience, for it represents a type of Judaism available to the grandparents of today but not to many children of today. It was perhaps noteworthy that there were almost no students in this audience.

At the very same time that the panel provoked me, negatively and positively, its historicity also made me alternately proud and sad. I was glad the Jewish women had excelled equally with men in academics, but I felt a real vacuum of religious belief. It was possible that some of the women were observant Jews, but the fact that they never mentioned it indicated to me that their religious belief was either problematic to them, a highly private matter, or had no bearing on their work as feminists. So, on the one hand, the panel made me aware of an even greater spectrum of contemporary Judaisms than I had previously recognized and of the different ways Judaisms might intersect with individual women's lives at different historical moments and in different generations. But on the other hand, the panel also troubled me because of its apparent secularism.

The panel offered various versions of one kind of narrative. But it was not mine. I tried hard to identify as talk after talk moved along. I too was a white, middle-class academic and in their age range, had finished with childbearing, was settled in my academic career, considered myself a gender critic, and had taught courses in gender and feminist theory and practice. Part of me longed to be even more like them, to have had foremothers and European Jewish origins about which to talk. I had looked into my family pasts to try to find a Jew, especially a woman, and found none. I fantasized that somewhere back in the Middle Ages or in the 1800s there must surely have been a Jewish woman in my family, maybe in Greece, maybe in Spain, maybe even in England. Her name, like my maternal grandmother's, was Sarah, but I just could not find her. (Early in the conversion process this psychological need for a real foremother would compel me to adopt a Jewish mother for myself.) But in the end the experiences of the women on the panel did not speak to me and I was left confused about the relationship between my experience of Judaism and theirs. I also wondered whether my story could hold meaning for anyone besides me and my family. My experience of growing difference compelled me to outline this book that afternoon.

Much later, with nothing of the book but the outline, I encountered a letter on the Web at "convert.org": "An Open Letter to Jews by Choice" written by Dr. Lawrence J. Epstein and reprinted from a 1994 issue of the magazine *Moment*. This letter encouraged people to share their conversion narratives for political and spiritual reasons. It began: "We who were born Jewish need you." Epstein explained that one of every 37 of the approximately 5.5 million American Jews was a convert. "We need you to tell us of your experiences," he wrote. "We need to hear your stories." He explained that Jewish identity is fragile, which I have come to understand firsthand, and that converts have a unique contribution to make because they have chosen this identity over all others.

More than anything else, conversion is a profound identity change. As such, it demands thought, time, dedication, and self-reflection. It cannot be rushed. Mine took eighteen years from the first vaguely expressed desire to convert to the first aliya (the first time a Jew is called to say the blessing over Torah). Conversion to Judaism requires study, as much study as becoming Buddhist or a member of any other religion would demand. Yet this study is aimed toward a particular end as well as a more general end. Conversion to Judaism also involves an oral examination to complete one's course of study. After full immersion in a mikvah (literally "gathering of water," a Jewish ritual bath with some of the water supplied from rainwater or a natural spring), one normally is questioned about the religion by the bet din, a religious court of three rabbis or learned Jews, who test one's faith and knowledge. The length of the meeting and the type of questioning vary depending on the group assembled. If one passes this examination, one normally moves on to a public ceremony, with a minyan present. Before the ark, one renounces former faiths, says the Sh'ma in Hebrew (the oldest and best-known Jewish prayer), and is awarded one's Jewish name.

Although the course of study is decided with one's supervising rabbi, becoming Jewish normally requires learning Hebrew, mastering the basics of the religion, having tutorials with one's supervisor, joining a prayer community, perhaps getting involved in a study group in Jewish texts or a synagogue outreach group, learning about the commanded observances (mitzvot) and performing them, and undertaking additional study if one is so inclined. Formal study usually takes between one and two years. I expected from the beginning, in September 1997, that it would take me a longer than usual time, partly because I am an academic who likes to read and partly because I felt profoundly ignorant. The more I learned, the more I wanted to learn and the less ready I felt. After ten months of intensive study, I still wondered whether I would ever feel ready.

My rabbi, James S. Diamond, director of the Center for Jewish Life at Princeton University, had supervised a number of conversions. Though he had targeted me as one who could happily study for a long time, he also had faith that I really would find an appropriate end. He was right. I arrived at a point where my desire to become a Jew became greater than my sense of unworthiness, the joy of study, or the deep fear holding me back. Urgency outran safety, and accepting imperfection and process conquered the sense of never being good enough. It took me seven months without a supervisor, followed by a year under his guidance, to reach conversion day.

My serious encounter with Judaism brought out those aspects of myself that I most valued and wanted to strengthen, and it rewarded me beyond words. I discovered new relationships to time, space, and holiness; wonderful friends and acquaintances with values in common; a legal, ethical, and religious code by which I wanted to live; and participation in a genuine community. I had experienced the warm ties of a group to this degree only once before in my life, with young colleagues in the early years of my professional life. Although the bonds and practices of a professional and a religious community differ in kind, I very badly wanted, in my middle-old age, to join a group based in service to others and spiritual values.

Judaism also introduced me to the challenge of Jewish as well as non-Jewish anti-Semitism and to the genuine surprise of my Protestant aunt and Catholic cousins. It provoked the disbelief of several Christian or agnostic friends and serious and probing questions from Jews about why I would do such a thing. It revealed aspects of friends I had never encountered before, because there had been no occasion for such discovery. Some friends expressed shock, especially at the severity of the halakhic (legal) strictures I was eager to embrace. Others were openly curious, and several engaged me in long, helpful conversations, in person and through e-mail, about issues of belief. These friends let me talk about my concerns and interests and discussed the vexed issue of spirituality with me. They joined me on a journey and shared their pasts and presents from within observant and non-observant Catholicism, Buddhism, Zen Buddhism, Protestantism, Quakerism, and Judaism.

When I seriously began study toward this identity change, however, I did not know how much inner energy I would need, and I was, as I've said, simply uninformed about many aspects of the religion I was joining. It became imperative for me to read about conversion and to talk about what was happening to me, particularly with other converts. When I had tried to meet converts and talk to them, however, in the earliest stages of the conversion process, I got almost nowhere. Nobody wanted to share stories or feelings. The only conversion memoir I found at that time, sent by a friend, was Nan Fink's *Stranger in the Midst*, which I devoured the evening before the first meeting with my supervising rabbi. Several months later, when I expressed my continuing dismay at not being able to talk with any other converts, my rabbi introduced me to another woman whom he was also guiding toward conversion. Although she was much younger and although she and her husband moved away almost immediately after her ceremony in 1998, she felt to me like a sister. I will always be grateful to her for our few but meaningful meetings. All these conversations, in which friends and strangers connected about one of the most important parts of their lives, remain a sustaining gift.

Likewise, I found myself sharing certain aspects of my journey with others, opening up more than I had done with highly personal matters in the past. I told some of the people around me partly because I needed extra courage. I felt that if others knew, I would stand a greater chance of following through to the end. There were times in those two years when I felt like giving up because I was overwhelmed by the work of inner change, the personal details of which I usually faced alone or with just my husband.

Although I had rarely discussed anything about my personal life with my students, I mentioned my conversion to my graduate students at Syracuse and at NYU and was touched by their support. In December 1997, the five non-Jewish graduate women who made up my nineteenth-century reading group, gave me a stunningly graceful Chanukkiya, with enough candles to last through two or three years of the holiday. I was deeply moved, and the feeling returns every year when I take it out for Hanukkah. Further encouragement came to me from an Orthodox student who was at NYU for the summer; though personally disillusioned with his faith, he was excited by my keen interest and supplied me with a choice reading list. He introduced me to the work of Rabbi Joseph Dov Soloveitchik and other important contemporary voices.

I think each conversion is very different, just as each of us is different. That fact has made me cautious in considering which details to share in this narrative, because I did not wish to project the outline of my life as any kind of guideline or truth for others. Nevertheless, there are emotions, situations, and commitments that converts share, no matter how different each person may be. Moreover, there are many issues that often remain hidden. One advantage of my study was that it enabled others to talk with me about their own experiences with religion. It even drew others to me. Ultimately, one can't predict what narratives may matter to what people. This came home to me most forcefully when several weeks after my conversion I discovered a conversion narrative that spoke to me so profoundly that it unleashed an hour of crying. In Julius Lester, a black man from the South, the son of a minister, and a civil rights activist, I found my conversion soul mate.

In his narrative alone of all those I had encountered, I found the vulnerability, the awe, and the personal wrenching closest to my own. Next to his life, of course, mine had been privileged and apolitical. I was never a minority before I converted. As an only child, I was the center of my parents' world. As a middle-class child, I did not suffer deprivation. As a young woman, I had been extremely lucky to have been enrolled at three prestigious all-women's schools. Throughout high school and college and while I studied for a degree from a women's college at Oxford, I had been under the impression that whatever I had to say was as important as what men said. Though this was not always true in the real world of men and women competing and living together—or in my own experience of two co-ed institutions, the marketplace, and the three academic departments in which I worked—I gained the impression that I had resources and power to equal men. I have been lucky in this regard—or I have made my luck. Although I have defended other women publicly and in private and spoken out against women's oppression throughout history and cross-culturally, personally I have rarely felt marginalized, silenced, or downtrodden. Thus, it was not a sense of marginalization or a desire to seek chosenness that drew me to Judaism. Just as Julius Lester's own attraction to Judaism was highly complicated, having much to do with a religious father and a son whom he deeply loved, so my attraction to Judaism was a matter of claiming religious values for myself, negotiating my relation to my father, and passing on values to my son. My conversion was also rooted in my need to claim for myself a relation to (a culturally constructed and a personal) femininity within a patriarchal tradition. Claiming femininity within and even through Judaism, I understood, might entail supporting some aspects of the religion I was embracing and critiquing others. I hope to clarify these statements in the chapters that follow.

Thus, in spite of the fact that Lester's life and mine were radically different and he in fact had experienced prejudice and marginalization from an early age, I was intimately drawn to his story. Even though Lester had felt a calling from God for something special, a calling that I had never felt, I found in his voice an encounter with Judaism remarkably similar to my own. His attraction to the Jewish letters of the alphabet dancing in his dreams, so "magical and alive," was my own. I understood his feeling that becoming a Jew is learning "a language of the soul." I understood his listening to an inner voice that told him he was a part of the Jewish experience. For both of us the inner voice was slow in making itself heard—maybe we were each the last to know! "Becoming a Jew is not memorizing a set of beliefs and principles. It is learning to feel as a Jew feels. If I were hearing that from someone, I would say he or she was crazy. But I am not." Every time I read the incredible section where Lester recounts leading his congregation in Hallel, the psalms of praise sung only on certain holidays or when Rosh Hodesh—the new moon—coincides with Shabbat, I am moved anew. The melody, he says, is sweet and mournful—the essence of Judaism, the essence of the joy and responsibility of keeping the covenant. This passage encapsulates Lester's conversion for me, for here he finds what his voice was always meant to sing.

In the height of the summer of 1998, ten months into my conversion study, I am riding the train from Princeton Junction, New Jersey, to New York City's Penn Station two days a week. It is an unusual journey for me. I'm used to traveling, since I've commuted for many years, by plane, train, or car, from Princeton to Syracuse, New York, where I teach

English and textual studies. But now I am on a relatively short commute to moonlight at NYU, where this summer I am teaching critical theory to a class of twenty bright, eager students from many different universities from all over the country. I leave behind my husband at his writing desk and my son at day camp, knowing I won't be home until after supper and that when I get home I will move directly into a talk about our day and getting my son ready for bed.

These hours of travel two days a week, at 10 A.M. and 5 P.M., are mine, and I look forward to reading Judaism on the way in and practicing Hebrew on the trip home. Coffee and doughnut in hand, I settle in on New Jersey Transit for an hour of total immersion and stimulation. When I get to Washington Square, I grab a lunch and head straight to a library desk and review the theory I will teach that afternoon. Sometimes on the way home during rush hour I sip lemonade, since it is a broiling New Jersey summer, and often have to stand for almost the whole trip. But I never stop reading—Rachel Biale on women and law in the Talmud, Rabbi Joseph Dov Soloveitchik's *Halakhic Man*, Judith Plaskow's *Standing Again at Sinai*, books on what it means to be Jew, on what Jews believe, on how they pray, on interpreting Torah, and more, many more.

During this part of the summer, my supervisor, Rabbi James Diamond, is teaching in Israel, and I am totally on my own for the first time. In the first days after he leaves, I am anxious that he will not return from the war-torn Middle East and scared that I will be unable to find my way alone on the most important spiritual journey of my life. It has taken me eighteen years, two earlier tries with rabbis, starting conversion without a sponsor this time, and then seven months to find a supervisor who is right for me. I wonder if I would have the courage to look again if anything were to happen to him. He does not fully realize, because he is so steeped in Judaism, that he is my most important living connection to a community of knowledgeable, observant believers and to a tradition that, with his help, I am only beginning to understand.

At this point, I am not able to separate faith, study, and action from my prime teacher. At the same time, I realize that my fears have less to do with him and much more to do with my conversion and the early death of my father. My father died suddenly when I was twenty-four and abroad. I saw him last at Logan Airport in Boston, as I set out on a new stage in my life, one that would take me to a job in journalism in London. I would mourn my father for many years. Only later would I understand that my cruel remark to my boyfriend at Newark Airport was related to that difficult good-bye. Displacement, reversal, fear of being hurt, issues of value, had all knotted themselves together in a tangle. In more positive ways, my conversion would come to mark a connection to my father and our shared values and a final farewell. But that summer, worried about my teacher, I watch the news on Israel every night for two weeks, apprehensive about bombings, until my husband, who is unusually receptive to the emotional complications and ups and downs of a conversion, though he's never seen one before, tells me that I am ridiculous to worry about the safety of my teacher, who is perfectly fine.

But I cannot really explain clearly or fully to anyone the uncertainties, losses, and transitions I am undergoing; the absence of my rabbi is in fact symptomatic of inner matters that are much more profoundly disturbing. I cannot fathom fully myself the shapes or depths of these inner collisions of past and present. They are intensely private, but, as I have read, they are also common to converts. Even though I know about midlife changes of all kinds, including those brought on by a new job, sudden disability, divorce, or the traumatic loss of a partner, parent, or child, and even though I hear that any worthwhile conversion entails a profound identity change, it is embarrassing to be in one's late forties and to feel so uncertain. Even though my rabbi has left me with good suggestions and assignments, I am simply at a loss, at first, as to how to proceed on my own.

Looking back for a moment on that summer experience, I think it was probably not surprising that having finally found a supervising rabbi, I would think of him as a father figure. Not every convert has a similarly complex psychological relation with his or her supervisor, though sometimes a psychological relation is played out instead with the religion, its laws, or one's relationship to God. Conversion raises critical unconscious and conscious issues of gender, authority, tradition, dependency, and love.

The projection of my father onto my rabbi, which became negative as well as positive, lasted about six months. I became acutely aware of it with the help of two friends and worked through it with counseling and an open talk with my supervisor. If it often seems that we go through life rediscovering, in new contexts, what we have already learned, I rediscovered the obvious point that even issues I thought I had resolved got stirred up again in new and old ways during my conversion. It was not surprising that my dead father made a reappearance: I'd been expecting him. What was surprising was how long it took me to figure out the insistence with which he was reappearing and to see all the ways he was present.

My father was a religious and ethical businessman who served his Episcopal parish as a lay reader, children's church service director, and vestry member. He was appointed to many committees and boards in our diocese and headed the Episcopal Charities Fund as well. He also represented our state at national conventions. During my previous two attempts at conversion and in the years following, I had been leery of breaking with my Christian past and my family, precisely because it seemed a betrayal and a rebellion. In the end, however, I was able to make my conversion into something else: a way to reacquaint myself with some of my father's deep religious commitment and to end my twenty-five-year period of mourning. In converting, I was both internalizing certain aspects of my father's character and saying good-bye to the remaining fragments of sorrow I had felt for many years. I had dealt with identity issues before, but the conversion resolved an as-yet unresolved strand of conflict and pain, connected with mourning and masculinity, I had long felt. Conversion granted me psychological as well as spiritual renewal.

The necessity of working out relations with family members, dead and alive, consciously and unconsciously, is often one of the key difficulties for a convert. It is hard to stay on track as one wends one's way through the labyrinth of feelings and memories and responses from family members. I think this can be as true for younger converts as for older ones. Sometimes conversion is paired with marriage or with a pregnancy—these personal events can, of course, offer sites for conflict or sweep it away in the joy of the moment. It all depends. I have been lucky that my relatives have generally responded favorably. Many of my cousins switched to Catholicism from Protestantism and to Protestantism from Greek Orthodoxy and thus have personally experienced a changing of rituals and beliefs. My decision to convert has been hardest on my mother, who feels that my becoming a Jew might distance us from each other.

In the summer of 1998, as I enjoy my commuting study periods, the other main issue for me, besides the absence of my supervisor and my relations with my family, is that I have never taken time away during a summer from publishing in my own field. That is, I have never taken time away from pursuing professional advancement of some kind during the months when I am not on duty teaching. I do not know how to relax fully. When I started the conversion process by taking courses in the fall of 1997, I was teaching at Syracuse University. In this summer of 1998, though, taking time for Judaism arouses feelings of guilt. In part professional work has been a joy, and in part it has been a defense against looking deeply within, a stay against changes that would be even more difficult than doing scholarship. At some point, then, I had to give myself permission to take time during this summer for other kinds of development.

Only vaguely do I understand that I am also giving myself permission to change how I think and act with regard to my profession, my schedule, and my life. Teaching the NYU course, itself a form of professional investment, is providing a psychological ticket for this larger summer journey. I am moonlighting because I want to do so, but the job gives me a chance to improve my professional skills while allowing me to do what I want in my free time.

Taking this time for the soul proves an important lesson, for I have not even started observing Shabbat, when I will set aside an entire day out of my week. Observance will, soon enough, profoundly alter the way I live and change forever the way I think, not only about my career but also about how I have always measured, managed, and valued time.

So in this summer I am making the beginnings of a commitment, visiting bookstores in Soho, using some of my earnings to start a Judaica library, devouring any book that looks remotely interesting, finding my way. I'm also writing three long biblical commentaries for my supervisor and sending them to Israel. My rabbi knows my seriousness, and he has told me to take a summer break while he is gone and to approach Judaism through films and museum trips as well as commentaries.

For better or worse, then, I approach this summer with longing—a longing to learn and a longing to be a valued student—and I find I cannot let up on the pace of study. I have moved well beyond my original sense of a duty to learn and curiosity about the religion into a state of hunger. It has been many years since I enjoyed reading texts so much. I start each ride eager and starving and arrive home sated, full of ideas, plans for what to read next, and new Hebrew phrases, and I sense that in some way the rest of my life will be marked by this journey and be the better for it. These six weeks, though relatively short, busy, and intense, become one of the passages in my conversion preparation that I will remember always with the greatest affection. For the first time in my life I have allowed myself to become totally immersed, with every part of my being, in something I am coming to think I will not be able to live without.

This summer is also an exploration into the contours of a Jewish female identity. It is the moment when I am beginning to feel that I am already a Jewish woman, grappling with the rabbinic sages, with the great twentieth-century thinkers, and with Torah itself—and to know that I am capable of doing so. The fact that I face a male tradition does not depress me; I am not yet confronting the status of women in Judaism, which I will later explore. I am reading Jewish feminists re-reading the rabbinic traditions, and my mood is one of excitement. I'm feeling challenged. I know already that I am trying to become a woman scholar of Judaism in one summer and that this is utterly hopeless, even absurd, but also that what is happening is enough for one summer. Another part of me, unaffected by the work ethic of mastery or the desire to stay deeply connected to my supervisor or my father, senses that I'm finding the areas that will continue to inspire me for countless hours in the days ahead—liturgy; the voice of a woman carving out a place for herself in a male-dominated system; the rabbinic shaping of the religion from Temple cult to the text-based re-reading that so influenced modern Judaism; the shape, feel, and sound of Hebrew letters.

During the summer I also review how I got to these train rides carrying Abraham Joshua Heschel and Franz Rosenzweig alongside Judith

Butler and Roland Barthes. It will be true for the entire conversion process, right up until the very day I write this, that I will ponder daily how I have tried to become a Jew, how I am becoming one, and, after the conversion, that I am one. It will seem a miracle to have converted, because I have wanted this for myself for so long but have not known how to acknowledge the wish, embrace it, make it happen.

The first time I even thought of converting was during the period of 1980–1981, a time when I became closer to the man I would eventually marry. In late 1981 we got engaged. It would be a long engagement— nine years. During the first years, my husband, Uli, had been divorced and had joint custody of his three children, Julie, Paul, and Daniel. In the summer of 1981, three of us—my husband, Daniel, then nine years old, and I—found ourselves on Bread Loaf Mountain at the Middlebury College summer campus where Uli was teaching at the Bread Loaf School of English. It was one of those idyllic periods of a lifetime—a summer with other teachers on a sun-drenched mountain, a summer of ideas, outdoor volleyball until the sun set behind the mountains, movie night in the barn, long walks, red lizards, the swimming hole, and my attempt to write articles, while Uli taught and conferenced with students.

It was there, in rather unusual and somewhat socially awkward cir-cumstances—I was an unmarried partner and not quite a stepmother— that I held my first talk with a rabbi about conversion. The conversation was short, friendly, and casual, almost offhand, though sincere. This rabbi had retired and kept a summer place on the mountain. He was a kindly man I met two or three times and I have now unhappily forgotten his name. I explained that I hoped to marry my soon-to-be-fiancé and that I thought I should join his religion but that I had some reservations about cutting myself off from my own past. I outlined the seriousness of my parents' religious commitment and my concerns about unity in any future family that Uli and I might have. The rabbi, an astute reader of situations, advised me that it was not necessary to convert and that if I wished to preserve my relationship and marriage, I would in fact not undertake a conversion at that time. He felt that I was too tied to my past to make the break and that, if I did so, these unresolved feelings could easily come between my fiancé and me. He tested me and then discouraged me—as a responsible rabbi is supposed to do in an initial conversation about conversion. In doing so, he would also have trusted that if the desire to embrace Judaism was strong enough I would find my way back again.

I found my way back in the autumn of 1984. By this time I was a regular commuter to my job in Syracuse and the children were growing up fast. Julie and Paul were in college, and Daniel was in middle school. I was on the tenure ladder. It was a time of intense self-reflection and various rapprochements with what was turning into a very long, seemingly permanent engagement. At Princeton, Uli had established a close relationship with the Hillel rabbi, Edward Feld. In turn, Ed and his wife, Merle, had invited us into their home a number of times for Shabbat, for holiday observances, or just to talk. Merle and I discovered that we both wrote poetry, so in addition to the family gatherings we used to meet in her backyard over coffee and go over poetic images or lines together.

During those afternoons and evenings in an observant Jewish household, I felt stirrings again of something larger that I wanted for my family and myself. I didn't and perhaps couldn't name it at the time (I do try to describe it in Chapter 2), but I could feel it. I thought it must be Jewish ritual and belief that gave this family a center and purpose. But my own birth family had had a center and a purpose, so why was Judaism any better than Christianity? Perhaps Judaism appealed because it was somewhat mysterious to me, and precisely because it was *not* freighted with the emotional intensity of the parental ties. It was clear to me that I wanted a family of my own and a living structure to unite it, but one that was different from what had bound my own together.

As I look back and try to identify what Judaism offered that my own family or traditions had not, I get lost in generalities and subjective impressions. I remember now many smells, experiences, and visuals of Christianity—what I loved and disliked most. The deep and beautiful colors of the altar cloths, especially the green and gold of Epiphany, the shine of the gold cross, my mother arranging flowers for the altar, the dark wood of the chancel, the congregation singing hymns together, saying the Creed and the Lord's Prayer by heart, the incredible beauty of

English cathedrals such as Canterbury. Then again, I was troubled by the cloying sweetness of the hundreds of lilies and other flowers amassed in the church at Easter; the worship of a dead man (which would have special resonance for me); kneeling and rising; the weekly, rote confession of sins; the sense that children should stay for part of the service and then leave; an overemphasis on surfaces in the congregations; Father, Son, and Holy Ghost; bringing money to church each week for the collection. I never understood what the Holy Ghost was; I imagined Him watching us from the ceiling rafters.

I went to Sunday School and learned all my lessons, was confirmed by the bishop, and even taught Sunday School. In retrospect, I think I was a believer at the time. But what I believed in was another matter. I knew very little about what or why—little history, little theology, only a superficial sense of how observant practice related to doctrine, and no sense of any other religion that I might find equally or more personally relevant. My religion, typically, was not really an informed choice; rather, it was a predetermined way of life. I went to church bazaars, church dinners, and church parties, enjoyed them, and became an Anglophile. When I was at school in England, I turned to the Anglican Church for a year of observance, and in graduate school at Princeton I attended a few Episcopal vesper services at the chapel. But I felt, once I left home, that while my relationship to God was intact, perhaps I was drawn more to the trappings of the Protestant religion than to its liturgy, its beliefs, or its theological tenets. I stopped going to church at all when I was about twenty-seven.

My religious and ethical training had not been confined to church, however. I think it is no exaggeration to say that I received more—and gave more—both inwardly and religiously when I practiced Quakerism at Lincoln School, my high school. Every Friday teachers and students attended mandatory Quaker meeting in the study hall. There were several Quaker teachers and enrollees, though the school population was mostly Protestant, Jewish, and Catholic. The Quakers, their tradition, and their meeting impressed me a great deal. Speaking about what was in one's heart, rotating the elders who led the meeting, the mixing of students and faculty, and the felt equality of race, ethnicity, the able-bodied and disabled, class, and sometimes sex (when there was a male faculty member to join us) mattered to me. Likewise, the plainness, the focus on social justice and social service, and the quiet ways and dignity of the New England Quakers whom I knew outside of school also impressed me deeply. The Quaker meeting at my high school was the closest approximation to the Jewish Conservative minyan, to which I now belong, that I have ever experienced.

In the early 1980s, when I spoke to the rabbis in Vermont and in Princeton, Judaism offered me a sense of the importance of this world, of how we treat each other on a daily basis, and of a sacred quality to each action, from setting a table to taking care of a pet or lighting candles. I have no wish to offend by implying that these features of religious life would be familiar only to observant Jews; I am sure that they are familiar to observant practitioners of other religions as well. I can only share what appealed to me about Judaism *at that time*. I believe that in my own case it was through my relationships with the Feld family and two other families with whom we spent time, building on my prior associations, that my interest in converting was piqued again.

What is remarkable to me as I try to find causes for my conversion is not only how random our lives can be but how accumulative they become. Small things mattered. Two Shabbat candles on a table. Holding hands before eating at the Felds' Shabbat dinners. Asking questions of the tradition and of each other as a way to keep the tradition alive. Three generations and three families at a Passover seder. The way she or he baked challah. It does not matter who. My reencounter with Judaism came through domesticity, ritual, and family Shabbat observance. It came with poetry, with backyard coffee, with the (sometimes messy or noisy) presence of children at services and at the table, and with learning and questions. These encounters accumulated and became increasingly important to me. Even missed.

I approached Rabbi Feld about conversion. If memory serves me correctly, I expressed a hesitant interest several times over several years. Then at one point in 1984 he gave me a list of requirements. I remember reading it, finding it too difficult, and tucking it into the glove compartment of my car for safekeeping. It disappeared, and I did not renew the dialogue about conversion. From time to time over the next twelve or thirteen years, usually on Passover at the house of Jews, I would articulate my interest again in conversion. The reception was always positive and warming, but I never followed through. Nor did I ever return to church or learn more about any other religion, including that in which I had been confirmed.

When I became pregnant in 1989, my husband asked me to raise our child Jewish, and I agreed. This was a pact we had made years before—any children would be raised Jewish. Our child would attend Hebrew school or be tutored, celebrate a bar or bat mitzvah, grow up attending High Holiday services, be given a knowledge of the Holocaust and family history, and share a heritage with his Jewish half-brothers and half-sister. I did not know much about what it meant to raise a child Jewish. I knew we and his first wife had done it with his three other children. I wanted a child; it did not seem difficult to agree to continue doing what we had been doing for a decade. He knew that my offspring would not really be Jewish, since I was not; I knew that too. But since we were not often observant and were not really in touch with halakhah (Jewish law), it didn't seem to matter much at the time. It came to matter to me crucially, however, after my son was born.

I view my decision to convert as the outcome of years of thought and years of forgetfulness, but also of one particular evening. In the autumn of 1995 we attended the Conservative Yom Kippur services at Richardson Auditorium on the Princeton University campus. The building, known as a Victorian extravagance—the kind one finds somewhere on every Ivy League campus, is round with dark paneling, gradated seating, and a large balcony around three sides, which makes it perfect for a concert hall. Its windows are positioned high up, and most of the light is artificial. The semicircular hall outside and around the auditorium features glass panels and various doorways. This grand building is elegant and formal, yet its dark main hall is intimate in atmosphere. Attending a concert there, one can easily feel like part of the orchestra and get swept up in the music with very little to distract. One can feel equally focused at a Jewish High Holiday service.

The Yom Kippur sequence of observance starts with a full meal, followed by fasting from sundown to sundown the next day. The holiday begins in the evening with the haunting Kol Nidre service, and the observance proceeds, throughout the entire next day until sundown, with the morning service, Avodah service, the Yizkor memorial service, the afternoon service, and the Neilah (locking) service. During the last hours of Yom Kippur in 1995, before the shofar was sounded, my young son Alexander stood on one side of me fingering Hebrew letters to find Alephs (A's), and my husband stood on the other side of me in prayer. Men and women I recognized from years of going to these services were moving and praying in front of me in words I did not understand, though I had tried to repeat the same words over and over by memory on High Holidays. The hall was full. We sat in a raised section, on the side, from where I watched a sea of blue and white prayer shawls and white blouses swaying before me. A visiting woman rabbi and the cantor, a man, led the service. I looked down the row where our good friends and their children prayed beside us, as they had done for over a decade at High Holiday services. I felt both peace and continuity.

The hall then became for me, suddenly and momentarily, all spaces in which all Jews had come together to pray for all time. Many different locations, in different historical moments, with thousands of Jews came to my mind's eye. The Jews in front of me suddenly were joined by their contemporaries and ancestors, across cultures, across time, and across space. I was overwhelmed. I did not mention this experience to anyone for a long time, but it spoke to me powerfully about my desire to belong to the Jewish prayer community. I had a very strong intuitive sense that evening that I wished to be part of this people, who were, I felt, my people.

That night I was transformed. In retrospect, I feel that this identification scene was also the moment when I stood at Sinai. Many times since this experience I have read that non-exclusive forms of Judaism consider all Jews from all time to have been at Sinai and that the souls of converts were also there. It is a highly abstract concept of faith, relying on a belief in the fluidity of time realms.

Although, as soon as this experience passed I judged my identification as incomplete or even fraudulent, considering my profound ignorance, I made myself a promise to become a Jew. Soon after, I introduced Friday night prayers and a Shabbat dinner into our home, and I reopened the issue of my possible conversion. I turned to Judaism on the holiest day of the Jewish year, fully conscious of my desire to take a place in the community.

PASSAGE 1

Who Counts?

THOUGHTS ON BAMIDBAR,
NUMBERS 1:1–4:20

*On the first day of the second month, in the second year follow-
ing the exodus from the land of Egypt, the Lord spoke to Moses
in the wilderness of Sinai, in the Tent of Meeting, saying,
"Take a census of the whole Israelite community by the clans of
its ancestral houses, listing the names, every male, head by
head."*

—NUMBERS 1:1–2

In the first class I took in Judaism, Rabbi David Straus, then of Temple
Har Sinai in Trenton, New Jersey, posed the central question: "What is
a Jew?" Embedded in this brief question were many others, and he listed them: "Who has the right or responsibility to speak as a Jew?" "What
does being Jewish mean?" "What role do birth, choice, and ethnicity
play?" "When did a patrilineal religion become matrilineal?" "Are questions of rights and responsibilities religious, universal, political, or historical questions?"

Rabbi Straus engagingly addressed himself to about twenty of us, men
and women, African American and Caucasian, Catholics, Jews, Protest-

ants, all of us between the ages of twenty-five and sixty-five or thereabouts, sitting together after a long January workday around a table in a nondescript meeting room of the Jewish community center. Exhausted but curious, we were all there that first week, and for many more to come, with one end: to learn more about Judaism.

We started with the issue of naming and identity. "Who is in and who is out?" as a fellow questioner put it. At the end of our class, we formed ourselves into discussion groups to decide on particular cases the rabbi had presented. I worked with a couple who were planning to be married within Judaism. The young man had studied in yeshiva and gone to Camp Ramah and was one of the most learned in our group; his Catholic wife-to-be, sincerely interested in Judaism and already knowledgeable about holidays and rituals, wanted to convert before marriage. The identity cases we were given to discuss were not all simple ones.

"What do you think? His father is Jewish, but his mother isn't."

"Well, he would be Jewish in the Reform wing but not in Orthodox."

"Yeah, but what about Conservative?"

"Probably not."

"Maybe it depends on the rabbi?"

"Or the congregation?"

"I don't know!"

We hashed them out, going back and forth and working out what the laws of various wings of Judaism would say today.

A Jew can be defined in more than one way: by citizenship, by religion through rituals and faith, or by culture and customs. Legally, one is a Jew if born of a Jewish mother or if converted. One is not legally a converted Jew to the Orthodox wing, however, unless one has studied intensively under the supervision of Orthodox rabbis. Yet Reform Jews, unlike those from the Orthodox or Conservative wings, count children born of Jewish fathers as Jews, as well as those born of Jewish mothers. Thus, even definitions that seem fixed are interpreted differently in the separate wings of contemporary Judaism. If one is a Jew, however, one is always a Jew, even if one changes to another religion later. A Jew can always return to Judaism.

Jews do not, however, constitute a race. Despite the still rampant stereotypes, Jews do not all share genetic characteristics of skin color or a type of hair or facial features. Ethiopian Jews, Argentinian Jews, Israeli Jews, American Jews, and European Jews do not all look the same. Nor do they act or sound the same. Jews all over the world keep cultural traditions unique to their own Jewish, ethnic, and national communities.

This diversity is not new. Ever since ancient times there have been many Judaisms and different ways to observe Judaism. There were divergent groups even during the rabbinic period, when, one could argue, a hegemonic Judaism was being established by the rabbinic quest for authority.[1] When we tried to define Judaism in Professor Peter Schäfer's class on rabbinic literature at Princeton in the spring of 1999, we discovered that there was no essence of Judaism in the ancient world. "Kashrut," said an Orthodox student. "It's gotta be circumcision," argued a Conservative. "Sacrificial offerings," said another. "Well," said the professor, smiling, "this is far more complicated than it seems." Even the rituals that we thought might have bound Jews together then, in postbiblical and prerabbinic times, apparently were not practiced or valued by all observant Jews, though they were certainly among the most consistent binding factors.

Despite multiple Judaisms and differences of beliefs within Judaism, then and now, several tenets bind Jews inclusively enough to be mentioned. A Jew believes in one God, creator and lord of the universe, the God with whom the people Israel have a special and enduring relationship. Indeed, one may argue that the religion is fundamentally about that relationship. Jews since rabbinic times have also revered a body of sacred literature: the Pentateuch (Torah), Writings, and Prophets (all three constitute Tanakh) and the Talmud (Mishnah and Gemara). All these writings can also be called Torah. In addition to these writings, there are many translations (Targum), mystical works (Kabbalah), and commentaries and midrashim on specific biblical books. Jews are also devoted to a sacred language, Hebrew, and a sacred land, Israel. These basic tenets of Judaism generally override cultural and historical differences. Within Judaism, being counted as a Jew matters, and this issue is of fundamental importance to converts as well. We seek to be counted in the minyan, or quorum, to take our places and become a part of the "holy nation" (Exodus 19:6).

Who is in and who is out? Who counts in Judaism? This problem is vexed, despite the laws of various movements in the religion. I tense up when I enter the discussion. Theologically and emotionally, as a Jew, I am aware of who is in and who is out; I know which movement counts for whom in contemporary Judaism. My love of Conservative Judaism and my sense of social justice and equality war with some rabbinic halakhot that still govern so much modern observance. As Rabbi Hayim Halevy Donin reminds us, halakhah, which makes concrete that which is abstract, embodies the Jewish attitude toward life. To disregard or reject it is to abandon the path toward holiness and to break the covenant. So if I call for the rethinking of certain aspects of halakhah, or for an adaptation of laws to current social concerns, I am instigating a questioning process that is itself part of the Jewish tradition. It is a call for further debate and justifications (responsa) and further inclusivity. It is not an arrogant renunciation of the authority of Torah, written or oral. My desire for social justice for women, the children of male Jews, and homosexuals puts me at odds with some traditionalists, but I err on the side of inclusiveness.

My view is that all Jews count—those by birth, those of fathers, of mothers, those by choice, women, men, children of age, the mentally and physically disabled, the sick and dying, white, nonwhite, and mixed races, heterosexual, homosexual, bisexual, transgendered, and gender-dissonant, rich and poor and in between, learned and not learned, religious and cultural and secular, Israelis and non-Israelis. Although the laws of Conservative Judaism would not agree with the size of my Jewish umbrella, and Orthodox laws would be more exclusive still, my reading of Numbers: Bamidbar tells me that, within the covenant, there are different ways to count. "The Children of Israel shall encamp, every man at his camp and every man at his banner, according to their legions . . . and the Levites shall safeguard the watch of the Tabernacle of Testimony" (Numbers 1:52–53). In this listing, however, to count means more than numbering; it also means that God has regard for each. Each Jew matters. We all, despite hierarchies and laws and separations in the religion, are potential equals on the path to holiness, as long as we know where we stand and are conscious of standing ethically and religiously in a place sanctifying place, time, and person.

We humans, not just Jews, harbor different gifts and weaknesses, interests and propensities, but we all start as equals. As I understand Torah, including Talmud, every human being, regardless of religion, race, ethnicity, or belief, is endowed with dignity, which is represented in Judaism by the halakhic principle of kvod habriyot—the dignity of man in the greatest universal sense. In fact, the guidelines offered by Torah for treating all people with respect are so strong that any commandment in Torah may be violated passively, shev v'al ta'asseh, in order to preserve the reputation and respectability of another human being. The dignity of men and women supersedes, then, every rabbinic law, whether we speak of a Jew, a non-Jew, or a nonbeliever. Moreover, the inherent dignity of each Jew as an "only child" of God, as my supervisor once put it in a High Holiday sermon, is not that of culturally constructed social roles or sexual differences. In this sense we all count. To be sure, recognizing the inherent dignity of all men and women is not the same as taking a census of Jewish men, as in Numbers, nor is it the same as judging who counts in a minyan or who shall chant Torah or be ordained. Yet for me there is a strong relationship in Judaism between who is counted, who is accountable, who counts, and why and how. These are the larger questions addressed by the census of Bamidbar.

The hasidic teacher Baruch of Medzibozh said that the world needs each human being because each one of us has the mission to make something perfect in this world. The mission is unique to the individual. If Bamidbar is concerned with numbering the Jews communally, by tribes, for a military campaign to claim land, it also is very much concerned with counting individuals and acknowledging their different positions and roles in a much larger enterprise.

When I was five years old, I let go of my mother's apron strings to go to school and out into the wider world. Like many girls in kindergarten at the Henry Barnard School in Providence, Rhode Island, in 1955, I had a boyfriend. Alan and I used to sit together on the school bus going home and hold hands. We did this every day for about half a year. He got off at a stop earlier than mine, and I was always sorry to see him go. Much of our kinship was unspoken—we just enjoyed being together. I told my parents about him. One day at a parent-teacher organization meeting, my mother met his in that way that moms do, their identities suddenly absorbed into those of their children. "I'm Alan's mother." "I'm Linda's mother." Well, Linda's mother was very surprised to discover, she reported at dinner, that Alan's mother (like Alan) was African American.

What happened after my mother and father told me how surprised they were? Given the tolerance for difference in my home, what could have happened? It was the 1950s, after all. I internalized the surprise; after I was five years old, I did not entertain the idea again of an African American boyfriend. The story became a family story and was repeated many times, with tolerance and some good humor. The story of the first boyfriend. Revelations at the elementary school meeting. But the telling betrayed some level of discomfort, as well as tender thoughts about a five-year-old's blindness to racial difference.

Many years later, when I was about eighteen, I worked at the library one summer. On my shift in the film and video rental department, I was making calls and I suddenly found myself connected to Alan, who was the contact person for a youth program. "Alan, that's you? Alan of Henry Barnard School? What are you doing now?" He was grown up. We were happy to hear each other's voice. We connected as schoolmates after many years. And there it ended.

Thirty years after my telephone conversation with Alan, on a Sunday afternoon over tea at my kitchen table, a dear friend inquires, "So what are your feelings about race anyway?" This is the story I tell her. "There is a lot in that story," she says. "You must have felt a knot inside when you heard his voice again." "I was glad to hear his voice," I say. I admit to not knowing more at eighteen, but now I feel sadness. It's a small story that is at the edge of a much larger one concerning history, social hierarchies and exclusions, cultural conditioning, conformity, and othering.

Before we even know how to think things through for ourselves, we are taught to "other" those whom we might love if only given a chance. How tolerant are the inclusive? And how tolerant are the exclusive? It is a deeply painful question not only for white Anglo-Saxon Christians, as I was, but also for everyone else, including Jews and Jewish converts, as I am now. One must think very hard, without making quick or ill-informed judgments, about hierarchies and the roles set aside for certain people but not others, both in a functioning democracy in a professedly egalitarian society and in an ancient covenantal religion based on social and religious hierarchies. If one wants to follow halakhah, loves Conservative Judaism, and respects orthodox Judaism but believes in social equality, one must struggle with incompatibilities.

Bamidbar is the first parasha of the book of Bamidbar, called in English Numbers; translated literally, "Bamidbar" means "in the wilderness." Its topic is a census—a numbering and a counting, near Mount Sinai, a year and a month after the building of the Tabernacle. God has called for a census of males above twenty years of age, tribe by tribe, except for the tribe of Levi, which will be singled out for special duty regarding the ark and the Tent of Meeting. Bamidbar follows narratively from the end of Exodus, which closes with the erection of the Tabernacle according to instructions given by God to Moses. In the pages of the Pentateuch, Bamidbar follows thematically and physically the end of Leviticus, where in the last section there has been a tithing of sheep, with every tenth sheep singled out as holy. Bamidbar concerns the counting of men. When I first prepared this parasha for discussion in our worship community, four issues caught my imagination: counting and what it meant, the spatial placement of tribes around the ark, the dangers of holy things, and the presence in the camp of uncounted women, children, and non-Israelites.[2]

Why would a census be taken thirteen months after the erection of the Tabernacle, when a census had also been taken, and how can we interpret it? I think the census is important emotionally, politically, and spiritually. On one level, it offers a chance for those being counted to remember the dead. Although I will not enter into the rabbinic debate about the miracle of coincidence of census numbers, from the exodus census to this one thirteen months later, I will note one point. Nachmanides suggests that the high figure of this census (600,000 men) is a sign. It is a miracle, he argues, that so many Israelites exist or have come of age after plagues, the Golden Calf, the battle with Amalek, and the difficulties of surviving after Egypt.[3] For later generations, the census is important emotionally as a genealogy: like so many passages in Torah, it offers a witnessing of ancestors through naming.

Politically the census serves as another transition out of the habits of slavery, as Rashbam argues, into a new kind of discipline and service.[4] It provides an opportunity for the leaders and participants to feel that each person and tribe count individually as part of a larger job and a larger holy nation. Most practically, a census is taken and physical places around the ark are assigned (for rest, march, and battle) to prepare a military campaign against the inhabitants of Canaan. The Israelites are encamped around the Tent of Meeting, with three tribes on each side. In addition, the tribe of Levi is counted separately. They camp on each side closest to the ark, forming a kind of protective barrier of holiness.

Spiritually, the census is also a moment of identity affirmation in relation to God. As Rashi points out, God counts His people frequently.[5] He counts them when they leave Egypt, after the Golden Calf episode, when He places His Tabernacle among them, now at the edge of Canaan, and when they cross the Jordan. The people give their names to Moses and Aaron, and a relationship is established between individuals and leaders. Although women, children, men over fifty or sixty (depending on tribe) and non-Israelites are not counted, the naming is representative of each person's *accountability* to God and of each person's *counting* to God. I will come back to the omissions.

What does it mean to count? "Take a census," says God. "Take a sum." "Number." "Lift the head up" of each (as literally translated from the Hebrew). I take it that "lift the head up" is an instruction to Moses, Aaron, and the tribal leaders to engage with each person and learn his name and therefore the virtues of which his name is representative. The leaders are thus forcefully reminded of the many attributes the names represent. To me, "lift the head up" means something more as well: you shall not allow anyone in the census group to be overlooked or forgotten. Nobody is unaccountable and nobody is uncountable.

When I prepared this parasha, I despaired at my choice. I could not at first connect to a set of passages that primarily features a list of men's names. I then ran across a thought on the Web in a parasha reading by a Rabbi Kraus of Belmont, Massachusetts, and it stopped me in my tracks. He asked: How does our society today count people? He offered various ideas, and I added a few more to them: demographics, gender, race, age, sexual orientation, political party, Fortune 500, and so on. In short, he listed the categories that seem to matter to us today. What would it be like, said this rabbi, if our leaders took a census that counted the kind, the generous, or the righteous? He was not equating those attributes or restricting them to men. What would it be like if our leaders lifted the heads of those people? In elevating them, society might be elevated. Since our leaders are not about to do so, Rabbi Kraus suggested that we do it individually in our own way as we think about who counts in our lives. Whom would each of us count?

This exercise was not intended to make any one of us into God, of course. Its purpose was to get us to think about this parasha in terms of our own lives and not as simply a counting of men with no relevance to us. Who was in our hearts, and why? Perhaps we could let these people know, in some way, that they mattered. Is this not what a biblical census also does? These remarks brought out well the meaning of what Rabbi Kraus illuminated for me: "spiritual mathematics." As I imagined beginning my own list, the names in the parasha suddenly made a different kind of sense.

This parasha is not only about counting, however. The tribes are organized. As mentioned, the tribes are placed in relationship to the ark by degrees of holiness and honor. They are given no choice in terms of where they are placed. The tribe that you belong to determines whether you become part of a first line of defense or a second line, or whether you fight at all. Maybe you are in the back, maybe in the front, maybe in the middle.

An essay by Martin Buber, "Where One Stands," suggests that each of us has been given a place, a little section of creation, in which to work and that something of meaning is to be found wherever we stand. But we must be aware of standing somewhere, of who and where we are, if we are to be, and to be for others. In fact, if everyone does her or his part where she or he stands, I can do mine. We are interdependent in this way. But where does the convert stand in Bamidbar? Or the woman?

A midrash on Bamidbar also comments on place by noting that when this parasha speaks about *place* in verse 1, it moves from general to specific, or from space to place—that is, from the wilderness to the Tent of

Meeting. "On the first day of the second month, in the second year following the exodus from the land of Egypt, the Lord spoke to Moses in
the wilderness of Sinai, in the Tent of Meeting, saying, 'Take a census.'
. . . " Yet, says the midrash, the sages taught that God's place, the Tent of
Meeting, is really the whole world and that the Sinai wilderness is the
specific locale. This reversal of what is general and what is specific also
asks the question: Where is God? Where are boundaries? What is place,
and what is endless space? What is secular and what is holy? Where do
we stand?

In our minyan service, a week before our discussion of Bamidbar, we
had opened the back door of the hall for the first time that season. Our
hall opened to grass, air, and more light. The specific place in which we
stood, before the ark, expanded. It seems a wonderful paradox of religious experience that being bounded in a place can lead to expansive
space. Within Judaism, as I understand it, God is not just in the world in
this place or that place, in this person or that one. Rather, this hall or
that, this soul or that, is in God. Place and space are dynamically related
in a spiritual sense. How could counting—determining placement in a
specific spot—or being in a place at all, matter?

One way in which placement matters is that it not only orders and
restricts but also honors, and thus awards or confirms identity. The
Levites, for instance, are specially chosen in Bamidbar to serve in a specific place and to perform a difficult job: they handle the holy vessels and
dismantle and reassemble the ark when it travels and rests. But they must
not gaze on the holy articles. The danger of bumping, touching, or gaz-
ing on holy things is described elsewhere in the Pentateuch and in
Haftarot (readings from the Prophets).

Crossing the line of holiness in this parasha continues to puzzle me.
What are the dangers of contact with holy articles? One danger that is
clear to me is the temptation to material or aesthetic treatment of spiritual symbols, a practice akin to idolatry. The entire Pentateuch can be
said to be a warning against idolatry. But beyond this warning, is danger
also present to keep the priests (Kohanim) and those who tend the ark
(the Levites) in their place and to keep them from pride of place? Or is
it that getting too close to or too intimate with holy things, like getting

too close to God, might break through a barrier that would make them lose their humanity through an obsession with holiness?

I marvel at this danger, which seems linked inextricably to placement and to identity. One must take up one's place or find one's place; one must see it as simultaneously fixed and always provisional. The issue of placement is critical for a convert. Because she has chosen the Covenant freely, she is said to be closer to God than God's own children. This is a gift and also a burden to me—one I especially felt in my first year as a Jew—to be worked through again and again.

The larger question I am left with regarding this parasha, a question directly connected to counting, identity, and placement, is the role of women and children and outsiders. What is the relationship between hierarchies of holiness and potential human equality? Or between Levites and non-Levites, or between men and women? These hierarchies are not limited to the sacrificial cult and Temple version of Judaism that we find in the Pentateuch or in a text-centered rabbinic Judaism. We still privilege men in subtle and not so subtle ways, despite the growing numbers of Reform, Reconstructionist, and Conservative women rabbis; despite the widespread use of the girl's naming ceremony (corresponding to the b'rit milah, or circumcision, ceremony for a boy); and despite the existence of Rosh Hodesh (new moon) groups and other female-centered events such as the bat mitzvah for older women. Despite all this, we continue to confront the omission in the liturgy of the matriarchs' names by many congregations, and discussions of Torah in which we omit women's experiences and voices. We often rely on masculine pronouns. Moreover, even though we do not need rabbis to lead services, we still often honor the hierarchy of the priests and Levites by awarding Kohanim and Levites, when present, the first aliyot, the honor of going up to Torah in synagogue to sing the blessings before and after a section is read.

The story of Korach's rebellion in Numbers 16:1–18:32 raises most directly the vexed issue of hierarchy and equality. Korach asks: If the nation is to be holy, as God says in Exodus, why do we need a leader, Moses, who is more holy than others, and why do we need laws of holiness anyway? If we are all equal, in other words, why are there hierarchies? "For the entire congregation is holy and God dwells in their midst; why then do you raise yourselves above the congregation of God?" (Numbers 16:3). The question is not answered directly in the Pentateuch and indeed is never completely resolved. Do we need hierarchies of holiness to create models, so that we will aspire to be better? Yet Judaism is not a religion of great men or heroes. Over and over one encounters the flawed humanness of Israelite leaders, priests, and Levites, who are sometimes not much better than the ordinary Hebrews. The hierarchies, it is thought, serve ideals of purity and holiness ingrained in the religion, which are utterly central to its practices. Maybe.

Women are considered separate but equal. They are never equal in Orthodox Judaism, however, or in some Conservative congregations. They are not bound by rules of public congregational worship; firstborn if female are not obligated to fast on the day of erev Passover; they may not approach the Torah or lead a worship service, as they do in egalitarian Conservative, Reform, and Reconstructionist minyans. Should there be hierarchical barriers between women and men in terms of privileges and obligations? Should women be separate but equal or special but not equal?

Writing on Bamidbar, the feminist Ellen Frankel notes in *The Five Books of Miriam* that not only are the twenty-two thousand Levites excluded from the count, but so are the children, women, and the erev rav—the mixed multitudes, the "strangers," the others—who accompanied the Israelites on their march out of Egypt. Although the population must have numbered about three million people, the rabbis talk about the six hundred thousand at the edge of Canaan and the six hundred thousand who stood at Sinai.[6] Who counts? What numbers matter and to whom? It is a historical problem, but also a metahistorical problem in an event that crosses time realms.

Weren't we all at Sinai?

Chapter Two

TIME, TIMELINESS, TIMELESSNESS

In each generation every person must act as if he or she personally had gone forth from Egypt.
—MISHNAH, PESAHIM 10:5

On the exodus out of Egypt, Moses carried Joseph's bones at the head of the people as they marched toward the Sea of Reeds with the intention of reinterring him in the Land of Israel. "Moses took the bones of Joseph with him, for he had firmly adjured the Children of Israel, saying, 'God will surely take notice of you, and you shall carry up my bones from here with you'" (Beshalach, Exodus 13:19). We carry the memories of those who came before us, and we carry their deaths and what survives them. They are part of us, literally and figuratively. It matters how we remember them, or do not forget them, how we honor them, how we carry them, and how we put them down carefully. As we handle memory and death, both through our actions and our identifications, we learn about living.

Converts renounce all former faiths, but they still carry non-Jewish memories in addition to new Jewish memories. They bear, arrange, and reinter the dead of various pasts and traditions. Placing those memories—separately, side by side, or in a blend—is part of the uneasy inner work of conversion. Often during my conversion study I reflected that had I only known about the Jewish handling of death, including the prayer Kaddish, and had I converted much earlier, my outlook on living might have been substantively different.

The Jewish tradition pays full respect to the dead while preparing those left behind to continue living. "You are the children of the Lord your God," says Torah. "You shall not gash yourselves or shave the front of your heads because of the dead" (Deuteronomy 14:1). Jewish rituals of mourning are framed by time. For instance, shiva, meaning seven, consists of a week of intense mourning for family and friends. Shiva is intended to help the bereaved to heal after the funeral by sitting through, rather than in, their grief. The mourners move through their grief with the community rather than alone, by reminiscing and sharing stories. Often a family member prepares a book or scrapbook or a set of pictures of the deceased, creating a pictorial and written tribute that visitors may also see. We cover mirrors. Friends arrive, and we come out of ourselves to greet them. They bring food. The rabbi visits. Traditionally, services are held each evening in the home. During this week mourners are exempt from normal duties and pleasures. Jewish law then requires a thirty-day mourning period, including the week of shiva; during that time normal duties may be resumed, but many pleasures are traditionally forsaken and grieving may continue. Some Jews wear black for a spouse or a child for a year. Jewish law also acknowledges the first year after a death. We say the mourner's Kaddish on Shabbat for eleven months. The stone marker is unveiled when that first year has passed.[1] Mourning does not end at this point, but remembrance enters a different stage.

Other aspects of the Jewish handling of death also felt instinctively right to me as I learned more about them. Jews prepare the body simply; we identify but do not gaze on the body; we drape the body in white, covering men with the tallit (prayer shawl), and frame the body in a simple wooden box; we try to bury the body as soon as possible. No embalming. No cremation. At the funeral we remember the deceased by honoring the soul of the person with loving testimony. For all a Jew may leave behind, the only important thing, besides children, is a good name achieved through deeds—how the individual moved through and handled time.

We take a year, then, to respond to a death; through a full cycle of regular observance and holidays, we recommit to life, though sorrow and memories last longer. Some prayers are explicitly for the dead, such as El Malei Rachamim and Yizkor, but Kaddish, the mourner's prayer, is not one of them. Referring neither to death nor to mourning, Kaddish is a prayer honoring God's name and his will, not for the dead but for God and the living who continue the journey through time. During personal loss, one publicly affirms one's faith in God. On the yearly anniversary of the death, the Yahrzeit, a Jew lights a memorial candle and rises in public to say Kaddish again. This ritual is required of a son, but in many congregations it is also acceptable for a daughter to perform it. We also say a full Kaddish for one or more relatives on Yom Kippur at the Yizkor service, on the last day of Sukkot (Shemini Atzeret), on the last day of Passover, and on the second day of Shavuot.

The Jewish handling of death appealed to me very strongly when I began to understand the beliefs I was embracing. Even in mourning one is charged to feel alive and thankful to be a part of God's larger plan, rather than emotionally destroyed. Had I only had these beliefs to live by before, perhaps I would not have spent half my life in circular motions of mourning. I say Kaddish for family members now.

My childhood was punctuated by a series of family deaths. I became used to hearing how people died and, I became used to visiting cemeteries. But I did not become used to funerals, because I was hardly ever allowed to go to them. I did not usually see the bodies of my relatives, and I did not say good-bye. Even as a teenager, I was considered too young. I assume my parents thought that I would have been frightened or traumatized. And so my relation to death, to loss, and to leavetaking became a relation to absence and to stone markers and to memories. Should children attend funerals? I don't know. I know only that my schooling in death was partial. The same is true for us all, I suspect, but in different ways.

Six deaths occurred in my relatively small family in eleven years. I cannot remember or imagine what I felt about this unusually large number, and I have no memory at all of the first two. I was too young, at five, to do more than register the deaths of my maternal great-grandmother and my vibrant forty-year-old uncle, though I felt my mother's deep sorrow.

The next year, when I was six, "Nana" died. She was my father's mother, and she lived with us. She had been bedridden for a few years, and I was quite used to climbing on her bed and chatting or sharing a radio program. One day I came home on the bus from first grade and jumped down the big, wide steps to meet my mother at the corner, five blocks from our house. On the walk home my mother explained that "Nana died last night in her sleep." She put her arm around me. "Does Daddy know?" I asked, apparently sensing that since Nana was his mother, he should be told first. My sadness over Nana's death was more lasting than it might otherwise have been at such a young age, because I had a conscience. I had been unloving to her the night before, had not given the requested kiss or said good-night. I had been bad-tempered, and I was now ashamed.

Her death left me fearful, at six, that I had missed a chance. Maybe she died upset with me, I thought. Or maybe she had not known I loved her. I did not remotely understand that I might not have been on her mind when she died or that adults forgive children these moments. I didn't know much about death, but I knew enough to feel shame. My mother's reassurances to the contrary calmed me, but a certain weight is still there today, made heavier through subsequent deaths: the lost chance to pay respect or give love.

Because the separation from my grandmother was irrevocable and she never returned, not even in a dream, that lesson remains after more than forty years: all of us miss chances, make emotional mistakes, or ignore, distort, or ruin moments of connection or potential connection. In one way or another, we pay for these errors. We can be sorry and atone; we can forgive ourselves; we can work through these errors. But they matter. My sense now is that nothing can be done to avoid making more such mistakes except to live in time differently.

Besides the deaths of my great-grandmother Sarah (in 1955), my uncle George (1955), and my grandmother Marguerite (1956), I also experienced the deaths of my grandmother Verna (1959), my same-aged cousin Christine (1962), and my grandfather Thomas (1966). I would like to think that all these deaths toughened me and made me more sensitive to the feelings of others and more aware that our family was just one of many families, that our deaths were no more important and no less important than any others.

But what these deaths did teach me as a child was different—that death comes often, when it wants and how it wants, both predictably and by surprise but very often by surprise; that children can die before their parents, and that those are among the worst deaths of all; that I would always be shocked by death and absence, no matter how well I might be prepared for them. The family deaths that punctuated my childhood taught me that love, which I thought was a great force, could survive death but could not stop it. I could easily have gotten used to death and become steeled to it, but I never did.

Perhaps because it was the last in a connected series, or because I was a young teenager, but more likely because I spent a long, close time with him, my maternal grandfather's death, when I was fifteen, made me question the presence of God. He died after a long struggle with angina. When we got the phone call from my uncle, I alternately prayed to God to protect him, for I believed he was going on a journey, and wondered if there was a God at all. I was relieved that my grandfather was not in pain anymore, but I could no longer believe that there was any meaning to life. Going to my room, I sat on the floor alone and hit out and cried bitterly.

My grandfather is one of the keys to my love of the Jewish people. He was strong-willed and the kindest, most generous, and most physically loving man I ever knew. His sturdy rugged body housed tremendous tenderness. A first-generation immigrant, he owned a neighborhood grocery store in the Greek community of Pawtucket, Rhode Island. The sights and smells and textures of that store, now long gone, come back and remind me of him.

As a child, every week I spent part of a day there. I see the cold soda chest that I would open so I could finger the large pieces of ice floating among the Cokes and root beers. "Bumpa, can I take down and put back all the soaps on the shelves?" I ask. "Sure," he says, "but don't miss out on what's new in the ice cream freezer today." I wander into the cozy darkness of the backroom where my grandmother is making succulent tomato, bay leaf, and chicken pilaf at a big black stove in the corner. I see the sun-struck vegetable garden out the backdoor where kittens run wild, the sawdust on the floor, the Kalamata olive and feta barrels, the large walk-in meat freezer. I see my grandfather behind the counter in his big white apron. He smiles back.

I also knew him from our many Sunday rides to picnic in the country. My grandmother would have been up at dawn to make pies and roasts and salads. My grandparents, Uncle Bill, Mom, Dad, and I would fill my father's Ford convertible. "Come, sit with me," he would say and have me climb up onto his lap in the backseat. As we traveled the country roads of New England, he made up stories to tell me and ran his hand through my hair. Stories made out of bits and pieces, like Ritz cracker crumbs lost in his vest. They were morsels of love, and I devoured them all. On the way home, we happily fell asleep together. Forty years later, wondering if I am blinded by sentiment or wishfulness, I ask my mother: "Was he as I remember him? Was he always so loving to everyone, so forgiving of human nature, so generous? Or was he just that way toward the granddaughter he prized?" "He was that way always," she says. Maybe she's blinded by sentiment too, or maybe this sentiment speaks truth.

My grandfather was special to me precisely because he was not special by any standards my society or I valued. Not refined or overly ambitious or educated or handsome or self-promoting, he was simply himself. I did not know him as a husband, a father, a brother, an uncle, or a friend. My memories are warped, partial, and few. He stands before me for his deeds, as someone who knew how to love openly and strongly. I carry his bones with me and lay them down gently.

My passion for Judaism is traceable in part to my grandfather, who was a devout Greek Orthodox. I don't know if he knew any Jews, and I have no way of understanding what, if anything, he knew about Judaism. He was born in a small village near Patras in Greece. Thus, by descent, he was linked to another ancient civilization that mixed with Judaism to varying degrees during the Hellenistic period.

Still he is part of my relationship to my Jewishness because his central values reflect some of the tenets of Judaism I most admire. He valued learning, and therefore books, as one of our most important cultural gifts, and he made sure his three children were well educated. He had great reverence for history and its lessons. Religiously observant, he supported his community, feeling it a moral obligation to take care of those worse off than himself. Week after week he practiced what we call mitzvot and tzedakah: he took care of widows, he was concerned for the sick and bereaved, he welcomed strangers, and he fed the hungry who could not pay their grocery bills. He acted on his knowledge that everyday life and everyday nourishment are sacred matters. He was not Jewish, and as a woman I am under no obligation to do so, but I say Kaddish and Yizkor for him.

It is January 1999, and my husband and I have taken our eight-year-old son Alex with us to San Francisco, where we are attending a conference. We have flown to California a few days early and are spending our first day there with my husband's second-cousin-by-marriage, Kathe Weiner, who first gave him a home when he came to this country from Europe and Bolivia. After lunch, we walk a few blocks to the Jewish section of the cemetery in Oakland. We are going to this cemetery to pay respects to my husband's mother, Hilde, and to the relations who settled in California after they left Europe. This is my second visit and my son's first. On the street leading into the cemetery there are several large flower shops. "Okay," says my husband, "we have to stop for flowers for her first. Let's see if they have her favorites." We look for ones she would have liked; she loved asters. "I want to buy something for her too!" says my son. These are Jewish lessons in honoring the dead passed from father to son.

My husband takes us to his mother's grave. "I want time alone," he says. So my son and I walk among the rows of markers and stones, and we try to find the names of others we know about—"Weiner," we say aloud. "Markus." It's a light-filled day, and the afternoon sun falls aslant on the graves as a light wind blows silk flowers along the ground. As we wander in the cemetery, we keep reading the names aloud together and look at the Hebrew letters, the dates, and the Jewish stars. We gather a few of the straying silk flowers and put them on the markers we know, trying to anchor them a bit with dirt.

When my husband is done talking with his mother, he calls us over. "There used to be a holder here," he says, "for the flowers. Let's try to find it." We arrange the asters in water. My son keeps one to press for remembrance, and we each perform the Jewish custom of placing a tiny rock on top of the gravestone. "Take a picture of Alex next to his grand-mother's grave," my husband asks me. I look at my son, thoughtful, respectful, and I see him making this journey, again, when he is a man, for the sake of his father. He will remember this day with his parents; he will return, stop at a flower shop on the way in, try to recall the flower she liked; he will search the names, and he will pay his respects. Someday, I trust, he will say Kaddish for us.

These memories, which stand out like islands in time, convince me of the importance of embracing the future and the everyday as holy. The aspects of Judaism that most centrally represent those values for me are Passover and Shabbat. They are especially important to me for their rit-ualistic nature and for the way they handle time and spiritual renewal. They reveal God to us in many ways but chiefly, to me, as the lord of time. As we read in one of the most famous passages from the scroll of Ecclesiastes on Shemini Atzeret (the last day of Sukkot, just before Simchat Torah), everything has its proper moment. There is a time to die and a time to live, a time to mourn and a time to dance, a time to speak and a time to be silent. God demonstrates to us that there is an appro-priate (and timely) time for everything, from rugged redemption to serene celebration. Moreover, the recalling of ancestors and the conti-nuity of their traditions are central aspects of Jewish observance.

The first time I defended Judaism to a Jew was on Passover. I struggle even to remember the year. 1982? I was preparing the seder table for Uli, my husband-to-be, and for his first three children at their home. I did not know the religious reasons for the specific rituals, and I had only the barest understanding of the spiritual and cultural aspects of the seder, but I had prepared Passover before, so I had the rudiments down. It was one of the more memorable Passovers, but sadly, it was memorable mainly for the fight I had with our houseguest.

A close friend of the family's had come to stay for several weeks because it was spring. The visit had nothing to do with Passover, though our guest was of Jewish descent. The air was full of a crisp, new spring that day, and he was a runner. As I set the table and put out the burnt, hard-boiled egg, the fragrant cinnamon, walnut, and apple charoset, and the rest of the seder plate foods, he jogged into the dining room to announce that he was going running for an hour with my husband's eldest son. "Hey, guys, Paul and I are going out." "But," I said, "you two can't leave now. It is Passover. We're starting early. We're starting soon." "Oh," he said. "I'll join you later. I don't celebrate Passover. It means nothing to me." I had no way to process this declaration and its nonchalance. I was surprised and hurt. I blew up. "You don't have to care about Passover," I shouted at him, "but this is what we are doing and you are our guest!"

I didn't have a clue. Passover was already important to me. My relationship to Uli and his family, past and present, included a nascent relationship to Judaism. My anger surprised me. At the time I felt no authority to speak. I was not a wife, a stepmother, or a Jew. My own uncertain relation to my roles and to Judaism must have impelled part of my confusion and anger. But what I read as the egregious disrespect and self-centeredness of our guest upset me. *How could he!* I thought. *If he has no feelings for Judaism, he should go away for the day, or at least respect the ritual we are committing ourselves to follow.*

I did not take our friend's response as Jewish anti-Semitism or as Jewish disaffection or as a refusal of distinctiveness or even as Jewish self-hatred, about which I knew next to nothing. I took it as thoughtlessness. "You may not take Paul out now. He is celebrating Passover with us," I said emphatically. Our houseguest left Paul behind and went running alone, I unset a place, and we held the seder without him. He prepared a supper for himself and ate alone, later.

I remain, even now, shocked at this argument and at my anger. I see rights and wrongs on both sides. Why should our friend have had to conform to our needs? Why should we have had to conform to his? Could each of us not have found a way to bend a bit? Why couldn't we at least have talked it out? Independence and conformity, departure and return, freedom and kinds of slavery—what great topics for a lively twentieth-century American seder! If only we had known to make these ideas our topic, instead of insensitively going on with business as usual that night.

Business as usual. I wonder. My relation to our friend, who returned several times afterwards to stay and visit, is still in need of repair.

While studying for conversion, I announced to this friend, in a letter on a variety of topics, "I'm becoming a Jew." In a return letter he wrote: "You are always re-creating yourself. You are one of the least boring people I've ever met! Tell me why. Explain it to me. I want to understand what this means to you." I did not write back with an answer for two years. I couldn't. I realized, too late, that my reference to conversion had been a kind of bait, as well as an un-thought-through invitation to renewed intimacy. I saw that we were in different places in our lives than we had been. We were both more settled, both married. Both of us had aging knees and couldn't run anymore. It was clear that he cared about learning what impelled my conversion. But I was scared to defend my choices. When I finally did, I was met with respect.

This Passover episode was a milestone in my continuing relationship to Judaism. On that day Judaism became for me a set of rituals worth defending, even if my knowledge of its beliefs was still almost nonexistent. By the time of the letter exchange with our friend, over fifteen years later, and as I approached conversion day, Judaism had become the molder of my identity at middle age. Only afterwards, when a Jew at last, did I realize that I would have to go through the more difficult struggle of explaining and defending my beliefs to those who asked, and that I would have to work much harder at openly granting others their belief or unbelief or disbelief.

No one Passover celebration stays in my mind above all others. We have always celebrated the first night of Passover at home with the family. Over the past twenty years, we have had the pleasure of celebrating the second night of Passover in the homes of five other families, sometimes several times. Each time was distinctive, as were all of our first nights at home. The point of the seder is to reconstruct the past but also, like conversion, to re-create us. There is no perfect or correct way to do so. Just as the seder itself has changed venues over the years—the Wilderness, secret cellars in medieval Spain, attics in Holocaust Poland, huts in Africa, dining rooms in Argentina—so it changes us as we celebrate it each year. No seder I've attended has ever been quite like another. In spite of the order of ritual in the Haggadah and in spite of the proscribed foods, the matzoh hidden away in exile for the meal, and the joy and sorrow expressed and felt, the guests change, the foods change, the reading choices, elaborations, and omissions change, the jokes and song tunes change, the children and the adults grow and change over the preceding years, and, through questions and discussion, the interpretation of the seder changes.[2] Every seder, like every ritual ceremony, is different.

One's relationship to aspects of the Haggadah and the seder also change over time. The epigraph to this chapter, a quotation from the Mishnah reprinted in all versions of the Passover Haggadah, refers to the need for each Jew to identify individually with the enslaved condition of Israel and with a state of redemption. We are asked to feel personally the precious gift of a journey out of bondage and into freedom. "I shall bring you out from under the burden of the Egyptians, and I shall deliver you from their bondage, and I shall redeem you with an outstretched arm, and with great judgments. And I shall take you to Me for a people" (Exodus 6:6–7). Such passages can be interpreted in different ways and with different inflections. The journey out of bondage can be physical, mental, and emotional. Before my conversion, even though I was safe, secure, and relatively happy with my life, I tried at Passover to identify with the travail and harsh burdens of Hebrew slavery, to imagine myself and my family in the biblical past. *What would it have been like to be a Hebrew slave?* I wondered. *To have such a different understanding of self and different relations to others?*

Sometimes at seders I have thought of more recent generations and tried to identify with those crushed by the slavery of poverty, political slavery, and anti-Semitism. Often this has led to thoughts and feeling about the African American experience of slavery, women's oppression— particularly in the Third World—the abridgment of the civil rights of homosexuals, and the social abuse of the elderly and the disabled. When I approach Passover in this way, I understand freedom as an expansive deliverance of the individual, of groups, and of a people, as well as the political deliverance of Israel into chosen-ness and the freedom of choice. I understand Passover as the deliverance into a new, more humane way of living—a release into a different set of perceptions and understandings.

On the other side of my conversion to Judaism, I now read the Mishnah and Torah passages with a somewhat different stress, one that emphasizes personal responsibility for action. I've given a great deal of thought to what the Hebrews had to do physically and mentally to get out of Egypt. By way of example, for the Sea of Reeds to part, the Hebrews had to dare to step into the water first. Faith was not enough; they had to act. Later, manna did not fall into their mouths; they had to get up every morning, except on Shabbat, and gather the day's amount. Hoarding was not an option, for the manna would not last but instead would rot; only a daily gathering between certain hours of the day, as stipulated by God, ensured food for survival.

During my first Passover after becoming a Jew, I read Egypt as a confining place, literally, geographically, and symbolically, where the Hebrew spirit, including mine, had been constrained and bound. I understood the going forth from slavery as a breaking not only of the shackles imposed on us but also of those that we impose on ourselves. "This reading," my supervisor told me, "is related to the commentary that notes that the consonants in the Hebrew word for Egypt, mitzray-im, a narrow place, are duplicated in the word for self-imposed constraints, meitzarim." Ah, then I saw that the rescue, redemption, and responsibility marked by Passover are not only about our relationship to the past and to others but also about our relationship to ourselves and our personal chains: life-denying impulses, mechanistic routines, bad habits, overindulgences, improper use of language, self-dramas, and other tightening, killing forms of bondage. These shackles keep us away from the best selves of other people and of ourselves.

In this sense, Passover, which promises renewal in the season of springtime, can be viewed in terms of active and willed, rather than natural, spiritual growth. It speaks to me now not only about God's rescue of us but also about our rescue of ourselves for God. Passover asks us which route we will take out of a withering form of life and how we will act on the journey—not only the springtime journey and the exodus journey but the life journey. The yearly celebration of exodus reminds us that it is a continuing journey, not a onetime event. Small, seemingly insignificant actions can affect eternity, and one never knows how and where they will resonate.

As Jews, we emerge not only into freedom of choice at Passover but, more important, into responsibility. During my first Passover as a Jew, I wondered about the nature of that responsibility, then decided that it is to "act as if" and then to act. To me, responsibility entails imaginative identifications transcending time, culture, and geography, but it also requires self-examination and hard work to alter one's mentality and habits. Without the latter efforts, all the words and songs and prayers of Passover remain only promises of growth.

The Passover ritual celebration is like a historical, temporal drama and even closer to a live theatrical performance. As the author Ira Steingroot suggests, we maintain the tradition by acting out the roles and parts that have been written for us and that Jews before us have recited and sung. We perform mitzvot (fulfill the commandments about Passover) throughout the evening: we hold the seder, eat symbolic foods, drink the four cups of wine, eat matzoh, discuss. To do so requires a form of self-suppression so as to become *like* another, whether that other "performer" be defined broadly or specifically, impersonally or personally— a biblical Hebrew, a modern Jew, a rabbi of the Yavne period, a Jewish parent or grandparent. We contemplate, through commentary and readings and memories, how others have interpreted these roles and parts, and our reflections shape and alter our performance. Sometimes we may think about our own prior interpretations. Yet the sense of performance as self-actualizing, not just as self-suppressing, is equally embedded in the Passover drama. We approach freshly the Haggadah text and the roles and responsibilities required of us in our own times and lives.

In other words, the status of performance is redefined through the Passover seder, continually shifting from the "act as if" to the act, from thinking identification to performing mitzvot, from repeating to renewing, from renewing a text and a role to renewing self. This redefinition is finalized on the second night with the counting of the omer. There are fifty days from the Exodus to Sinai.[3] At this moment in Passover, we might say that the "act as if" and the act find the fullness of the why. For the exodus is never an end in itself, but merely a preparation to accept Torah at Sinai (on Shavuot). Counting the omer puts us into the realm of teleology: it makes clear a sense of direction and sets out a goal.

The section of the Passover seder on the four children has remained for me the central moment of this teleological and living narrative. My reading of this part of the Haggadah, however, has also changed over time. When I first experienced Passover, I was a literalist and a monologistic reader. Children were children. At that time I used to read the Haggadah midrash on the four children as advice to adult Jews about how to tell the story to their children of different talents and different ages. After all, the narrative requires a telling, which the seder does, but not all children who need to learn can absorb or need to be told the same things. The type and age of the child would dictate what part of the story was told and how it was told. I figured some generational and psychological mediation was required for such an important story.

The rabbis distinguish among the children who receive the story: the wise, the wicked, the simple, and the one who does not know how to ask questions. The wise child is curious and asks lots of questions and must be given the story in its entirety. The wicked child scoffs at the rituals and should be told that God worked miracles. The simple child does not understand what is happening and should be given clear and uncomplicated explanations. The one who does not know how to ask may be too young and should be told one idea: "We celebrate because of what God did for us when we left Egypt." The segment of the four children always initiates a conversation, a give-and-take, at the seder table. Each child present can decide to which group he or she belongs.

Later on, having been to several Passover seders, I came to see those children as being there for reasons of adult identification as well; I began to understand that the Haggadah is not talking about just those Jews twelve years old and under sitting around the table. *I'm a child*, I thought. In fact, I felt like a child as a non-Jew in my thirties and forties and totally uneducated in Jewish matters, sitting at the seders of my friends. Thus, I always used to read this section and find myself in one of the children. *I must be the simple child!* I'd think.

At that time it did not occur to me that my adult identification with a child might be probed further. Nor did it occur to me to question how the four "types" of children are set apart from each other and what those types might conceal or how they can be interpreted in multiple ways. I did not think about typing as negative in any way, nor did I think to honor the midrash's recognition of the blessing of diversity in humans or in narrative.

Over time I decided that I could not merely abandon my literal understanding of intergenerational mediation, since that fact is central to the seder. But I could absorb it into a larger explanation. Now I tend to read this pivotal narrative moment as also doubly dialogic. That is, I read children as the children inside us all, not only those who are chronologically children. I read the rabbis' mediation as one that instructs us to take ourselves as we are—at different levels of inquiry or understanding—and to treat ourselves appropriately and with kindness as we try to assimilate and learn from this important narrative of deliverance. Thus, for me since conversion, the child section inaugurates a literal and a figurative dialogue both between children and adults at the table and within each of us.

I also read the four children as holding a perpetual dialogue with each other, within each of us. We are all at times wicked, or wise, or simple, or unquestioning. Sometimes we demonstrate more than one of these traits at the same time. Presumably, we react differently to different moments of the service as well. Perhaps the meanings of the four cups are clear to us but we have no clue about what the omer means. Perhaps we turn the meanings of the seder outward but not inward, thinking about the oppression of others but not the ways in which we oppress others or are oppressed ourselves. Perhaps we question some parts of the holiday but not others. We are never only one thing.

Moreover, each type or response or trait can be used for different ends, so we can use the wisdom, simplicity, ignorance, or wickedness we find in ourselves for good or for evil. Perhaps the Haggadah asks us to inquire into these aspects of ourselves at a time of potential redemption—to weigh the story, one might say, four ways at the same time.

To welcome and know oneself as a child, without mastery or power or authority, is rarely easy. Our cultures of control and management provide us few models to develop such necessary retrospection and integration. Yet from this side of conversion, Passover offers me an ongoing dialogue, in an oscillating movement of time frames and identities, between historical and personal, between biblical narrative and present reality, between self and others, between acting and being, among past, present, and future, and within the self, as it helps us all explore ways of knowing time and responsibility, alone and together.

Shabbat, the Sabbath, is the day mandated by God to be set apart from the weekdays. Lasting from sundown Friday night until sundown Saturday night, it is the day to spend with family and friends, or with members of the community, to eat together, talk together, take walks, slow down, reflect, read Torah, and examine one's self and relations and religion anew. Shabbat is "a palace in time," in Abraham Joshua Heschel's terms.[4] It is a commandment that I find most beautiful and most difficult. "Shabbat is anachronistic," say some of my acquaintances. Otherwise traditional and observant Jews, they don't keep Shabbat. They mean that the laws one must follow to "keep" Shabbat are relics, as thin as a lintel worn down by generations, with no good foothold. "The laws are out of touch," they argue. These acquaintances do not want the point of Shabbat to be its irreconcilability with our times, and they do not keep Shabbat. "Who can live today," they ask, "without driving on Shabbat, without writing or computing or shopping?" But that is, I think, the point. It may also be that the difference, the separation, between Shabbat and other days has become all the more acute in the twenty-first century.

To do work, melakhah, is forbidden on Shabbat. It is important to understand why Torah forbids melakhah, which refers to more than just physical effort or labor. The thirty-nine categories of melakhah, taken from the Mishnah, Tractate Sabbath 7:2, include such activities as sheepshearing, cutting to shape, writing, erasing, kindling a fire, baking, and tying a knot. Lighting a fire, for instance, includes the manual turning on of electricity, heating water, turning on your furnace, turning on a light, washing clothes, and more. The Jew refrains from human creating and any purposeful control over nature on Shabbat. The Torah forbids the accomplishment of a directed purpose by practical skill and intelligence. The purpose, as Dayan Grunfeld explains, is what matters.[5] What this means is that we are asked to refrain from making significant changes in our environment on Shabbat. We are asked not to create.

Shabbat, then, is a stopping point—the crown of the week and a time to remember God's beneficence. But it is not just that. Nor is it a time for total passivity. As Abraham Joshua Heschel conveys throughout his book *The Sabbath*, we try on Shabbat to become attuned to the holiness of time. It is the day on which we are summoned to share and actively respond to what is eternal, not to what is time-bound. We turn from the results of human creation and of history to the mystery of God's Creation itself. The mood on Shabbat is festive, calm, and loving. It is a time to make love with one's partner and a time to express one's compassion for and closeness to others. The Sabbath is the nefesh, the soul of the world of matter, the dimension of the wholly spiritual in our lives.[6]

A midrash, as reproduced in Gunther Plaut's edition of Torah, constructs a dialogue between Israel and God on the value of observing commandments. God explains that if the people of Israel are faithful, he will give them the gift of the future world. Israel replies: Is there no reward in this world? God explains that Shabbat will be a foretaste of the future because it is one-sixtieth of the world to come. The rest we take on Shabbat is not only a refraining from work but a positive, active effort to devote ourselves to a higher reality, a world of the spirit.

Shabbat is enjoyed by the Israelites after they leave Egypt and when they receive the gift of manna. It is also the fourth commandment:

> Remember the Sabbath day and keep it holy. Six days you shall labor and do all your work, but the seventh day is a sabbath of the Lord your God: you shall not do any work—you, your son or daughter, your male or female slave, or your cattle, or the stranger who is within your settlements. For in six days the Lord made heaven and earth and sea, and all that is in them, and He rested on the seventh day; therefore the Lord blessed the sabbath day and hallowed it. (Exodus 20:8–11; see also Deuteronomy 5:12–15)

I have read that Shabbat is considered inherent in the process of God's creation. Separating us from the man-made world, it connects us directly with God's creation of the world in Genesis (where the word *shavat* means "rested") and asks us to imitate His own seventh day of contemplation. The separation of Shabbat from the rest of the week is thus both part of and the outcome of other separations made by God and recorded in Genesis, such as those between darkness and light, between good and evil, and between the Tree of Knowledge and eternal life. Although Shabbat is not given to the Israelites until the Ten Commandments, recorded in Exodus, the idea of it was coexistent with the act of creation, and the people of Israel were probably already observing it as a special day before they entered the wilderness.

To make a day holy is to fulfill our duty to honor its sanctity with blessings and to observe it by changing secular time to holy time. The second version of the commandment concerning Shabbat (Deuteronomy 5:12–15) is not identical with the first. It opens with the words "Observe the Sabbath day, to keep it holy, as the Lord thy God commanded thee." Where the first version, stressing remembering, offers a theocentric reason (remember the Sabbath because God made it), this version, stressing observance, offers an anthropocentric reason—because we were liberated from slavery. The first version stresses the spiritual, and the second stresses Jewish history. Pinchas Peli reminds us that the Babylonian Talmud, Shavuot 20, explains that "remember" (zachor) and "observe" (shamor) were uttered as one word by God, impressing on us the twin aspects of Shabbat. We are to experience God's creation as well as our own freedom from slavery and work, both longing for Shabbat as if she were our bride and honoring her as if she were our queen.

Before I decided to become a Jew, I neither kept Shabbat nor knew about its laws, in spite of having been to Friday night Shabbat dinners at the homes of friends. Even when my rabbi suggested it was time to start regular observance at Shabbat services, I did not know about the halakhot that I would be expected to remember and observe as well. *Sure,* I said to myself, *go to services, no problem. Then go home and get to work.* I was a slave to work and still am. Thus, it was a total jolt to my system to discover that the central fact of observance involved carving out a day of the week and, as it were, giving it up. *No way,* I thought. *There's no way I want to do this, and there's no way I can do this!*

Nevertheless, in the beginning of my observance, starting in August 1998, I tried very hard to follow the rules. And I found it impossible to do, because other members of my family, both those living with me and those living away, did not observe many of them beyond attending services sporadically. During these years the older kids would call on Shabbat, oblivious to anything but weekend time. In addition, the majority of my family did not go to services or think in terms of Shabbat as a day of the week that was in any way different from any other. In the beginning I went to services alone. Suddenly I was a zealot! I had already asked a lot of my husband and son by getting us to services; my conversion study had significantly altered our lives and schedules. And of course, worship conflicted with my son's soccer practice on Saturday mornings every fall and spring. "You take him to soccer." "No, you take him to soccer." "I did it last week. I want to go to services today." "You always go to services. I want to represent the family today." Over the course of that first year my husband had become very keen to go to services too. On and on it went. We had to work out a trade during fall and spring; we three negotiated and had to be flexible with each other and with the soccer coach. Even on the day we hosted a lunch for our worship group, my son had to be taken to soccer to get team assignments and pictures taken, so he came to services very late, just in time to say a prayer and then leave to set up kiddush at home.[7]

My occasional insistence on certain Shabbat rules sometimes produced quarrels, tears, accusations, and hard feelings—even illness, as happened when I firmly maintained that we had to walk to a friend's bar mitzvah in the rain. Because there's to be no driving on Shabbat, we three trudged for two miles, without umbrellas (no carrying on Shabbat), instead of going by car. The dominant mood that day was resentment. I would discover that keeping Shabbat can be divisive of family life, not unifying. Surely, disunity is not the fundamental idea behind Shabbat.

I was torn between divine laws and human needs. To be torn by a love of God's laws and a love of one's ties to the human realm is one of the central issues of a life within religion. The difficulty of this dual allegiance is registered in our response to the Akedah, in which Abraham's love for God and his faith are so strong that he is willing to sacrifice his son Isaac when asked to take him up Mount Moriah (Genesis 22). And the difficulty is equally felt in small daily decisions—such as deciding which parent will go to services and which parent will go to soccer practice.

Despite my wish for piety and my desire to follow mitzvot faithfully, I quickly discovered that I was no Abraham. The human realm would sometimes have to come first. Any imposition of Sabbath rules on my family became increasingly out of the question. Nor did I want to leave them and go my own way alone. I was unwilling to give up family times when the older children and our grandson came home, or events like my stepdaughter's wedding shower in New York, scheduled on a Saturday. I was just as unwilling to sacrifice my marriage to my faith. My husband had been a Jew long before me and was happy with his slowly increasing level of observance; my son would not benefit from seeing his parents argue about religion. I did not mind struggling with these issues, but I did not want Judaism to divide us when one of the key reasons I converted was to strengthen the bond we already had. Thus, for a while I contented myself with trying to keep Shabbat rules and realizing that observance would increase over time.

It was hard enough, it turned out, not to shop, drive, or create in the kitchen or garden, and even harder to reorganize the week so that all shopping and cleaning and preparing were done on Wednesday and Thursday, days when I was often away in Syracuse at my job. It was even harder for me not to do academic work or answer phone calls or read mail. The easiest and most beautiful Sabbaths consisted of services all morning, with a cold lunch at home, followed by going to the Princeton Jewish Center for a late afternoon Talmud group. By the time it was over, it was four or five o'clock—dusk. And soon after that, time to separate the holy from the profane by reentering, through the Havdalah ceremony (the braided candle, spice, wine, and prayer ceremony to end Shabbat), the workaday world of the week ahead. Those were my ideal Sabbaths. There were just two of them in the first two years. Later, when I found a regular reading partner, I could attain this inner freedom and happiness twice a month.

There were other days that approached these special Sabbaths, especially when we opened our home for large or small groups to share lunch. The rest of the time in those first years, I erred and strayed, some-times in tiny ways, sometimes in large ways. Often I had to drive across town for my son's play dates or sports games or take his friends home when their parents could not collect them. Even on Yom Kippur after-noon, the most holy day of the year, I was not keeping holy time between two-thirty and three-thirty, when I might have been resting between services. I was driving to pick up my son from the house of our only non-observant Jewish friends, who graciously offered several years in a row to take him in for five hours. I had to bring him home to feed him an early supper so that he could attend the evening service with us, as he had the Kol Nidre service the night before. "Had to . . . I had to . . . did I have to?" I wondered aloud as I drove. "Was there really no other way?" "I don't know how they do it," my husband would say of our very observant friends. "I don't know how they are able to keep Shabbat so strictly." One thing I did learn quickly was that if you break a rule on Shabbat, it becomes not only easier to break others but also much easier not to keep rules week to week. In turn, if you keep rules on Shabbat, the best you can, it gets easier to keep them week to week. After a while the issue of "ease" becomes irrelevant.

Given different needs and routines in our family, I tried to divide up Shabbat for myself and think about it in manageable units, at least some of which I could observe. Friday night candles, prayers, and family din-ner. Torah study alone or with the family. Time with my son and my hus-band. Saturday morning services for three hours, sometimes with family and sometimes without. Often a Saturday afternoon discussion of the Torah portion with my husband after we had discussed it in services. Sometimes a study meeting on Talmud with a reading partner or in a group. Saturday early evening. It was a trial as to how long from Saturday services until dark I could last. Usually until about two or three in the afternoon.

Almost always my Sabbaths were imperfect, but better than none. And when I went to soccer practice instead of to services, trading off with my husband, I found myself missing services so much that I'd sing parts to myself the next day, as if my system had to have the tunes and words. I heard my husband doing the same thing on Sundays if he had missed

services. In a matter of a year, we were in as much need of Shabbat services as we were in need of going to the gym during the week. "Given
your situation, just try and do a little more each month," said my supervisor. "Just take it slowly. You have the rest of your life to improve. At
some other time in your life it will be easier to keep Shabbat as you'd
prefer." I nodded. Shabbat had begun to keep me.

Although the Sabbath is an island in time, untouched (whenever possible) by routine, daily business, it changes with the seasons and our locations in the world and the times in our lives. It is never exactly the same,
and this is one of its greatest joys. For me, Shabbat takes on a different
flavor through the year, depending on the calendar, the relationship of
light to darkness, and the Jewish holidays. A Shabbat near Yom Kippur,
for example, is highly serious, long, and introspective as the community
prepares individually and communally to repent during the penitential
season, whereas those near Purim go quickly and feel festive. Some
Sabbaths bring the children and grandchildren home; other Shabbats are
for celebrating the couple or the young family, for friends or the single
individual. Some are full of talk about the Torah portion and others are
not. Contrary to what I ever imagined, Shabbat is never dull.

Week to week, the membership at Friday evening or Saturday morning services changes. Those going to Torah to chant or receive an aliya
change. The readings change. The names of the sick change. The conversation during kiddush changes. The food and wine are different
from one Sabbath to the next; even the type and taste of the challah
changes. The level of commitment, the strength of song, and the blessings change. Sometimes the services lead to a social occasion at kiddush
for its own sake, a get-together that goes on and on, touched with good
feelings; sometimes the kiddush and sharing of food is quick, and people peel off to continue Shabbat alone or with others; sometimes the
social occasions are not so sharply divided from the services themselves, but an extension of them in a real sense. Every now and then
there is a large minyan occasion: a bar or bat mitzvah, a funeral, a circumcision or naming ceremony, a conversion ceremony, a group lunch-
eon, a lecture, a departure as members go abroad, or a return. One may

have intuitions about a Shabbat, but one never knows what it may become.

To be sure, Shabbat also changes every week with our readiness or unreadiness to receive her, and with our experiences of her. In summer Shabbat comes later and seems to last longer as we absorb every drop, like the sweet juice of a ripe berry, late into the evening. June bugs light the way in the garden. In October she lingers radiantly with the warm light and full colors and textures of fall. Golden leaves blanket the last summer geraniums and vinca. In December we make a trip to Friday night services as well and light more candles at home, getting closer to them, hoping they'll help carry us through spiritually as the winter deepens and we take the passage of Hanukkah. In spring, after reading Exodus for parts of January and February and March at morning services, Shabbats are crowned by the grandeur of new birth and the journey of Passover in the month of Nisan. They move toward it and recede from it, leading to Shavuot. Always, no matter the season, the smells of Shabbat—the fresh bread, the grape juice and wine, the dying flame of the candles in hot wax—fill the halls as we climb the stairs to bed.

The Shabbat rules, the thirty-nine categories of prohibitions, and their gift of reflection, peacefulness, and community stay the same over the months and years. So much else to do with Shabbat is subject to time's passage, however, that Shabbat is not just an island in time, if that means a separation from temporal or cyclical patterns, but also an intersection of timelessness and the timely. It is a meeting point of godliness and the human, of continuity and change.

For all the change I find in the institution and privilege of Shabbat, I have come to associate it in particular with a prayer, the Amidah, which reflects and continually reframes for me the personal struggle and sublimity of Shabbat. One might say that if the Sabbath is the high point of the Jewish week, so the Amidah is the high point of the Shabbat morning service. It is that moment when we are allowed a communal and then a private talk with God. The Amidah comes again in the Musaf, an additional service after the Torah service. It is not surprising

that we say this prayer one extra time, a fifth time, during all day services on the holiest day of the year, Yom Kippur, when we are communally closest to God.

One could talk about this differently. One could say, as did my supervisor, that the Sh'ma and the Amidah prayers are two points in an ellipse
and that the foundation of the Shacharit service rests on them as if on
pillars. Or, thinking of who speaks, one could say that the Sh'ma is the
word of God, while the Amidah is composed largely of our words to
God. There is thus a conversation between God and the Jews built into
the very structure of the morning service.

It is noteworthy that, as Reuven Hammer notes, in traditional Jewish
usage "prayer" and the Amidah are synonymous.[8] "Tefillah" always refers
to one specific prayer, which the rabbis called ha-tefillah, the Prayer, as
if all others pale by comparison. It is the prayer that falls into three
parts—three blessings on praise, sixteen blessings of petition, and three
blessings of thankfulness—although on Shabbat the petitions are omitted because Shabbat is a time to honor and thank God, not to make
requests.

The Amidah is the prayer with highly specific rules: it is said while
standing, facing Jerusalem, and not moving. One does not walk out in
the middle of it or stop to scratch one's nose; one does not shift or turn
around or sit. If my son forgets and interrupts me during the Amidah, I
feel conflicted, but I usually turn back to the beginning page and point
to the word "Amidah," and then he knows to wait.

The obligatory actions we perform before and while saying the
Amidah both heighten the importance of the occasion and sharply delin-
eate us as subservient. We move back three steps, step forward, bend the
knees and bow, as if we were subjects in the presence of a human king or
a master. And we remove ourselves at the end by stepping back and bow-
ing, not turning our back as we leave our Maker's presence. The rabbis
also decided that the Amidah must be said three times a day as well as on
the Sabbath and holy days—reflecting the times when sacrifices were
given at the Temple—and that the middle section, omitted on Shabbat,
is flexible.

The point, however, is that feeling as though one is in the presence of God is not easy to achieve. Like Shabbat, not only does this prayer have specific rules, but its purpose—speaking to God—also requires memory, effort, kavanah (focus), and renewal. This prayer demands paying attention and making the effort, physically and spiritually, to know before whom we stand.

"But what does it mean to stand?" I ask. Torah helps me understand a bit better. When we think of the Genesis stories in particular, of creation, of Adam and Eve, of Noah, of Abraham, of Jacob and Esau, of Joseph and his family, we may be struck by the horizontal nature of the human journey. In Genesis, we are given our first mitzvah: to increase by multiplying. Fertility leads to humans' spreading out in space and to their journey from place to place—to chronological and horizontal movement. We are born horizontal, and we die horizontal. I do not know whether Adam and Eve were created standing or lying down, but it is significant that the punishments they and the serpent receive in the Garden of Eden relate to the horizontal: experiencing death as dust to dust, bending down to toil on the land, lying down or squatting in the pain of childbirth, and, for the serpent, living on the ground. So we are born horizontal and die horizontal; between these moments, we walk upright. Those of us who bend, crawl, hobble, or get about in wheelchairs often wish we were walking upright. And yet to stand upright is not the same thing as to walk upright. To walk is to journey; to stand is to stop.

To stand is certainly not only to reach for the vertical and get closer to the Divine—to stand or reach upward—but it is also to stand apart, to stand out, to mark a separation. A midrash on creation, cited by Rashi, posits God's saying that if he creates man, wicked people will emerge, but if he does not create man, righteous people will not stand apart from the wicked. It is also clear in God's handling of very righteous bodies, such as those of Moses and Isaiah, who ascend vertically after death, that decomposition to dust is not required for those exceptionally worthy human beings who have stood apart. In Judaism we do not have heroes, yet some are rewarded for the way in which they have moved through time and stood.

The Amidah prayer, which takes us as close as we get to God on Shabbat by requiring us to stand up and even rise on our tiptoes, makes us stop in one place to think about our place and placement in the universe. The Amidah is a prayer of humility and thanks, but it is also a prayer of potential and yearning. It affirms aspiration, as Lawrence Hoffman puts it; it is a "conversation" with God about "what matters most in the grand scheme of things."[9] To rise and stand, to abstain and desist, to be stable and durable, to be permanent and enduring—these are the meanings of Amidah that Maimonides isolated from his knowledge of Torah for *The Guide of the Perplexed* I.13.[10] He explains that the last two meanings apply to God. We cannot be permanent and enduring in the sense of outlasting time or being eternal; we gave that up when we ate of the Tree of Knowledge and lost the Tree of Life, but we can try to be stable and durable in time.

The opening blessings of the Amidah serve not merely to praise but to prepare us for a personal encounter with God. Like other parts of the morning service, but here compactly, these blessings remind us of how Judaism understands God and a relationship to him. In the blessings, God is known in many ways. He may be felt intimately, as close by, or as beyond human thoughts and feelings. The blessings move in intensity from the God of creation, history, and redemption to the God of wonders and miracles and the God of awe. We move toward the concept of holiness as the essence of God. In other words, the prayer helps us make a mystical ascent, from chaos to time and timeliness to the holy, which is also signified in the Prayer of Holiness, the Kedushah, especially with the antiphonal section: "kadosh, kadosh, kadosh" (holy, holy, holy).

The final paragraph of the Amidah proper, which reminds us of the conclusion of the Temple service as well, recalls the Temple priests' blessing for the people who were about to depart. The blessing comes from the Book of Numbers 6:24–26 and evokes the essence of Shabbat: "The Lord bless you and keep you! The Lord make His face to shine upon you and be gracious unto you! The Lord lift up His countenance to you and grant you peace!" As we leave our most direct encounter with God in the morning service, the word we internalize last is shalom, peace.

The personal prayer included in the Amidah is also a petition for this greatest gift—wholeness and completeness within ourselves, in our relations to others, and in our relation to God and His world. We let God in, Martin Buber says, "only where we really stand, where we live, where we live a true life." Standing upright where we are during the Amidah, knowingly and feelingly, we reestablish a place for the Divine Presence in our lives.

PASSAGE 2

So God Turned Them

THOUGHTS ON BESHALACH,
EXODUS 13:17–17:16

It happened when Pharaoh sent out the people, God (Elohim) did not lead them by way of the land of the Philistines, although it was close; for God said, "The people may have a change of heart when they see war, and return to Egypt." So God turned the people [led the nation] by way of the wilderness at the Sea of Reeds. Now the Israelites went up armed out of the land of Egypt.

—EXODUS 13:17–18

The first time I led a Torah discussion in my worship group, I had chosen this passage from Exodus. Because I was still studying for conversion and felt nervous about my lack of background in Torah, I read commentaries, but I also relied on what I knew from training in literature—narrative structures—to think about the two roads out of Egypt as different ways of reading and two kinds of narrative structure: linearity and framing devices. Beshalach means "to send out," so two questions about the title and the first sentence interested me: *Who* sends out the Israelites, and into *what?* I knew that they are being sent literally toward a desert and Sinai. But into what else are they being sent? Moreover, I knew that on a historical level Pharaoh sent the Israelites out from Egypt, but what interested me was the religious level: God's sending them forth and leading them into some new state of being and toward a new commitment, not just into some new place.

In general, this parasha seemed to me to be about the replacement of man's history by God's time, the replacement of one kind of power (military) by another kind (spiritual), the replacement of one sovereign by another, the replacement of a state of slavery by one of freedom and redemption, and the replacement of God's miracles by reliance on God's voice and the written word.

The opening verses, reproduced in the epigraph, stress direction. However, the entire section is full of geography—roads, routes, and stops. Linearity is stressed in this panoramic epic movement of a people, and it is easy to follow the plot in a straightforward manner. Before the discussion, our family had just seen Steven Spielberg's *Prince of Egypt*, with the dramatic climax at the sea, and I could visualize this route through the wilderness. As I discovered, this first set of verses, concerning roads and direction, has received an enormous amount of commentary. Rashi, Maimonides, and Nachmanides all spend time on the opening paragraph. They debate what "nearer" or "close" means (close to Egypt, suggests Rashi; close to Israel, suggests Maimonides). Does "close" refer to geography or psychology? What does "armed" mean? What would it mean to go back to Egypt? To become slaves again, to seek protection as vassals, to be weak and lack courage? They question the reasons for going back to Egypt and the ramifications of such a return. They ask why "Elohim" is used to nominate God instead of "Adonai." Elohim is God in His personage as a strict dispenser of justice; it is also the general name of God that is known to all nations, including to Pharaoh, who gives them permission to leave.

Commentators puzzle over the meaning of "seeing war," and the *Mekhilta* of Rabbi Ishmael, a midrash on Exodus, also has a great deal to say about a putative prior leavetaking, some thirty years earlier, which had failed. Rabbi Ishmael makes the point that if Moses had led the people by the land of Philistines, they would undoubtedly have seen the bones of those who had died in that first exodus. Dispirited by the sight, they would have turned back to Egypt. The rabbis see the meaning of return as submission to the yoke of Egypt, and they repeatedly counsel, "One may not return to Egypt to live there, but one may return there for trade, for business, and for conquest" (Talmud, Sanhedrin 10). Modern commentators suggest that God's intention was not to spare the Israelites war but to lead them right into it, to force a sense of liberation and a victory song and add mental and emotional liberation to their physical liberation.

My own direction, after seeing the film twice and reading so much fascinating commentary, was to think about the meanings of "turned" and "change of heart," as these words relate to the whole parasha and to two ways in which we might read the material—reading routes, rather than just to the geographical or emotional issues suggested in the first few verses. God seems concerned more broadly in the opening with the effects of the route, both spiritually and geographically. The route is neither direct nor fast, but roundabout and difficult. Perhaps the verses are asking us to think about how the Israelites experience not only the road of leavetaking but also the road by which they will come into a new state of being when they are offered, at Sinai, the gift of becoming a "holy nation."

It seems that the roundabout route must ensure, not that the people will entirely escape war (they will confront Amalek at the end), but that God can bring them through miracles to a new conception of God and their duties. Indeed, He will use war to that end. The process involves leaving slavery and rebellion and moving into the state of freedom and faithfulness. The Israelites are being sent out by Pharaoh, but brought into a new mentality by God.

If the roads mentioned may also be thought of as reading roads—one teleological and straight, one roundabout—then we can travel the road to Sinai either linearly through the narrative or via the longer, roundabout route. The form of the book of Exodus drives it forward from slavery to freedom, from history to miracle, from individual to nation, from intercession through Moses to God's involvement in the building of the Tabernacle. Movement is always forward and upward. If we take the direct route through the parasha's structure, then crossing the Sea of Reeds is the climax, as it is in the Spielberg film and in many interpretations. We also then read an additive collection of amazing miracles, and we come away with a number of parallel situations as well: God appears in a cloud, water is significant, and there are two enemies: Egypt and Amalek.

But I chose in my discussion to stress the nonlinear or roundabout shaping of this parasha and a different central event. Reading through patterns other than linear or teleological reveals somewhat different emphases and leads to other conclusions. Looking at the structure in terms of frames or circles, we have an outer frame of two enemy army attacks and defeats. Notably, each army attacks from the rear, aiming for the weakest, most tired, and most vulnerable of the Israelites. It is as if to say such wars and sneak attacks on Israel are always possible. The Israelites show their faith in God by entering the sea and by following Moses' hand, maybe an ensign, during the daylong battle with Amalek. There is then an inner frame of two thirst and water miracles. At Marar the water becomes sweet and the people drink. At the rock Moses strikes and water flows. God takes care of His people, even when they whine and complain. The central event in this reading is the miracle of the manna and quails as God provides food.

This interpretive route finds support from Ibn Ezra, who remarks that the manna is arguably the greatest miracle of all.[1] For manna is food from heaven that is provided not once but every day for forty years! This beautiful and mysterious food appears overnight and can be gathered only during certain hours every day, after which it evaporates or dries up or otherwise disappears. Rashi compares manna to a coating of ice, a beautiful substance.[2] In addition, the miracle comes with the revelation of God's presence in a cloud. Manna links human time—daily existence—and God's time—eternity. It is the conjunction of the two as miracle and revelation.

What, I wondered, *would it have been like on the exodus?* I was on a journey myself when I first read Beshalach, returning from San Francisco via Dallas to Newark. Because of high winds on the East Coast, my family and I were delayed on a Texas runway for three hours.

The trip grew to twelve hours door to door, so journeying was on my mind. Inconvenience was on my mind. Obtaining food and water was on my mind. Getting out of where we were was on my mind. I could see this would be a long sit on the runway. So I hauled out the Torah and the commentary I had brought with me—packed precisely for such an eventuality. Might as well dig in! Both my husband and I had discussions coming up; I gave my husband a photocopy of his, and I started reading Beshalach.

I easily identified with the Israelites, who listen to all the rules about manna and then break them. In fact, I realized rather quickly that I would have failed God's manna test on day one. With my Girl Scout's mentality, I like to be prepared, as the carrying of the photocopies indicates. My cupboard is always well provisioned. So there I was, thinking about how I would have responded to all the rules and regulations about the manna: it's available only during certain hours; it's to be gathered every morning; only a certain amount can be gathered, no more or less; two portions can be gathered on Fridays, but no collecting on the Sabbath. I would surely go out there and collect a week's worth for my family anyway. I could just see myself serving boiled manna, manna cakes, leftover manna bits with veggies, manna on matzoh. To me, stocking up on manna would have been the right thing to do, the natural thing. But I would have failed the provisions test. Such a mentality and behavior would have been profoundly wrong.

I asked myself why. Why did God not permit planning ahead and leftovers? It seemed very unkind. Why get us up every day at dawn except on Shabbat? The miracle, I surmised, was supposed to teach me something. So I reviewed what the prior miracles had taught me and what I, as an Israelite, have learned but still not internalized. I have learned that God rescues us from slavery, that God rescues us from enemies, that God can light the dark, that He can split a sea, that He can provide nourishment, and that He can be present in the desert. But what I and the other Israelites do not know is anything about His constancy or ours to Him. We know how to serve Pharaoh, but not how to be obedient or grateful to God. No longer slaves, we do not know what to do every day, nor do we understand that God can provide, every day. Maybe God insists on *daily* collection of His gift, the gift of nurturance and survival, to teach faith, gratitude, and the importance of ritual, observant action. He seems interested in leading us not only to a geographical place of freedom but also to a change of heart and an awareness of relationship or partnership with Him. I know about God's tests, but this seems to be asking a great deal. Here faith is structured and ordered but not to be taken for granted. How, then, does God ensure that faith is renewed but not thoughtlessly so?

Two details suggest that God is taking the Israelites from here into a faith that keeps manna collecting alive but *un*routine. One of the commentaries suggests that the word *manna* is related to a question the people asked when they first saw the fine and flaky substance, as delicate as frost on the ground: *Man hu?* What is it? What is it called? Gunther Plaut explains that this is a popular etymology, assuming that *man* (not *mah*) could mean "what," though it has no precedent in Hebrew.[3] Later Torah records what it is like: "The House of Israel named it manna; it was like coriander seed, white, and it tasted like wafers in honey" (Exodus 16.31). It is *like* coriander seed, it tastes like something we have eaten before, but what it is remains unclear. We are left to question the inscrutability of God, the why of events and the what of elements. We are left, in other words, wrestling with ultimate questions.

Despite the simile, Torah treats manna not as a natural phenomenon, available only when there is rain in western Sinai (which is how it has been historically explained), but as lechem shamayim, the bread of heaven, a gift of God, a miracle, a reminder to the people of God's constant caring for them. It must remain a mystery, not a thing. As Plaut and others have noted—and as came up in discussion of the passage in our minyan—the manna miracle connects the creation of the nation Israel with the creation of the world in Genesis. In Eden, Adam and Eve are given food without toil, then are punished with labor (toil and childbearing) after being driven out of the garden. Forever after, people have to earn their food by labor—except for the forty years of manna. Here, then, is a second Eden in a post-Edenic world. Manna continues the story of matzoh by supplementing and replacing the food of slavery and redemption with the food of creation and sustenance. On the one hand, God provides—and

Beshalach records—the restoration of a pure relationship, if a different one, between God and man. God feeds the Israelites, in this view, until their creation as a people is complete. On the other hand, God makes them get up every day but one to collect the manna. They are made to adhere to a routine and to take responsibility for the gathering of the miracle. God's gift connects time, timeliness, and timelessness. The manna is collected in a timely fashion; it lasts only a certain time; it connects us to eternal favor. But we have to *think* about it every day.

Shabbat, a day of rest from creation, is a day of worship and responsibility and the only day we do not labor to collect manna. Shabbat itself is the nourishment instead. In the minyan discussion, there was much debate over the issue of labor and this post-Edenic story—precisely over whether labor is required at all in collecting manna and how the Eden and post-Eden stories are alike or different. My view is that Beshalach is very much concerned with kinds of labor—physical, mental, spiritual— and that as it documents a redemption from slavery it also redefines structures of labor. The effort one must make is not so much the effort of tilling the earth or building it up as it is the effort of thinking and being receptive.

The second detail that piques my interest is God's saying to Moses in Exodus 17.14: "Write this." Even as Moses's role as a miracle maker will be superseded soon enough by his roles as lawgiver and teacher, so too God no longer offers His laws in terms of "signs" (as in Genesis with regard to tefillin, circumcision, and Shabbat). The people hear God's voice at Sinai: "And God spoke all these words" (Exodus 20:1, 19:4–6). Even before Sinai, God has the Israelites moving into a written Torah, but also into that which keeps Torah alive: questions (What is it?), debate, and text to be interpreted and reread. He does not just institute faith and constancy in Beshalach, teaching a way to be through manna collection, but seals His relationship with the gift of Shabbat and establishes the importance of memory, recording, and text for reinterpretation, all as ways to continue the act of creation and re-creation through time.

In the chapters concerning God's revelation to the people, the word *devarim* is frequently used to mean "speech" or "words." Later, Moses reminds the people: "God spoke to you out of fire. You heard the sound of words; you saw no image, nothing but a voice" (Deuteronomy 4:12). The response to that sound is the victorious Song of the Sea and the dance and joyous music of Miriam and the other women. It seems that Beshalach inaugurates the important journey of God's turning the Israelites to the word and into the word.

Chapter Three

GOD, WOMEN, AND GENDER

❧

*With regard to women, Torah does not say No to the practices
of the world as they are found in actuality; here alone
Torah confirms the world, denying the meaning of its own
Covenant.*

—CYNTHIA OZICK,
"NOTES TOWARD FINDING THE RIGHT QUESTION"

*We can not impose a monistic frame upon this material and
assume that all the Jews of antiquity, most of whom knew no
Hebrew and had no contacts with Palestine, adhered to the
rabbinic piety which was being codified in the Talmudim and
later works. . . . However, as Conservative Jews loyal to rabbinic Judaism, we must justify our decisions by appeal to
sources within the rabbinic tradition.*

—SHAYE J. D. COHEN,
"WOMEN IN THE SYNAGOGUES OF ANTIQUITY"

The status of women within Judaism, in law, practice, and in representations, is an issue that has energized and divided men
from women, women from themselves, men from each other,
rabbinic authorities, the various movements within the religion, and
male and female feminists at certain historical moments in the last twenty centuries. The above epigraphs, one by a learned woman and one by
a learned man, illustrate just one such division. Cynthia Ozick takes on
Torah and the rabbinic legal tradition from a position of moral outrage.
Her devotion to social justice and equality overrides what she perceives
as the absence or unequal position of women sanctioned and sometimes
promoted by Torah and the laws of Talmud.[1] Professor Shaye J. D.
Cohen acknowledges the archaeological evidence of women's participa-

tion in some ancient synagogues and distinguishes such Jewish practices from the later codified rabbinic laws that more narrowly circumscribe women's roles, but he remains loyal to rabbinic tradition.

Specifically, Cohen argues that evidence of the high status of a small number of women leaders in ancient synagogues does not constitute a precedent for admitting women to the Conservative rabbinate. His argument against using this particular archaeological and historical evidence in a debate about contemporary seminary admissions is, I believe, correct.[2] At the same time, the delays of the Conservative movement in admitting women to the rabbinate were, as I see it, highly unfortunate.

Still, Cohen's comments are very important for other reasons. He presupposes that halakhah and mitzvot (law and sacred commandments), as instituted in the Torah, including Talmud, take precedence over ancient practices of greater equality for women, which were not supported by ancient Jewish law, and over modern practices of social inequality. In other words, for Cohen, religious law overrides social practices or historical precedent in this instance and possibly in other instances. He would, I suspect, demand a very thorough analysis of modern issues in light of ancient laws—for example, an analysis according to conservative (in its nondenominational sense) hermeneutic and legal methods used by the Committee on Jewish Law and Standards of the Rabbinical Assembly.

Despite their differing institutional and personal locations and political and social agendas, Ozick and Cohen are paired here to raise some important questions. What is the relationship between religious law and social change? Between ancient practices and modern times? What is the status of sacred books among Jews in a post-Holocaust, post-Zionist, postsecular moment? Another important issue is the relationship between two revolutions: the shift from a sacrificial Temple cult to a book-centered religion, based on oral and written Torah, during the Yavneh period (73–132 C.E.), on the one hand, and the development and spread of post-Enlightenment feminisms, on the other.[3]

Both Ozick and Cohen speak to me directly, representing well the passion and the reasonable caution I feel with regard to how we go about changing the legal status of women, with how and why we go about rereading Torah, with how and why we alter or adapt halakhah for modern times. The debate bothers me, even tortures me. At bottom, however, I think we need to rethink, both communally and individually, the relations among law, modernity, social change, and justice and reconsider how far we are willing to go ethically as Jews to repair the modern world. Ethics and repair are not divorced from law in Judaism, nor are multiple interpretations; indeed, they are the backbone of the religion.[4] Yet, if we are to act on central issues of equality and justice for all people, are there not reasonable limits to how far we can go as a group of men and women to honor Torah to the letter? Could we not honor the spirit of Torah, when the letter leads to severe exclusivity and rigidity? Which is the dynamic element in halakhah—legality or the spirit behind the laws? Holiness is no more achieved by a technical compliance with halakhot, by strict observance, than righteousness is achieved by asceticism within Judaism. It can be argued that forms of excessiveness, including rigidity with regard to the letter of the law, inflict more spiritual damage than lapses in observance.

This question is not just religious. It is broadly sociological and therefore transcends in importance the local rabbinic domain, where the rabbi, in consultation with his or her congregation, establishes practices of equality; those practices may then be rescinded by the next rabbi of that congregation. I am not suggesting that we should ignore the ebb and flow of congregational opinion or of rabbinic appointments, but I do believe that human equality is simply too important to be left to the vicissitudes of local decisions.

In contrast to the Orthodox or Reform approaches to halakhah, the Conservative movement has stressed the need to conserve Jewish law but has also recognized that halakhah has changed and developed over time in response to historical and social circumstances.[5] Significantly, the Conservative movement changed the name of its law committee to the Committee on Jewish Law and Standards in order to recognize that law can be equated with standards and not rigid formulas for behavioral practices. Standards are gradational norms that we try to meet, not external forms or legislations.

Nevertheless, as thirty-five years of debates from the Conservative movement's Rabbinical Assembly show, rabbis are divided about the limits and possibilities of the halakhic process (how to handle Jewish law). In particular, they question the degree to which ethics should govern law. They are divided over whether or not halakhah can be altered and adapted, and over who can authorize change, whether the Committee on Jewish Law and Standards, local rabbis, or the assembly. For sixty years they have disagreed about the irreconcilability of an ancient covenantal tradition of mitzvot and a modern Western philosophy and tradition of law mandating individual rights.[6] It is unlikely that such divisions will be easily healed or even breached, particularly when they are lauded as a tolerance for diversity of opinion.

Meanwhile, we need and want more advances on social issues from progressive, visionary, and courageous leaders within the Conservative Rabbinical Assembly, from leaders within the new Orthodox movement, and from laypersons through national and international meetings of Jews from all walks of life and movements in the religion. Besides further education in Talmud and Torah, we need ideological, theological, intellectual debate so that we may inform ourselves better about adapting or changing halakhah, especially on issues pertaining to bioethics, sexual orientation, and gender. The Conservative movement has not yet resolved critical issues relating to the family and to women; patrilineal descent; the status of homosexuals; egalitarian language in marriage contracts, ceremonies, and liturgy; women on the bet din; divorce; and equal participation of women in all synagogue ritual. Yet much of the debate of such issues that we read in journals and newspapers remains woefully popular, intellectually thin, or religiously uninformed. There are hundreds and thousands of us eager to study and learn more, to think, to argue, and to work for social justice. Who will lead us?

The questions raised here have been the most wrenching ones for me, and this chapter has taken the longest time to write, aware as I am of the complex difficulty of reconciling contemporary ideals of social justice with ancient Jewish laws, or even of reconciling passages of Torah with each other. Yet it would be profoundly irresponsible of me as a woman and a convert, but also as a human being and a Jew, to ignore the position of women in Judaism or to fall silent rather than discuss the kinds of further change that are possible.

Women in the Jewish community supported my conversion desires from the start, and I came to depend on them for inspiration and support. They invited me to reading groups, to schmooze sessions, to lunch. They explained the Havdalah ceremony, gave me Passover recipes from their grandmothers and mothers, and taught me to sing the blessings over Torah. I loved their warmth. But they weren't easy on me, either. Especially the feminists and social justice activists. "How can you embrace such a brutal, cruel, and patriarchal religion?" some asked. I wondered if this was a test. "Are you aware that every interpretation of Torah supporting its holiness is just supporting the holiness of men by men and for men?" I wasn't sure—wasn't interpretation open within certain limits? "Do you get it?" "Do you see," they persisted, "that the relations between men and women in Judaism are totally distorted?" "The treatment of women in Judaism," said a smart writer in her thirties, a Conservative cantor's daughter, "is the reason I left the religion."

I listened carefully. One day one of my close Jewish friends did her duty by me. She sat me down and handed me a list of references from Torah she had written out for us in her spidery handwriting. Part English, part Hebrew. Part names, part numerals. It was a windy, sunny afternoon. Through the windows I could see ochre and red leaves falling and imagine them gathering on the ground in layers. "Here's the Tanakh," she said, handing over a book. "Look up the passages and read them aloud. You won't get this in your tutorials." Murder, rape, humiliation of women. She'd found the most offensive and denigrating passages on women available in the Hebrew Bible. There were more than just a few, recounting far more than just a few tales of terror. We sat together working on this project a long time. She watched me look them up and listened to me read them out. She asked me to read and confirm every book, chapter, and verse. "I just want you to be minimally educated in Torah's brutality," she said.

I listened just as carefully to women who do not object to such parts of Torah. These women prefer *not* to assume equal roles within Judaism, which I see as a totally valid personal and religious choice, though it isn't mine. Later, when I sat apart from men at an Orthodox bar mitzvah and did not participate equally, the experience was not wholly undesirable to me either. I could see pros and cons.

Still, before I converted, it was difficult to hear about women's humanity being stripped from them by men bound by tradition; women who say blessings over Torah, I was told, are like apes. I read about the women pushed away from the Wailing Wall and the women who have read Torah defiantly in public in Jerusalem. Yes, I did feel this scandal within Judaism, as Ozick refers to it, and it increasingly became deeply painful to me as an issue of social justice. Judaism was itself not flawed. Its institutionalization was. What we had done to it, how we had read it, why we had taken the letter and not enough of the spirit, and how we had misread it—all this I saw as terribly, painfully wrong.

Is Torah at fault? In fact, although oral and written Torah are seen as a continuum to be read as universal truths apart from historical and cultural locations, I treat the Pentateuch as far more open and multifaceted than many more traditional readers apparently do, and I view rabbinic oral Torah and medieval commentary not only as coming out of particular historical circumstances and agendas but also as helping to shape particular historical circumstances. Torah does not include guidelines on how it is to be read. Rather, it challenges us to figure out how to read it. It is our task to reaffirm Torah's covenant by continuing to interpret Torah in our times and for the future.

In this chapter, I tell of my preconversion encounters and temporary reconciliations with these issues and my conflictual postconversion relationship with issues of social justice within Judaism. I then review some of the important feminist interventions by both women and men in our readings of Torah, including the biblical Pentateuch and rabbinic Talmud, and I make suggestions about how to advance social change while keeping the covenant. To do so, I will also have to take a stand on what I believe to be the essence of Torah, itself the subject of rabbinic debate.

About eight weeks after conversion—pious, Torah-loving, so wanting to be a good girl, a Jewish mother, a Jewish wife, a nurturing friend, a strong teacher—I was being called to say the blessing or to roll, tie, and cover Torah at least twice a month in the small, egalitarian worship group I attended. I was completely in love with Judaism. Every morning I woke up filled with pleasure at being a Jew. It took two idyllic months— an experience akin to what I imagine the best moments of narcissistic infancy must have felt like—before I discarded my preconversion accommodations and confronted the irreconcilable contradictions I was living in my new position as a Jewish woman.

Like many before me, I had initially sought a new identity that was conflict-free. "Identity," as Trinh T. Minh-ha has written, "has long been a notion that relies on the concept of an essential, authentic core. The search for an identity is, therefore, usually a search for that lost, pure, true, real, genuine, original, authentic self, often situated within a process of elimination of all that is considered other."[7] If passing is about trying to appear as someone of higher prestige or someone who better fits the norms, I'd reversed this entire notion for the eighteen years I'd lived in a Jewish family. Observant Jews are considered marginal in our culture, and many consider Jews worthy of othering. Moreover, our numbers are certainly modest compared with those of the other major world religions. But I had imbued Judaism with a kind of prestige it did not hold in my WASP circles, and, as Trinh T. Minh-ha suggests, I began to see Jewishness as my original, authentic self. From one partial psychological point of view, I had become the other, but merely by changing the location of my authenticity from Christianity to Judaism, from WASP to Semite.

This erasure of conflict through simple replacement, I discovered, would not work. My identity as a Jew, as I saw, was not only far from whole but also riven with contradictions: my feminism and my deep love of Torah; my sex and gender; my observance and my tolerance of others' non-observance; my strong belief in upholding traditions and my belief in questioning legalisms; my small acquaintance with Eastern European and Sephardic cultural Judaisms (which I loved nonetheless) and my post-Holocaust, postmodern historical location; my ability to lead and my ingrained desire to follow; my belief in the centrality of teshuvah (turning in repentance) and tikkun olam (repair of the world) and the dignity and equality of each human being; my ideals and my failures to

act on them; my faith in a supremely caring but also strict and just God—
all these contradictions landed me smack in the middle of conflicted loyalties and responsibilities, with no easy way out.

Friends and strangers have asked me why the status of women was not
more of a problem for me during the two-year conversion process. In
spite of my desire for unproblematic wholeness of identity, I knew this
issue needed some kind of resolution before I converted. At some point
in my study I was sharply attuned to such problems, and I reconciled
myself to them through one line of mainstream feminism, which was one
of various options.[8] I might have been persuaded by the hermeneutics of
recuperation, which is a first-wave (circa 1970s) feminist reclamation of
female images and stories in the Hebrew Bible. I therefore could have
focused my fears and desires on heroic pictures and narratives of women
in Torah—Deborah the judge, say, or Hannah, who teaches us how to
pray—to prove to myself that powerful and spiritual women were present in Torah as role models. I did not take that route, though I admit that
I tried. I bought the picture book on famous women from the Hebrew
Bible, which highlights their admirable traits and contributions and features artworks that depict them as beauty queens. This approach forti-
fied me only briefly. The scandal of oppression remained.

   This method is not a form of critique but a celebration of individuals.
It essentializes women cross-culturally, historically, and socially and
ignores the historical embeddedness of power relations, gender and sex
ideologies, ethnic difference, and other systemic social inequalities. It is
an important political move within religion by women, because it
attempts to rewrite the tradition from a female point of view while keeping that tradition, and it can be used to carve out models of religious
leadership within institutions. But it was not my move.

   So too I might have eased my mind by reading Torah symptomologi-
cally, that is, focusing on women's absence and the unraveling effect on
the text of their absence. This reading can be seen as a Marxist-inspired
form of ideological criticism linked to a womanist-centered deconstructive critique of Torah. Here is a set of questions, for instance, that a visiting Conservative rabbinical student offered our worship group one

Shabbat when he led a discussion on the Akedah, the binding of Isaac from Genesis: Where is Sarah when Abraham, assuming he will sacrifice their son, takes Isaac up Mount Moriah, and what do you think she feels? How would you have felt? What would you have said to your husband if he had done such a thing? What caused Sarah's death? This was a politically correct approach by a seminary student sensitive to women's issues. Yet, as an English professor who teaches narrative and feminism, I found this tack to be as essentializing, loaded, and perversely wrongheaded as the first, which just celebrates women's achievements. It seemed to me to violate the text by treating gaps solely as empty places to be filled with personal feelings and fictions. I was reminded of that mode of criticism that wants to investigate how many children Lady Macbeth must have had.

This is modern midrash, but it is not congenial to me in its handling of Torah. It does not bother me because it diagonally and rather surreptitiously calls into question biblical authority or because it emerges from a midrashic impulse. It bothers me because it essentializes women and because it becomes equally one-sided in its attempt to see the "other" side of the event as if there were two. Just as it reads gaps monochromatically, it does not attempt more than one kind of interpretation of absence: Sarah must be left out because she is considered inferior, her husband excludes her, God excludes her, and it is our job to give her sympathy and a voice. Nor does this critical view focus on the other absences in the text or on the ways in which these absences might be connected: Isaac does not go with his father down the mountain, and God is not present in this narrative at the end, except by implication when he sends an angel as intermediary.

To deepen his point, the speaker might at least have ventured, with Alicia Ostriker, into the concept of permanent absence in the next parasha, which involves Abraham's arrangement for Sarah's burial in a cave "out of sight" or "away from my presence" (the cave at Machpelah in which the patriarchs of Genesis are buried).[9] This narrative of negotiation for a burial place immediately follows the Akedah. Ostriker, who is sensitive to multiple reading strategies, interprets Sarah's elimination from Abraham's presence as equivalent to the elimination of maternal power, a critical stage in the development of monotheism. She suggests that the absence of maternal power is the *condition and consequence* of the male covenant. She then locates her interpretation in relationship to the medieval midrash that explains Sarah's death as caused by the Akedah. Ostriker's formal and interpretive analysis of important verses in Genesis evokes work done by other feminists on the relationship between monotheism and goddess cults or religions including goddesses. I do not agree with this reading either, but I also don't know enough history of religion and archaeology to dismiss it. In any case, I find it far more interesting as an example of feminist critique than being asked to identify with Sarah's feelings.

Why else might Sarah be absent? How else could we think Torah on this issue? Since her absence is blatant, perhaps we are asked, through an internal Torah critique, to wonder why women are not tested on mountaintops in the presence of angels. Perhaps we are invited to see that even at one of the founding moments of Jewish identity, there are problems within the system of earthly responsibility and power. Perhaps Sarah's absence is a reaffirmation of the traditions that place women at home to bear and raise children but restrict their duties in the public realm. Or perhaps her absence and silence is to be read as an internal critique of Abraham's monomaniacal devotion to God. There are examples of Torah's critiquing excessively rigid patriarchal positions through the figures of women.

I do not endorse whitewashing Abraham or the foundation of the covenant on father-son relations, by any means; nor do I, however, endorse whitewashing Sarah or Israelite social relations. I encourage multiple views. I warm to the rabbinic statement that each passage in Torah has many "faces" or meanings, because as a postmodern (but also as a Jew!), I read for multiplicity and debate, not monologically. As Mieke Bal and other postmodern narrative theorists show, any interpretation of a text that claims completeness or truth or purity is to be suspected of an analytics of domination. As such, it would be distinctively un-Jewish, since Judaism promotes an exegesis of dialectic and debate, of questions leading to new understandings and to more questions. Indeed, this is the fundamental mode of rabbinic commentary and should be the mode of modern analysis as well.

Thus, I take the Akedah as a highly complex narrative about different kinds of faith, with multiple viewpoints that comment on each other. The feminist tack that searches out women's absent experiences does not teach me anything, raise my consciousness, challenge or increase my faith, tell me what to do with a Judaism that takes this narrative as central to its identity, or lead me in the direction of social change. In short, the critical agenda of simple "identification" with women holds little for me, though I appreciate the strategic value of opening up gaps, silences, and absences.

The wider-reaching version in Jewish studies of this mode of interpretation, which I did not study until after my conversion, retrieves the silenced lives and recorded historical experiences of women in biblical or rabbinic times. This version of feminism is thus related to the recuperative hermeneutical move and to a deconstructive move, but it is grounded sociologically and historically as an act of reconstruction that aims to set the record straight by uncovering more factual evidence. The studies of Carol Myers and Bernadette Brooten on ancient women, including those who were leaders in synagogues, fall into this category.[10] Their work and that of others illustrate the partiality of the historical record, question the agendas of history writing, and seek to restore a fuller view of the traditions. It tests biblical texts against social practices. This method, akin to the opening of the literature canon inaugurated in the 1970s by critics like Elaine Showalter and Ellen Moers in women's studies and literature, might have been congenial to me had I known more about it. It would have allowed me to take the next step to question the historical record, the text of Torah, and modern adherence to rabbinic halakhah—and more fundamentally, to question the relationships of these nodal points in Judaisms, so largely constructed, written, and controlled by men.

I took a third, common, feminist way. Before conversion day, I reconciled myself to the status of women within Judaism by accepting that men have written and reinterpreted Torah (and Talmud) in different and changing cultures and historical moments and that men have controlled the religious institutions, but that Jewish legal history has been rewritten to increase the rights of the oppressed. At that time I was studying the rabbinic interpretations of Torah and their institution of halakhah more than the many faces of Torah or the silences of history itself. I under-stood that rabbinic interpretations after the destruction of the Temple and the end of the sacrificial cult late in the first century were made in a quest for dominance and authority, at a critical time when Judaisms were in contention with each other and with Gnostic sects. It was a time when Judaisms were under threat of extinction. These rabbinic interpretations and their agenda of authority-building have importantly shaped modern Judaisms and continue to shape different aspects of them.

In focusing my attention on the development and changes within rabbinic writings, I was also hoping to find at least a broadening of legal rights for women. A Jewish patriarchal institution of any era, defined by what the political theorist of modernity Carole Pateman calls "the sexual contract," seemed unlikely to me to offer *equality* for women under any name.[11] I was a realist. Jewish patriarchal institutions seemed to me more rigid in the highly limiting roles they carve out for women in the religion and in society than those of other institutions—say Christian ones. Nevertheless, even though I did not expect to find legal equality, I hoped that rabbinic literature would offer an increas-ing consciousness about the lesser position of women and a will to change that position.

Since one can find, within thirty or more years of Jewish studies, almost any argument one wants to find, I was not surprised when I locat-ed what I came to think of as the historical broadening of the women's rights position, a stance taken and "proved" to varying degrees, with varying feminist and religious agendas and with very different emphases by Conservative, Orthodox, and Reform Jewish thinkers, such as Rachel Biale, Judith Hauptman, Blu Greenberg, and Rachel Adler.[12] While preparing for conversion, I read selectively in the work of those scholars, and chance led me to focus most on the work of Hauptman.

The feminist-Talmudic scholar at the Jewish Theological Seminary, Judith Hauptman, following Biale and others, argued in the 1980s and 1990s that some rabbinic authorities actually did increase women's rights within halakhah over time. "The Rabbis," Hauptman wrote in 1998,

upheld patriarchy as the preordained mode of social organization, as dictated by the Torah. They neither achieved equality for women nor even sought it. But of critical importance, they began to introduce numerous, significant, and occasionally bold corrective measures to ameliorate the lot of women. In some cases, they eliminated abusive behaviors that had developed over time. In others they broke new ground, granting women benefits that they never had before, even at men's expense. In almost every key area of law affecting women, the rabbis introduced significant changes for the better.[13]

This observation, grounded in Hauptman's extensive research, provided enough consolation for me to get to conversion day.

One example of this kind of encouragement was the rabbinic change concerning divorce cited by Hauptman. This change increases protection for women and children. We find a ruling by Rabbi Gamliel the Elder in the Talmud M. Gittin 4.2: A man can no longer cancel a get (a bill of divorce) already granted by a bet din (a court of law), without informing his wife of such a cancellation. He thus cannot void his ex-wife's second marriage and make her children from a second union illegitimate. The point of such a legal change, as Hauptman notes, is to make the man more responsible to the woman, to make the husband think twice before issuing an invalid get or canceling one, and to safeguard her freedom to remarry. One can applaud such legal changes. Nevertheless, the woman, the object of the get delivery, remains inferior.

As so many feminists argue, the major source of female oppression is the male othering of women. It is instructive to take a textual example from Talmud to see this process at work in a representation of an intellectual woman. The ancient world, we find, may well have offered at least limited opportunities for the expression of the female intellect by letting women head synagogues and learn Torah, but the ancient Jewish religious worldview could not offer emancipation of the female intellect. Nor could there be a widely advertised or recorded acceptance of women's leadership or intellectual accomplishments. Indeed, when a woman's intellectual authority was accorded honor, the tradition normally worked to erase or diminish that reputation.

A case in point is that of Beruriah, a scholar, and reputedly the wife of Rabbi Meir. Tal Ilan, in her brilliant summary and analysis of the

Beruriah materials, demonstrates that as the redaction of the Mishnah continued into the Gemara, and into medieval commentary, the role and representation of women, if not their rights, were often circumscribed even further. In light of Hauptman's argument, this constriction is illuminating and important. Ilan makes this argument with reference to Beruriah because she alone of the prominent modern commentators (David Goodblatt, Rachel Adler, and Daniel Boyarin) on this figure views Beruriah as a historical figure about whom legends later grew up. The others either do not make this claim or see her as primarily a legendary figure.[14]

Although Beruriah is the most prominent woman mentioned in rabbinic literature, the critics tell us, she is not referred to in the Mishnah; a ruling attributed to her, however, is repeated there. As Ilan reports, Beruriah is named once in the Palestinian text of ritual law, the Tosefta: "A *claustra*—R. Tarfon declares it impure, but the sages declare it pure. And Beruriah says, one removes it from this door and hangs it on another. On the Sabbath these matters were related to R. Yehoshua. He said, Beruriah said well" (T. Kelim Bava Metzia 1:6). Thereafter, she appears named in the Babylonian Talmud (B. Berkhot 10a, B. Eruvin 53b, B. Pesachim 62b, B. Avodah Zarah 18a). Thus, for instance, we find her portrayed in Pesahim as having learned three hundred ritual laws in one day from three hundred rabbis. And yet sadly, as Boyarin notes, her appearance in medieval commentary is negative in what can only be described as a misogynistic narrative. The brilliant and highly regarded eleventh-century commentator Rashi offers this view of her reputed seduction and suicide:

> Once Beruriah made fun of the rabbinic dictum, "Women are light-headed [licentious]." He [Rabbi Meir, her husband] said, "On your life! You will end up admitting that they are right." He commanded one of his students to tempt her into transgression. The student importuned her for many days, until in the end she agreed. When the matter became known to her, she strangled herself, and Rabbi Meir ran away because of the shame. (Rashi on the Babylonian Talmud, Avoda Zarah 18b)

Scholars who have written on Beruriah have wrestled with the interpretation and dating of the "Beruriah traditions." Is she a legend or is she real? Might she be a historical figure overlaid with legend? Rachel Adler asks: If Beruriah is a legend, who would have invented her, and why in the form of a woman?[15] How we interpret Beruriah matters, but how we interpret the rabbis also matters. For the male-authored tradition explores, with the figure of Beruriah, the highly problematic nature of woman: her intelligence, her virtue, and her authority in relation to men. Why do we have a Beruriah story at all? And what are we to make of the variations in her representation? Why, as Cynthia Ozick wonders, does she come to us as a bluestocking *and* reinterpreted in another tradition as licentious?

Even though they instituted correctives that worked to increase the rights of women, the rabbis appear fundamentally, indisputably sexist. Rachel Adler believes so. Her feminist interpretation reads Beruriah as representing extreme male ambivalence about woman. Women clearly threaten male study partners and male rabbis because their sexuality is in some sense constructed as something that cannot be controlled. It seems that, when they are in touch with such female excess, men are led astray from the proper study of Torah. There is no suggestion in the rabbinic tradition, however, that women might be led astray from the proper study of Torah if exposed to a male study partner. Nor is there a suggestion that men fear their own powerful sexuality, not that of the woman, as an impediment to study and project that fear onto her.

In an interesting reading, Daniel Boyarin sees Beruriah as a "cultural fantasy" concerning Torah study.[16] He looks at differences among the sources to find the various readings of the signifier woman. In the Palestinian Tosefta, he finds no repugnance at a woman's studying and no suggestion that her love of learning might in any way be wrong. In the later traditions in Babylon, he finds a developing connection between sexual immorality and female learning, as if the male homosocial study partnerships cannot accommodate a female partner (Adler's point). He believes that the tradition both acknowledges and denies female access to Torah study, which we know some women had engaged in during the rabbinic period.

Still the ambivalence about women is not restricted to the reading partnership with a male rabbi, as Boyarin notes. Even worse, woman's presence is considered to interrupt the erotic connection of each male student with his female lover, which is Torah. Are we to understand, then, that, at the least, female intellectuality is to be firmly discouraged? Apparently so. Boyarin argues that the Beruriah materials support the specific point of Rabbi Eliezer that "anyone who teaches his daughter Torah, teaches her lasciviousness," as understood in the Babylonian Talmud. Thus, Beruriah's fall into licentiousness, as portrayed by Rashi, is a narrative necessity. Otherwise, it would be a refutation of R. Eliezer. Indeed, the intolerance of a learned woman is so extreme that her husband must be shamed as well.

Boyarin goes on to develop a case that Rashi's narrative is no fluke but rather follows from analogous stories in the Babylonian Talmud about Beruriah's sister, who was a prostitute. Tal Ilan, by contrast, suggests that many additional legends of Beruriah were transmitted but now are lost, between the Babylonian Talmud stories and that of Rashi.[17] Whichever interpretation one chooses, it seems probable that women are confined to the procreative role in rabbinic Judaism, not only because of a male discomfort about sexuality (male or female), but also because that valued resource needed to be reserved for the home. Moreover, both women and Torah are highly valued, but they need to be kept apart, one for physical procreation and one for spiritual growth. Thus, rabbinic culture—and certainly that culture within Babylonian culture—enforced separate spheres for women and (feminized) Torah and separate responsibilities and access for women and men. Any women learning Torah as study partners with men would have been exceptions.

After conversion, I was moved to reconsider my position about rabbinic changes that increased the rights of women, the representation of women, and a feminist defense of that position. Encountering Cynthia Ozick's 1970s attack on such a feminism stopped me in my tracks: The defense of the *leniency* of tyranny honors injustice nevertheless, she argues. It is not good enough that the ancient rabbis were not as bad as they could have been, not as oppressive as we thought they were. Thus, while Hauptman's type of argument carefully modifies our sense that the rabbis always worked from a position of patriarchal misogyny (which they often seemed to do), and while discussions of Beruriah point to a cultural ambivalence toward women who exceed the roles carved out for them in Judaism, not total gynophobia, one must still beware the seductiveness of this feminism's consolatory power and the limited reach of its political agenda. The basic system was still unjust toward women and in many ways remains so.

Judaism did not immediately welcome the challenges of feminism, yet it now houses a varied and vital feminist movement. The historical intersections of feminism with Jewish studies are not easily separable from the sequential analytic moves in the history of modern feminism generally (the phases have been: recuperative, historical reconstruction, questioning-deconstructive, critique of systems of domination and ideological agendas, identity politics, global). I would like to address two of the many varied issues within Jewish feminism and gender critique and locate myself in these debates as a new convert. Two key sites held up by different feminists for critique and change are the adaptation of halakhah (law) and social practice and the interpretation of Torah in the light of modern social history.[18]

It is worth raising again the now-classic debate between Cynthia Ozick and Judith Plaskow over how to identify the problem of the oppression of women within Judaism, if only because a number of thinkers come down on one side or the other, seeing the issue of oppression through either a sociological or a theological explanation, when in fact such explanations must be connected. To summarize, Ozick begins by asking how we can include in Jewish thought an adumbration of divinity as also female, nodding to those women's groups that seek to reestablish a female-centered theology. She concludes that such a move challenges monotheism and that the status of women for Judaism must be understood through a sociological lens, not a theological lens. She notes correctly that Judaism does not have a theology.

In turning to the sociological explanation, instead of the theological, Ozick implies that the honor of the community—that is, protecting male prestige—was the justification for excluding or denigrating women and their status, whether in the synagogue today or in the ancient rabbinic academies. Citing the case of Beruriah, Ozick argues that the dual reception of her as scholar and whore is overdetermined and paradigmatic: "There is no doubt we are meant to see a connection between the two."[19] In Ozick's view, the lesser status of women and the higher status of men emerge from human decisions and are therefore amenable to repair by human institutions. For her, repair of inequality must emerge out of halakhah, as Blu Greenberg (whom I treat later) also advises. But that is only half the story. Ozick knows that women's essential otherness is laid down in Torah itself from Genesis, without any large principle of justice or commandment that views woman differently. In Torah women are persistently seen as "lesser, and are thereby dehumanized."[20] The relation of Torah to women, she argues, "calls Torah itself into question." She claims that the covenant and Torah are "frayed" with regard to women.

What is her remedy for this social and textual oppression at the heart of Judaism? Ozick reminds us that when the Temple was destroyed, the Jews redirected the religion, at Yavneh, to become a text-centered one. We invented the synagogue, she says, to save Torah by transmission. Historically, this deduction is not quite accurate—synagogues were in evidence during the Second Temple period—but her tracing of the shift from Temple cult to textual transmission in the Yavneh period certainly holds. She invokes it to serve a larger point. She believes that, as once before in a historical crisis of delegitimation, the Jewish response today must be to strengthen Torah. She argues that strengthening Torah is necessary, not for modern times, for a more harmonious social order, for the sake of women, or for the sake of the Jews, but for the sake of Torah, to preserve it.

I am not sure how preserving Torah is to be distinguished from these other issues, nor am I clear on how, in Ozick's program, we are to strengthen Torah unless it is by changing or adapting halakhah. She seems to call for a re-reading of Torah—some existential way of making Torah become its best self. However, instead of looking for analytical programmatics in Ozick, I read her statement as a powerful literary essay, and I believe its structure and rhetoric go hand in hand with its complex message. I therefore do not expect its message to come through as if it were a prescription for change. I feel most keenly Ozick's anguish and devotion, even as I come away from her work with no sense of a specific agenda.

Therefore, it is with some concern that I read what I take as Judith Plaskow's partial, strategic misreading of emphases and complexities in Ozick's essay. Plaskow asserts, in response, that the subordination of women is rooted in theology, in the very foundations of the Jewish traditions, not in law or social practice. Plaskow writes: "The subordination of women, [Ozick] argues, is not deeply rooted in Torah but is the result of historical custom and practice, which can be halakhically repaired."[21] This is clearly a very partial reading (Ozick does note the roots of women's subordination in Torah), and indeed, Plaskow admits in her next sentence that Ozick does cite Torah; she complains, however, that Ozick treats theology only at the end as a kind of addendum. In reply to Plaskow's criticism, I would suggest that Ozick raises the issue of Torah at the start, throughout the essay, and most forcefully at the end, since the end is where the point or topic receives the greatest rhetorical weight in a traditional literary essay. I would have to fault both writers, however, with never clarifying what they mean by "Torah." It matters historically which Torah one is talking about.

The major aim of Plaskow's attack on Ozick's position is to link her with a mainstream Jewish feminism interested in *repair* but not in *overturning tradition*. As I read Plaskow in this instance, she is using Ozick as a foil. Yet Plaskow actually agrees with Ozick's argument about the assumption of women's otherness and develops the point into a politically harsher attack—and here I believe she is correct. "Underlying specific *halakhot*, and *outlasting their amelioration or rejection*, is an assumption of women's Otherness far more basic than the laws in which it finds expression."[22] This otherness must be addressed and defeated.

In seconding Ozick on the cause of otherness, Plaskow stands in a long line of other feminists and gender critics, male and female, before and after her. Plaskow assumes the otherness of woman reflects a male need to control female sexuality: "The need to regulate women is articulated not as a general problem but as the need to control their unruly female sexuality because of its threat to the spirituality of men."[23] Is woman's otherness a subjective, internalized result of cultural conditions? Is it a male projection? Is it based on inherent objective differences in her biology and nature, which are then transferred to her social possibilities? Is otherness awarded by God or by man? Legal change alone, argues Plaskow, will not restore humanity to Jewish woman.

Moreover, disagreeing with Ozick, Plaskow suggests that woman's otherness is directly related to the imagery and language we use in attributing maleness to God, because of the powerful and *seemingly* irrefutable binary of sexual difference, which defines one sex as always *against* the other (male versus female). Plaskow calls for not only a restructuring of halakhah but also an acknowledgment of the injustices of Torah, a recovery of the femaleness of God for reintegration into the Godhead toward a plurality of images, a new understanding of Israel and expansion of Jewish history and memory that allows women a voice. Important changes in all these directions have occurred and continue to happen through the efforts of feminists and others who want equality. But the pace is not fast enough, I believe, and the changes do not go far enough.

The importance of the classic debate between Ozick and Plaskow lies, in fact, not in their different emphases but in the intertwining of the issues they raise. I am not convinced that, as Judith Wegner states, feminists adhering to the less rigorous Conservative or to the Reform traditions see the status-of-woman question as theological rather than sociological because they do not deal as much with actual exclusion as do Orthodox women. However, she is correct when she notes, "In the last analysis, the distinction between theological and sociological questions is not as clear-cut as either Plaskow or Ozick would have us believe."[24] I would only modify this statement to "not as clear-cut as *simplistic readings of Plaskow or of Ozick* would have us believe," because I read both feminists as recognizing the interpenetration of what I would call the religious and the sociological, but as differing in how and what they make the basis of their political arguments.

Another major sticking point among feminists, besides that of the debate over sociology and theology, has been a particular contradiction of Torah: the two different explanations of woman's relationship to man offered by Genesis. We find dual accounts of the creation of humanity and sexual difference in the first two chapters of the Pentateuch. In the first story, the original creation of humans included both sexes: "And God created the earth creature in His image; in the image of God, He created him; male and female He created them" (Genesis 1:27). In the second telling, by contrast, woman emerges as a secondary creature from the rib of an original man: "And God formed the earth-creature of dust from the earth and breathed in its nostrils the breath of life, and the earth-creature became a living being. . . . And the Lord God constructed the rib, which He had taken from the earth-creature, into a woman and brought her to the earth-man. And the earth-man said, this one at last is bone of my bone and flesh of my flesh. This one shall be called woman, for from man was she taken" (Genesis 2.7, 22–23).[25]

This seems contradictory, but as Thomas Tobin has shown and Boyarin has seconded, the first narrative concerns ontology and the second concerns division into sexes.[26] For many Hellenistic Jews, like Philo, oneness of pure spirit is ontologically prior to division of bodies. The "self" exists prior to gender. This historical view, as Boyarin explains, is related to a narrative of "fall" (known to us from Christianity) in that the two stories apparently inscribe a hierarchy of value in which the "spirit" is superior to the "body." Moreover, the aligning of the spirit as masculine and the body as feminine is established by this order, as well as by this gender narrative.

Rabbinic literature, however, refuses this hierarchical view of spirit and body, as does normative Judaism. Gunther Plaut suggests in a commentary that Genesis 1 describes the ideal relationship between man and woman—equality, with "man" as generic—while Genesis 2 describes the actual social relationship—inequality, with "man" as concretely human and sexed. Because rabbinic Judaism demands the biological importance of woman and universal marriage, the sages insist on the roles of wife and mother as primary for women. There are few other options, and there is no way, it seems, to transcend female sexedness within Judaism. For example, there are no saints and no priestesses who join Aaron and the other Temple functionaries within the religion. By contrast, there is at least some opportunity within Christianity for women to play such roles, to transcend gender, as it were, within some asexual or androgynous location, but within Judaism there is no such opportunity. Thus, Jewish feminists struggle with the apparent contradiction of Genesis that seems to award woman secondary status.

No Jewish feminist I have read duplicates Philo's reading, but they often take sides or make choices about which "version" is correct and what to do about it. Some critics side with the explanation offered in Genesis 1. They support a traditional reading that if men and women are both created in God's image, then God is neither exclusively male nor exclusively female but must encompass images of both. However, this reading does not tell us about men and women. Rachel Adler reads human sexuality in Genesis 1 as a metaphor for an element of the divine nature. In other words, something in God illustrates itself as varied and as unified. This element—God's sexuality—is reproduced in men and women. We are various and different, but our desire for sexual union makes us capable of unity with the other. Adler reads Genesis 2 through the patriarchal perspective, but she refuses to take it as normative because she refuses its injustice and its perspective as necessarily con-nected to binding law.[27] She sees Genesis 2 as a social construction of the inequality of the patriarchal social world and hence as something that need not be upheld.

A reading of the Adam and Eve story proposed some years ago by Phyllis Trible has influenced other depatriarchalizing feminist read-ings.[28] She points out that the creation of Eve implies superiority in the use of the word *ezer* (helpmate), a word adopted frequently in the Bible for the relationship of God to Israel. In creation myths we often find the culmination of human creation mentioned last, just as in Genesis 1 humans come after animals. Thus, in Genesis 2 Eve's coming last does not necessarily make her inferior. John Milton, a strong and brilliant reader of the Hebrew Bible in *Paradise Lost*, certainly draws out Eve's superiority and her relationship to God. Moreover, while it is obvious in various ways that male and female were ideally equals, it is also clear that men master women outside of Eden only as a result of sin. The question is: Why does female subordination have to be part of the non-Edenic reality?

The seemingly contradictory accounts of creation raise important questions: Are the two sexes different or are they alike? Is woman an agent, a person with equal rights, responsibilities, and obligations, or is she fundamentally different in a world of male norms and lesser in a theologically ordained hierarchy? Or is she really the superior? If so, does she have to be mastered? Is it really necessary to reduce everything to power and hierarchy?

The system of ancient rabbinic polarities, which was influenced by Hellenistic thinking, treats woman as "other," and woman is thus, as Wegner argues, a hybrid: ontologically equal and socially inferior. As Tikva Frymer-Kensky points out, it is a paradox in ideology that Israel's gender system combines the social inequality of the sexes with an ideological construction of the essential sameness of men and women.[29] This, then, is a central paradox in ancient Israelite ideology: human beings occupy a socially hierarchical relationship with respect to gender while remaining ontologically equal. That equality is insufficient, however, for modern women who remain the product of male ambivalence or misogyny and dominance. When we do not resist that view, we internalize it.

What is the essence of Torah? This too is debated. I think it is important that those asking questions about social justice generally and questions about female equality specifically understand the debate. In Bereshit Rabbah 24:7, we find:

> Ben Azzai said: "'This is the book of the Descendants of Adam' is a great principle of the Torah. ["In the day that God created man—in the image of God he made him" is the continuation of the verse; see Genesis 5:1]." R. Akiva said: "But 'Love thy neighbor as thyself' (Leviticus 19:18) is an even greater principle." Hence, Ben Azzai continues, you must not say, "Since I have been put to shame, let my neighbor be put to shame." R. Tanhuma said: "If you do so, know whom you are putting to shame. In the image of God He made him."

In the Sifre (Kedoshim 4:12) the order is reversed. R. Akiva's view is first. Ben Azzai maintains that Genesis offers the greater principle.

Wherein do they differ? Rabbi Akiva's view is similar to Hillel's in Talmud Shabbat 31a: "What you would hate to be done to you, do not do to your friend. This is the entire Torah, all the rest in commentary. Go learn it." What this means is that we should love our neighbors as ourselves, but it gives us no specific reason why. Because we are all equal? Because this is the nature of love or friendship? Is this admonition premised on the neighbor as stranger or on the neighbor as like a family relation? Should we treat our neighbor as we would want to be treated because we are commanded to do so? This principle is similar to Mishnah Avot 3:18, where Akiva says, "Beloved is man for he was created in the image of God."

But the issue is women. The problem is that Genesis 5:1 continues the sexed differences of Genesis 2. Or does it refer back to Genesis 1? Are women to be included in the biblical term "man" for "mankind"? Some say no. Yet surely the greatness of Torah lies in its ideals, not its narrowest depiction of a patriarchal, social reality. To be created in the image of God, male and female, is to carry within the divine spark. We are equal creatures.

Two of the most eloquent feminist commentators on the status of women within Judaism have emerged from Orthodoxy. Both are learned women. Each is a mother, and each is devoted to social justice; one is married to an Orthodox rabbi, and one is the widow of an Orthodox rabbi. Both are conflicted, sensitive, and forward-looking. Both advocate revision, but their marvelous analyses are located differently, created in different media, and carry different political agendas. In her now classic book *On Women and Judaism: A View from Tradition*, Blu Greenberg stresses a combination of sociological issues and women's psychological internalization of long-held norms.[30] She cries out for revision and halakhic change, balanced with the retention of tradition. In her art installations spanning the 1990s, "The G-d Project," Helène Aylon wrestles more radically with the Jewish religion. She focuses on the passages in the Pentateuch that denigrate women and on the oppression of real women over time from within Judaism; she calls for a re-reading of sources and traditions and a major rethinking of priorities.

Blu Greenberg usefully suggests why the more traditional Jewish communities in America, Israel, and elsewhere, both men and women, reject challenges from feminism. In her account, Orthodox women feel that they have, by and large, been treated well by Orthodox men, in spite of the fact that in this century halakhic authorities have largely resisted change. Moreover, she notes, feminism raises fears about Jewish survival among many Orthodox women, as well as among men, particularly when it seems to threaten the family unit and the continuity of the people of Israel. In addition, because of the importance of the institution of the family in the Jewish religion, many Jewish women are as wary as men of any change that might redefine the family or women's roles.

One of Greenberg's most important chapters concerns the role of women in the minyan or in congregational prayer.[31] She explains women's exemptions from certain mitzvot that are incumbent on men, such as leading the congregation in prayer or reciting certain prayers at certain times of the day. "Women, slaves and children are exempt" (Talmud Kiddushin 1:7). The principle, as here stated, does not equate women with slaves or children, but it does indicate that the free male is set apart, and along with many other statements in Torah, it suggests that he is of the highest status. Moreover, slaves can be freed and children will grow up, but women remain in the same "unaccountable" category, as Greenberg calls it. Any mitzvah (commandment) that one must perform actively within a certain time limit is not binding on women. So, for example, women are not required to hear the shofar, recite the Sh'ma three times a day, and don tefillin (and thus be counted in a minyan). Although the Talmud gives no specific rationale for the exemption of women, scholars have offered interpretations.

Greenberg helpfully identifies various schools of thought that have made their appearance in Judaism from the thirteenth to the twentieth centuries.[32] I review them here, though not in historical order. The "sex-hierarchy" theory with men assigned the advantage (version 1) argues that men are masters and women need to be free to serve them, which they cannot be if they are conflicted about serving God and husband. God thus exempts woman for the sake of the domestic harmony that is essential for Jewish survival. The "sex-hierarchy" theory with women assigned the advantage (version 2) argues that women are spiritually superior to men, and this fact exempts them. They do not need the refreshment offered by such mitzvot. The "lack of control" theory suggests that women, like children and slaves, are fools because they are controlled by their impulses. The "time control" theory proffers that women are more sensitive to time than men anyway and don't need the temporal reminders offered by mitzvot. The "private-public" theory maintains that the nature of the ritual is the key. Women may engage in economic exchange in the public sphere, but mitzvot in the public domain, such as serving as a court witness or a minyan member, are not acceptable and are restricted to men. As in the first interpretation, women belong in the house serving the family.

Greenberg calls for a dialogue between feminists and the upholders of key Jewish values, especially in areas of halakhah that she believes can be altered while traditions are also preserved. This puts her in direct conflict with voices such as that of David Klinghoffer, author of a recent conversion narrative (actually conversions narrative: to Reform, to Conservative, and then to Orthodoxy). He maintains that amending mitzvot and "inventing a new regimen more in keeping with modern assumptions about spirituality, gender roles, contemporary lifestyles, and so on" is nothing more than "breathtaking self-confidence" by a human saying "he knows better than God."[33] This is one Orthodox point of view: Klinghoffer valorizes an "unambiguous" Judaism in which there are monolithic answers, and it disdains the Conservative rabbinate as cynical or unserious about mitzvot. Klinghoffer defends the oral and written Torah as the word of God—not dictated by God, not written by Moses, not edited or redacted except through God's intentions. For this he relies on one authority, Rashi, who presumably speaks only truth at all times, to make his case. Klinghoffer takes Rashi's statement that we must obey the rabbis of our day, no matter what, as a dictum that the alternative to living by *fixed* rabbinic law (that is, Orthodox) is indeterminacy (read chaos). The fact that Torah itself shows the imperfections of Levites and priests or that Talmud has passages in which it mocks its own rabbis is ignored by Klinghoffer, even as Rashi's agenda (and perfection) goes unquestioned.

Greenberg, by contrast, values tradition, debate, and change. Her position, with which I am in sympathy, calls for Orthodox rabbis to alter their views and to amend oral Torah *where necessary*. To leave halakhah unamended is to retain a legal system unfair to women. Rachel Biale argues, from a far more liberal position, that new authorities must emerge and that Jewish women must become versed in halakhah so that they can contend with men on equal ground. I completely agree. Our daughters need educating in Torah. Some Jews argue that it is enough to let congregations do what they please about women, that the problem is entirely sociological and local and up to the rabbi of the individual congregation. In current practice, this is the way change usually occurs. Importantly, however, we depend on a legal system, not human conscience, to set ethical standards and to uphold, alter, argue, dissent from, or even nullify laws.[34] I am not content with a system that relies on individual rabbis' adjustments, because these changes are not only often ad hoc but also can be ignored by the next rabbi.

Greenberg goes further, as do many Conservative rabbis and congregations, and argues that there is a precedent in rabbinic tradition for changing halakhah—indeed, that there is a history of halakhic change operating in tandem with the preservation of tradition. She contends that numerous laws would benefit from revision with no loss of spiritual seriousness or transgression of the commandments. She refers to the areas of divorce law, prayer and synagogue responsibilities and rights, education of women, and community leadership roles.

In glossing Greenberg's words with those of a Conservative rabbi who spoke before she did, I mean not to diminish the force of her argument and voice but to supplement it. Rabbi Phillip Sigal, of blessed memory, of the Conservative movement's Committee on Jewish Law and Standards, wrote in 1984 (a year before his death) the memorable Responsum on the Status of Women, which considered issues pertaining to serving as prayer leaders and as witnesses to divorce. Although the Responsum was tabled and not passed, it is worth comment. It opens with a respect for the present historical situation rather than an adherence to the past. "The preferred path for the Rabbinical Assembly Committee on Jewish Law and Standards in this era would be to issue a comprehensive resolution, a *takkanah* that would serve as an halakhic ERA. This would state that women are to be considered equal with men in all aspects of Judaic religious life, that no prior statement of the Torah, rabbinic literature, medieval or modern commentaries or compilations, whether aggadic or halakhic, should be construed in any manner as valid to prejudice this equality."[35]

How could a halakhist make these statements? Because he believed that a historic precedent should reflect the spirit and not the letter and that halakhic theory can include radical shifts from the past. He also contended that not all generations are equal in their ability to see, hear, and understand Torah. Thus, some generations fail, while others are privileged to understand certain issues on wholly new levels (see Isaiah 6:10). So it is with the status of women. Moreover—and here I find his point of view most compelling—Sigal argued persuasively that our task is to return to classical sources and not get bogged down in the constraints of a closed medieval society, constraints perpetuated by post-Enlightenment anti-reformers. Medieval halakhists, he showed, reversed certain advances made for women. Some of these inequalities have been addressed during the last century, such as the education of women in Torah, but others have not, such as the complex set of menstrual halakhah.

Sigal's important paper has been partly superseded by the acceptance of women into the Conservative rabbinate, but the point of his paper remains important. Sigal argued that the oppression of women within Judaism derives from male psychology, cultural conditioning, and historical circumstance. Now shut away, the issues tabled, and the author dead, the essay nonetheless deserves a careful and wide re-reading. Sigal closed his paper with a call for "a faith which upholds the dignity of the human person" to remove all indignities and inequities. Not surprisingly to me, he quoted Genesis 1:27: "male and female alike created in the image of God."[36]

Also unwilling to separate psychology from the sociology of women's oppression, Blu Greenberg asks us to consider the subtle messages that have been conveyed to women and men over centuries by women's lack of participation in certain mitzvot and by the restrictions placed on them.

What has been the impact of such messages on our daughters and on the possibility of change? Redefining role and function and viewing privileges as moral and spiritual responsibilities, Greenberg charts a new course for Orthodox Jews and thus for inegalitarian Conservative Jews as well. "Given the new reality of women today," she writes of the eighties, "it seems that this is perhaps the right moment in history to chart a more demanding spiritual course to give women equal status and equal access that comes with obligation."[37]

Greenberg's emphasis on social change as a holy responsibility, not an abdication, links her writing with the art installations of her contemporary, Helène Aylon, who also comes from an Orthodox background. An avant-garde artist and ecofeminist liberal since the early 1970s, Aylon has spent the most recent decade of her thirty-year career creating a Jewish anti-midrashic response to Torah. Perhaps more than any other living Jewish woman artist dealing with the tradition, she understands the immense powers of ideology, which is based in language, both present and absent, as well as in visual symbols. Looking to name her mode of installation art, one could call it an ideological, feminist, ethical, humanist critique. For she reads Torah against itself, challenging viewers and readers to rethink power relations and to take responsibility for the world in which they live and that they will pass on to succeeding generations.

The most notable and monumental project of her career to date, reaching a level of "spiritual sublimity," is that of the 1990s—"The G-d Project."[38] Aylon here expresses her ambivalence about Orthodoxy and its dogmas. Her installation project comprises four parts. "The Liberation of G—d" interrogates a male-centered Torah projected onto God and searches for the feminine principle. "The Women's Section" depicts the misogyny directed at the foremothers and questions what Aylon's "Babas" would have said about her critique. "My Notebooks" expresses her sorrow about her fifty-four school notebooks devoid of any woman's commentary and the perpetuation of the sex/gender stereotypes in modern yeshivas. "Epilogue: Alone with My Mother" dramatizes the wrenching pull of her mother's Orthodoxy and the loneliness of following another path. Each installation combines text and architecture. Each is imbued with holiness even as each critiques: Aylon neither abandons the Jewish tradition nor wholeheartedly endorses it.

The first of these installations, "The Liberation of G-d," housed permanently and exhibited magnificently in the Jewish Museum in New York City, has been the most widely viewed and publicly debated. Notably, it has brought rabbis from all wings of Judaism into the museums where it has appeared, and it has brought Aylon into synagogues and universities to discuss the issues raised by her art. In this installation Aylon places a sheet of vellum over each page of selected Hebrew and English versions of Torah. She highlights in pink those passages that offend, that are violent, restrictive, denigrating, or support only fundamentalism. She opposes the all-pervasive patriarchal code in Torah, its barbarity by modern standards, and its continuing (conscious and subliminal) influence on men, women, and children. Aylon's intention is to liberate God from man's violent projections onto Him and His Name, for in Judaism, the religion more opposed to any form of idolatry than any other, are we not free to make God what we will? Aylon calls on us to change our deeply flawed relationship with an exclusionary and patriarchal God. We are at fault, not God.

Actively participating in the rabbinic tradition of midrash—through anti-midrash—Aylon constructs a feminist art of blessing that re-reads, questions, and reinterprets Torah for our time as a gesture of tikkun, or repair. Although some would argue that her art walks a very thin line between heresy and reverence, I agree with her that human constructions of God used to dominate or do violence to others are profoundly wrong and that fundamentalism is the key problem for the new millennium.

Aylon's installation includes notebooks in which viewers can write. And they do. They come from all over the world—rabbis, children, adults, men, women, believers, unbelievers, nonbelievers, Jews, Muslims, Christians, from different backgrounds, with differing relationships to Judaism. The majority of writers are awed, amazed, and moved by her work—some to tears. The day I took my ten-year-old son to see the installation, he wrote her a note: "I like the way you stand up for what you believe in." He gets it too.

Over five thousand comments have been collected from viewers of this installation, nearly all testimonials of wonder and gratitude at the mixture in her work of observance, critique, sanctity, and longing. One of the most meaningful responses to me comes from a Los Angeles rabbi: "Encountering Helène Aylon's remarkable 'The Liberation of G-d' envelops one in the mystery of Torah, in the Jew's weekly engagement with its ancient parchment text, and in the persistent pulsing Jewish questions—Jews, after all, answer questions with questions!—which all end in more questions: 'Where is God? Who is God? What is God? When is God? Why is God?'"[39]

In October 1999, I spent a weekend with Helène Aylon at the MacDowell Colony in New Hampshire, where she was resident artist for six weeks. I drove all day Friday from New Jersey, through New York, Connecticut, Massachusetts, and Vermont, fighting traffic, a slight collision with a truck, and the sun's going down, thus the approach of Shabbat. After quickly dumping my belongings at a motel, I found the colony, just as the red sun started to settle among huge and fragrant pine trees and birches.

Helène and I quickly created a special Friday night Shabbat dinner, as outsiders are not allowed at meals with the MacDowell fellows. A Shabbat like no other before or since. Dinner for two Jewish women in a hallway on a little table next to a bay of windows with views of the New Hampshire fields and hills. Two glasses of deep red wine appear in her hands. A small standing lamp casts a pool of light. We can barely see each other, but it is enough. At the last minute, before leaving New Jersey, I had run back into the house and grabbed a loaf of challah from my freezer, on a hunch that none would be available in Peterborough, New Hampshire. I carefully unwrap it—you can still smell its freshness, as if it had been baked that morning. We each take it up to our faces to smell the yeast. Nothing else like it in the world. Helène draws two white candles from her bag, not regular Shabbat candles, since none are available in the area, but tall white ones. Our Shabbat is wobbly and makeshift, but the sacred smells of yeast, flame, and grape began to encircle us. We put our tall imperfect Shabbat candles in glasses at a rakish angle and try to anchor them with a bit of wax at the bottom. As she says the blessing,

"Baruch atah Adonai," Helène draws the light to her face, as thousands of Jewish women do each Friday night all over the world. We alternate reciting the other blessings. She brings her plate of food to our table and divides it in two.

The braided challah, says Rabbi Lynn Gottlieb, is a heritage from ancient times and the worship of female deities. Sarah, our matriarch, reports the midrash, undertook the lighting of candles, long before Torah was given at Sinai. That Shabbat evening, Helène and I perform male and female duties, two Jewish women alone in the middle of New England darkness in a pool of Jewish light.

Of course, this was not a traditional Shabbat. The only services in the area were almost an hour away—it was already too late to start—and there were none at all in the area on Shabbat morning. It seemed that there were no other observant Jews at MacDowell either. Yet it was a special and memorable Shabbat, created by two women out of necessity and love. Was God present? Undoubtedly. What, I wondered, would the second-century rabbis or today's fundamentalist Jews have said? Would they have condemned the patchwork quality of this Shabbat meal, or instead, would they have understood and valued the respect and holiness and love of tradition that made it happen in the middle of nowhere with no service and no minyan?

In her studio at MacDowell, Helène was still working in October 1999 on the installation "My Notebooks," which was to be shown at the Aldrich Museum in Ridgefield, Connecticut, in January 2000. All around the walls of the studio were blackboards with Torah quotations and with the aleph and bet of the alphabet: A B; AB; ABBA (a, b, ab, abba = father). On one wall there was a sample notebook, like those Helène might have once used in her Jewish girls' school, with the pages blank and each page curled inward to the inner spine. The notebooks, placed one above the other, looked as if they were columns with black edges. Fifty-four of them, all blank and rolled in, serve as reminders of the fifty-four "books" of Moses. A photograph of Helène's eighth-grade graduating class at Shulamith School for Girls is superimposed on the wall of blank books. What did these girls learn in school about women in Torah? Was it nothing or was it the content of the blackboards? Certainly there was nothing positive worth writing down, as the notebook pages remain blank. Three school desks of increasing size face the viewer of the installation in the foreground. A quote on a blackboard reads, "searching for a word from my foremothers . . . I found no woman's explanation to tell me, tell me . . . no woman's commentary to teach me, teach me. . . . "

Aylon probes the relationship of Jewish women to their past, to the religious past, to the sociological past, to the historical past, to their individual pasts, to their cultural pasts. As Yosef Hayim Yerushalmi argues in his stirring book on remembrance, *Zakhor*, the Jewish faith is based on memory and on historical rupture and loss. Yet for the graduating class of 1944, for whom no foremothers' commentary existed, memory flows back into absence in a particularly poignant way.

I have not seen the installation whole except in photographs. Yet the conception alone leads me to mourn the inequalities perpetrated on women within Judaism. It cries out to me: How much longer? Twenty years? Forty? One hundred? And what happened to these women, to so many women before us? What did they pass on to their sons and daughters about Jewish women? How much did their daughters have to learn for themselves? Whereas modern women are the products of the same historical ruptures, breaks, and losses as are Jewish men, the men do not confront the same ignorance, misogyny, and inequality that Jewish women must face, work through, and endure.

For Hélène Aylon, the greatest issue of the 1990s and the 2000s is fundamentalism. Her desire to free God from the framing of patriarchs and from the projections of fundamentalists is a desire to free God from the agenda of those who wish to be chosen above all others, to be chosen above all others in the most damning sense of all—as dominating through othering. What a profoundly limiting and damaging notion is chosenness, how anti-Semitic, when it is used to unholy ends in a non-Jewish way by Jews and non-Jews. "There is enough patriarchy in institutions around the world," argues Aylon in her book manuscript, "without having to swallow it in the holiest of holy books, all in the name of G-d."

What can we do? The most progressive leaders of Conservative Judaism in America should be teaching Judaism far more aggressively to its adults, not only its children, and, even more important, staging a series of *focused debates* at universities, in the media, in the press, in synagogues, among Jews alone, and with interfaith committees, precisely on the issues of our day and the twenty-first century: post-Holocaust genocide, the status of women, abortion rights, moral global leadership, gay rights, the scandalous treatment of the disabled and the aged in our communities, forced child labor, the ruination of the earth, an inability to share Jerusalem, fundamentalism, all forms of terrorism, and other critical issues. The list could go on and on.[40] The Dalai Lama's call for a World Council of People, representing the moral and ethical conscience of the world, is an important step in the right direction. Helène Aylon's request for a worldwide conference in Jerusalem to address the liberation of God is another important step in the right direction, as is Blu Greenberg's call for changing specific halahkot. It is time for the progressive groups among the new Orthodox and Conservatives to make good on what it means to be a "holy nation" (Exodus 19:6) and to repair the world (tikkun olam) in modern times. This may mean a shift in emphasis so that Torah lives differently than it does now.

Although I am deeply appreciative of careful deliberation before adapting or changing religious halakhah and I understand the legal arguments against alteration, I do not accept the snail-like movements within modern Conservatism or Orthodoxy toward change in this historical moment. I am calling on the liberal and the nonliberal leaders of these movements to act more quickly from within the halahkot requiring Jewish social justice on the issues I have mentioned, but also on specifics such as: the approval of patrilineal descent; the acceptance of openly gay rabbinical students at the Jewish Theological Seminary; the acceptance of Orthodox women into cantorial schools; the endorsement and performing of gay marriages and commitment ceremonies; a mandate for synagogues to reach out to the disabled in our communities with ramps at the *front* doors and Braille sacred books for each Jewish place of worship; improvements in the specifics of divorce law; a wider interpretation of the need for a woman's right to choose abortion; and stronger state-

ments about the rights, responsibilities, and privileges of women in synagogues and congregations.

Which God do I worship? Do I worship one of dominance, exclusion, and dogma, or one of law, yes, but also of equality, a God who judges, forgives, and has love for all mortals made in the image of God?

The Two Tamars

Thoughts on 2 Samuel 13 and on Vayeshev, Genesis 38

A person is obligated to teach his daughter Torah.
—BEN AZZAI, M. SOTAH 3:4

During the summer of 1998 I wrote three long biblical commentaries for my conversion supervisor. The last, selected from a list he was also giving to students in Israel, was the story of Tamar, the daughter of King David and Maccah, from the book of 2 Samuel. It was not a narrative I wished to treat, and I wrote on two other passages first, before finally confronting the brutality of incest and rape, a legacy of Davidic transgressions. When I finally did get to Tamar, I wrote over thirty pages on her story, about which I had initially thought I would have little to say. I was very interested (not surprisingly perhaps, given my reluctance to comment) by her defense speech and subsequent silence, or silencing.

Once, long ago, I studied dramatic monologues in a poetry writing seminar whose director, Pamela Hadas, instructed me always to assume the voices of the figures that seemed most alien, or most difficult, or most different from me. That, she knew, was where one would find fric-

tions leading to self-discovery. My encounter with the Tamar of 2
Samuel turned those summer weeks into a passionate engagement with
Torah, the most meaningful encounter yet. Tamar's story was also the
first one with a woman that I had read up until that time, and so it
plunged me into issues of gender identification as well. I fell in love with
Tamar and in love with Torah at almost the same time.

That early love for Torah has matured with time. As a Jew, I understand that Torah elicits many interpretations, but as a textual critic, I
find myself judging some interpretations as better than others.
Following from issues I raised in the last chapter concerning women in
Judaism, I turn here to reading the representation of two women in the
Hebrew Bible. I juxtapose the story of Tamar in 2 Samuel with that of
another Tamar, the heroine of Genesis and of the Israelite people.
Indeed, Torah itself suggests a connection between these women, for
the striped tunic worn by the royal child Tamar in 2 Samuel (one of her
only distinguishing traits to be mentioned) echoes the striped tunic
worn by Joseph in the Genesis story cycle, into which the Tamar and
Judah story is inserted.

I want to stress first that all biblical narratives have gaps, silences, and
absences and thus that all are ambiguous. Moreover, units that seem to
have nothing to do with each other appear alongside each other. Yet, in
its sum, Torah is a great poem that has to be read with a sensitivity to its
poetry and its structure. Its ambiguity, I suggest, is deliberate. We can
read teleologically, backward, up and down, just as we can read and connect Hebrew words through patterns of root, grammatical form, repetition, or verse placement.[1] At the same time, we must try to remember, as
we read, what came before and what will come after, mindful of simultaneous and multiple time frames, including the frame of mysterious holy
time that obeys none of the rules of standard chronology.

Much of the patriarchalism that we associate with Torah, as Tikva
Frymer-Kensky argues, is the overlay of later voices.[2] Thus, we do not
have to read the Pentateuch only for patriarchy, even if its frame and its
society are clearly patriarchal. Rather, we can attend to struggles within
patriarchy, to contradictions, to other voices, to rebellions. Nor do we
have to read all women as victims, just as we do not have to project a fun-

damentalist God onto Torah. Let's see what happens when we turn around what have been called "texts of terror," a term coined by Phyllis Trible in her book of the same name.[3]

Texts of terror, such as the two that follow, are not simple narratives. They force readers to see Israel at odds with itself, and they should make readers very uneasy. Just as only fundamentalist readers could not be shocked by Abraham's unquestioning readiness to sacrifice his son Isaac, so too only fundamentalist readers could not be shocked by the wrongs committed against the two Tamars, as well as against many other women in Torah. What is so interesting, as Frymer-Kensky points out, is that Israel apparently does no better in this regard in the absence of a polity in Genesis than it does under the localized government of the judges or under a monarch.[4] Regardless of the form of government, power wielded in a certain way always yields results that are unjust and deadly.

This first Tamar enters the narrative in Genesis 37, which features the story of Jacob and his sons but is mostly the story of Joseph. We read about the favored child, indulged and arrogant, his "coat of many colors," his dreams, his brothers' hatred of him, and even his father's growing concerns about his egoistic boy. Joseph's brothers, as we recall, throw him into a pit. On Judah's recommendation, he is sold to traders. He ends up in Egypt with Potiphar: in Genesis 39 we find the story of Joseph and Potiphar's wife, the attempted seduction, Joseph's resistance, his imprisonment, his eventual reading of dreams for Pharaoh, and his rise to prominence in Egypt.

But Genesis 38 interrupts the Joseph cycle with a story of Judah, Joseph's brother, and his family—a story that seems fundamentally out of place. But of course, anything "out of place" in Torah begs for scrutiny, not to force teleology but to look for analogies or other types of relationship. Not surprisingly, then, some have argued, including Menachem Lorberbaum, the discussion leader on this parasha in our minyan, that the Tamar episode not only is critical at this point in Torah, but also is the key episode in the entire Joseph cycle. I would go even further to claim that it is the key to much larger patterns concerning men and women in Genesis and even a window to the treatment of women in Torah in its entirety.

In discussing the two Tamars, I ask a large question: How are we to read women in Torah? And by taking each Tamar as not only a woman in a specific narrative who is misread and misused but also as the figure of the text itself (Torah is gendered female), I ask: How are we to read Torah itself as a text? Thus, I am writing partly about meaning in these two narratives—what happens to the women, what they do, and what effect they have, what the women mean, what narrative structures harbor them or confine them, in what ways they are silenced or fall silent and why. More fundamentally, however, I am writing about how each Tamar's speech connects her with Torah as text and how these figures are used dramatically to critique or improve patriarchal social relations, while not undermining the word of God, law, or the nation of Israel. Indeed, the voices of the women here are linked to morality and to the Divine.

In connecting the Tamars with Torah, however, I do not want to lose the specificity of the female figure. Rather, I'm keen to show that these women are instructing both those around them in the narrative and us as readers in how to read them properly, since they are themselves the objects of profound misreadings. Moreover, they offer a corrective in how to read society and law, and their examples illustrate how to misread and how to read Torah itself.

A few words on the name *Tamar* are in order, because in biblical interpretation names often signify inner qualities. If we look at the simple definition of *Tamar*, we find "date, palm tree." But looking at the root and at the word in its various parts, we find the stories of these women encapsulated in their name. Each appears first as a virgin, each is misused by a man, and each stands upright in the face of such misuse. *Tameem* means "whole, pure, and faultless." *Tamare* means "erect as a tree." Within the name *Tamar* we find not only *tam*, which means "pure," but also *mar*, which means "sad, sorrowful, bitter," a reference first to the purity of their natures and to the sadness we should feel at their mishandling.

Genesis 38 involves the humbling of Judah. It reminds us of the failures and evils of a blind patriarchy. Judah's daughter-in-law Tamar shows these "righteous" Israelite men the failure of their laws and the errors of a human justice system. Her presence as a figure of critique and instruction in Torah is not singular. Indeed, the critique leveled at the patriarchs in Genesis and Exodus and other books shows time and again that the Israelites must not be myopic or exclusive in their interests but must instead draw in women and non-Jews to help redirect them, whether the patriarchs' wives, Moses's father-in-law, Jethro the Midianite, Ruth the Moabitess, and the mixed multitudes who join the Israelites at Sinai.

Women are deeply influential in directing and redirecting the history of the Israelite people. Incited by Rebecca, for example, Jacob displaces Esau. Joseph marries an Egyptian. Because of the intervention of non-Israelite midwives, Moses is saved. Israel survives not because of the often deeply flawed rule or governance of men, such as Judah or David, but because God invests in us in ways that often take unpredictable turns. In Genesis 38, Tamar teaches Judah so that the Hebrew law can be fair and productive. It is no accident, but overdetermined, that she herself produces Judah's new twin boys.

At the start of this chapter, Judah has fallen into moral decay. The verse says that he "went down from his brothers," in the sense of leaving them, but also, as Rambam notes, in the sense of falling spiritually. It was Judah, we recall, who proposed selling Joseph into slavery. Not a patient person, as Tamar will be, Judah quickly marries the daughter of a Canaanite. His marriage to this foreigner produces three sons, Er, Onan, and Shelah. Yet the births bode ill, for with each one there is a lessening of Judah's interest.

The symbolism is significant. Judah is not taking care of the future generation any more than he nurtured his brother Joseph. Judah names his first child at the birth; the second is named by his (unnamed) wife; and he is not even at home for the birth of the third child but in Chsiv (from the Hebrew root for "deceit"). His wife names their third son as well. The names of these last two children foreshadow an increasing remove from holiness and from God: "Onan" suggests grief and "Shelah" suggests error.

When his first son is ready to marry, Judah arranges a marriage between Er and Tamar. The narrative handles the subsequent years with speed. When Er is found evil in God's ways, he dies and Tamar is left a widow. As the male head of the family, Judah owns Tamar, so he then tells his second son, Onan, to marry her and asks him to help raise children with her. However, Onan, realizing that children would carry his brother's name and not his, wastes his seed whenever he lies with Tamar. This activity is an affront to God—both the waste of seed and the non-consummation of the marriage. Onan pays with his life.

The commentators ponder the fact that the complicated story of Judah and his sons temporarily halts the flow of the Joseph cycle. Rashi questions: "Why is this story brought immediately after the other, such that the Torah interrupts the story of Joseph?" In answering, he looks to the death of Judah's two sons as a divine punishment of Judah and his brothers for having cut off the beloved son from his father Jacob and for having been deceitful. Yet it seems to me that there is far more going on than the imposition of divine punishment: for one thing, Judah does not connect his own behavior to the deaths of his sons. Instead, he begins to have suspicions about Tamar. It would appear, from his next action, that he blames her, for he sends her back to her own family, explaining that his third son is not yet ready to marry. He is not eager to lose his last son. Tamar does not respond but simply waits to see what will unfold next.

At the end of the prescribed mourning period for his own wife, Judah goes to shear sheep at Timna, where Tamar lives. Hearing that her father-in-law is coming, she takes off her widow's dress and covers herself with a veil and sits on the road. She sees that the third son, Shelah, is grown, yet has not been given to her, as Judah had promised. Judah then catches sight of her and, because she has covered her face, "sees" her as a prostitute, a zonah. Done mourning, he's ready to lie with a prostitute. When she demands some payment, he promises a kid from the flock. When she demands surety for the kid, he provides her with the markers of his identity: his seal, his cord, and his staff. He then lies with her; she leaves him and again dons her widow's clothing.

Judah tries to fulfill his promise of payment. He sends the kid to Tamar and asks a friend, Chira the Abdullamite, to retrieve the seal, cord, and staff. But Chira returns empty-handed, and Judah comes to terms with the loss of the symbols of his identity. Not wanting his reputation ruined, he inquires no further. He would not wish it known that he gave away such important items just to sleep with a woman. Three months later he is told that his daughter-in-law has become a whore and is pregnant and that he must put her to death.

Here we have the crux of the story. Until now, Judah has taken no time to find a wife for his third son or to mourn a day longer than necessary for his own wife. That he has never tried to understand Tamar and has jumped to conclusions about her gives the ironic twist to her tricking him. She exposes his double standard. His quick, thoughtless actions continue. By so freely jeopardizing his reputation for momentary pleasure, he shows that his identity is forged not inwardly but by outward signs—there is little substance to him. Judah's sin is not a momentary loss of control but moral superficiality, precisely the qualities we saw when he decided to sell Joseph. Whereas the other brothers could be said to have been swept up in the confusion of the moment, Judah's decision to sell his brother was rational and wrong.

Judah does not care about others, and he has no feeling about anything he does. He reads situations and people with profound inaccuracy. He makes no inquiries about what his sons might have done to merit sudden death, nor does he inquire about the woman with whom he sleeps. He does not bother to bring her the kid himself and retrieve his identity markers. It is difficult to imagine how he could have been less caring about himself and others, short of committing crimes against them.

Other stories from Genesis share similarities with this one: Esau's selling his birthright for a meal, Jacob's using the skin of a kid to deceive his father, licentiousness in Sodom and Gomorrah, Joseph's brothers tricking him and deceiving Jacob. Each time it is not absolutely clear that the history of the Israelites will continue.

Many commentators continue to focus on Judah in this narrative because he has the opportunity to change, yet Tamar is just as important, if not more important. Without her, Judah would never have understood what he did to Joseph or to her. When the right moment finally presents itself to confront him with his insensitivities, his moral failures, and misreadings, Tamar acts. "Identify these, recognize these," she declares in a message sent to her father-in-law alone, accompanying the signs of his identity, as she is on her way to be burned to death. This confrontation between Tamar and Judah is one of identity—the woman asks the man to identify himself, to identify the trappings of his worth, and, more important, to be the man he should be and own up to his misdeeds, even at the cost of public humiliation. Notably, he is able to read the situation and understand the justice of her trick. In doubting her worth and in not giving Shelah to her, he had broken faith and Jewish law.

Judah realizes that there are kinds of exposure that lead to teshuvah—repentance and a turning back to God. Later in Genesis, when he and his brothers stand before the not-yet-recognized Joseph and are faced with the prospect of losing Benjamin to Egypt as surety, Judah, now schooled in betrayal and surety issues, gets his second chance. This time he can right the wrong against his father and his brother Joseph. In a lengthy, moving speech, he offers to sacrifice himself for the sake of his half-brother Benjamin and out of love for his father. This is the turning point of the Joseph story. At this moment Joseph knows his brothers have truly repented. Because of the intelligence and compassion of Tamar, the natural order of life is restored and the history of Israel is able to continue.

Tamar does not call Judah to account until her own life is imperiled. Although some commentators speak of her seduction of Judah, as if her trick is ill intentioned, her deception, unlike Judah's, is in the service of good. It shows up the flaws of a patriarchal system run by selfishness. It proffers justice and reconciliation in place of male thoughtlessness and immorality. Through the figure of Tamar, Torah offers a critique and correction of its own foundational patriarchy. Tamar's story is essential to Genesis and to the future of Judah, Joseph, and the Israelites.

Such inner critiques or countervoices in Torah lead me to read the Israelite God as nonpatriarchal. Seen in the context of critique and countervoice, God is not identical to the patriarchal society of Torah. Indeed, divine and human checks and balances seem built into this deeply flawed human system to make it often unpredictable, nondogmatic—and finally, mysterious.

Through the particular motherhood of Tamar, Torah rebalances a specific flaw in the system—fraternal rivalry—that had so often led to pain and error. It flows through Genesis as a mighty subtext: quarreling, mortal struggle, and fraternal deceit in the figures of Cain and Abel,

Isaac and Ishmael, Jacob and Esau, and Joseph and his brothers. When Tamar gives birth to twins (recalling Jacob and Esau), the two fight in the womb, pushing to see who will get out first and earn the rights of the firstborn. One of her twins thrusts out an arm, and the midwife ties a red thread on it to identify the firstborn, yet when he pulls that hand back in, his brother pushes out first and is named Peretz. Judah then names the second boy Zerah. As was discussed in our minyan, however, we do not have a duplication of the birth scene of Esau and Jacob, but its opposite. Esau was the "red" child who emerged first, inappropriately, but here the "red" child comes out second, so there is no necessity to restore the order later on. Judah also has some consolation for having lost two of his sons by his Canaanite wife. The line of Tamar, Judah, and Peretz is an honorable one, leading through Moses to King David.

The story of Tamar and Amnon in 2 Samuel is the negative legacy of the story of David and Bathsheba. The later tale also echoes the Tamar and Judah story in its misreading and misuse of the woman. The woman's presence in the earlier account serves as a corrective, but in the story of David and Bathsheba the man will not be corrected, and the result is familial and national tragedy.

The chapters of 2 Samuel start with the death of Bathsheba and David's firstborn, continue to the rape of David's daughter Tamar, and end with the death of David's son Absalom and parental mourning. This is the extent of God's punishment of the House of David: He will not remove His favor from David, but He will also not let him go unschooled in suffering.

The story of Amnon and Tamar commences in 2 Samuel 13. Amnon lusts for his lovely half-sister Tamar, a virgin and an innocent versed in laws of Torah who is indisputably moral. Her striped tunic connects her in this characterization with Joseph. Amnon's friend and cousin Jonadab, intuiting Amnon's lust, solidifies male bonding with a violent plan whereby Amnon can force Tamar into having sex with him. Amnon follows the plan to the letter. He lies to his father, saying he is ill, and explains that only Tamar can make him feel better if she cooks for him. Tamar is summoned and cooks dumplings for him. Amnon sends away his retainers and rapes her, despite her pleas, committing incest in the process. Tamar is taken into her brother Absalom's home for protection. What follows is grim: Absalom bears a secret grudge against his half-brother Amnon for two years; he then deceives his father, David, and murders Amnon according to yet another secret plan. Short indeed is the distance between private and personal sinning and that which implicates families, friends, and, in the case of princes and kingships, nations.

Once again a Tamar is misread and misused. Unlike the first Tamar, the second Tamar, once violated, has no resources—no power, no status, no security symbol of any kind to redeem that could serve as a corrective to the men around her. Amnon's refusal to heed her pleas to spare her results in family humiliation, fraternal ill will, fratricide, a train of more deceptions, and eventually Absalom's death at the hands of his father's army. Her enforced humiliation in a state of semi-isolation is in marked contrast to the men's self-assurance, their speeches, and their murderous behavior toward each other through trickery and battle.

The rabbis view men as the active sexual agents in sexual interactions and as the necessary protectors of female family members. They have greater physical power, greater social power, and the social permission to initiate sex. An Israelite man's role toward the woman in his immediate or extended family requires him to protect her. Amnon violates this commitment to protect the woman in his immediate or extended family. The Bible, the rabbinic sources, and the postrabbinic sources all condemn his act of rape and incest as a sin of wide physical, mental, personal, and public implications. According to Rachel Biale, the broad biblical definition of incest includes many relations outside of the immediate family, including half-sisters. Moreover, the rabbis define the violence of rape as not only physical but also psychological, for it begins under compulsion. Maimonides takes this further, suggesting that a woman compelled to have intercourse is exonerated from any charges that might be leveled against her; only the man is at fault. Thus, the woman is not subject to fines, making sacrifices, flogging, or death.[5] Moreover, her male relatives are also considered victims: rape and incest are sins not only against a woman but also against the family authority figures as well.

If a woman is a virgin when she is raped, the act is considered to be a crime against her father, because she is now worthless as marriageable property. Because the father incurs a financial loss, the rapist is fined. Normally, the rapist should also take the woman in marriage and never be able to divorce her—hardly a punishment for the man, but surely a horrifying punishment for the woman. It is possible that when Absalom tells Tamar to keep quiet because it was her "brother" who did it, he is not simply trying to plot revenge against Amnon in secret but also trying to avoid bringing dishonor to his father, the king, and his house.

Yet the rape of Tamar critiques all the men in the house of David: Amnon, Jonadab, David, and Absalom. Amnon calls Tamar to feed him but then rejects the dumplings she has made for him. He spurns what she can give and sees no meaning in her coming to him; he is blind to her dutifulness, her promptness, the gift of preparation, and the deliverance. He does not see, does not know, and does not care to know goodness.

Amnon then comes to hate Tamar: "And Amnon hated her with a very great hatred, for greater was the hatred with which he hated her than the love with which he had loved her." This narrative voice, which reports love, is either ironic or reporting Amnon's delusions, since love does not lead to rape: One does not commit crimes against a loved one. Amnon never loved her. But perhaps the narrator means that his hatred was even greater than his lust. Either way, the narrator judges Amnon harshly. Amnon hates Tamar because, once having had her, he sees her as a reproach. Had he been neutral toward her, he might have tossed her out like a melon rind. But he hates, presumably because she resists, tells him what he is, and is no longer a virgin. A more generous reader than I might argue that Amnon hates himself. My take is that any self-hatred is as shallow and perfunctory as his love; the man toys with feelings as much as he toys with women and then rationalizes his behavior.

Not only is Amnon condemned, through the figure of Tamar, but so is his conniving cousin and friend, Jonadab, who bears an eerie resemblance to Judah's friend Chira. Jonadab, however, is given a character shading that we can only infer about Chira from his actions. The penetrating mental and intuitive skills of Jonadab, which could have been put to good use in the insightful instruction of others, are instead turned to evil ends—playing games with people's lives.

Nor is King David free of guilt. He fails to respond to Amnon's rape of Tamar, neither counseling his son nor rebuking him. Ultimately, his inability to act on what he knows (of Amnon and of himself) leads, indirectly, to murder. Had he punished Amnon, Absalom might not have been compelled to kill his brother nor to pursue fraternal rivalry. At the least, David should have rebuked Amnon, since the righteous man should protest the actions of the wicked. Since he does nothing, one can only wonder whether he learned anything from his own deeds. David's silence is echoed by Absalom's silence about his plans and by the horrific inverse: Tamar's silence after she is raped.

I want to focus for a moment on her speech, however, for her impassioned plea begging Amnon not to rape her is one of the most poignant moments in the Hebrew Bible. Robert Alter has argued that "the relatively lengthy reply is a kind of panicked catalogue of reasons for Amnon to desist, a desperate attempt at persistence."[6]

She is, he notes, like Joseph before Potiphar's wife in Genesis, responding to attempted seduction with elaborate protestations. I would not disagree with Alter on the issue of the catalogue or the comparison to Joseph. In my view, however, this is not a panicked speech. It is impassioned, rational, and lengthy, delivered from a position of moral authority. Tamar couches her appeal on the grounds of law, kinship, status, rank, morality, ethics, respect for her individuality, respect for his individuality, and the lack of necessity. This is a voice of reason. Basically she is saying to the man: You do not really need or want to do this, and here are the laws you should follow to prop up your better impulses.

She is appealing to the other, not just to save herself, but to save him, too, because she sees that the redemption of the one is intertwined with the redemption of the other. It seems indisputable to me that Tamar automatically sides with Amnon's better self to protect it. Yet even as Tamar offers Amnon at least five sites for his identification, at least five reasons to turn away from his deed, he does not locate himself in any of them and rapes her.

The fact that Amnon does not listen to Tamar illustrates his abject refusal to read her as anything more than a female body. I cannot agree with Rabbi Joseph Dov Soloveitchik that Amnon's hatred of Tamar comes from shame and remorse.[7] The powerful moral critique leveled at Amnon in this story and at Judah in Genesis is achieved through the contrast of the two Tamars. Both demonstrate patience, logic, and duty.

Considered side by side, the stories startle us by showing male authoritarian identity in need of repair by women to redirect Israel. Each features patriarchal power and a critique of that power. Such negative treatment of women in Torah becomes, as Frymer-Kensky suggests, "the clue to the morality of the social order."[8] Each story invites us, as have feminists, not to focus on the men or on the women as mere victims of these men, but to depatriarchalize the Hebrew Bible. It is time to turn to other stories and look carefully at them for the mixed ideologies that so often pit Israel against its own best interests.

Chapter Four

POLLUTION AND HOLINESS: THE BODY

❧

You shall separate the Children of Israel from their contamination; and they shall not die as a result of their contamination if they contaminate My Tabernacle that is among them. This is the teaching concerning the man with a discharge, and from whom there is a seminal discharge, through which he becomes contaminated; and concerning a woman who suffers through her separation, and concerning a person who has his flow, whether male or female, and concerning a man who lies with a contaminated woman.

—LEVITICUS 15:31–33

You shall not lie with a man as one lies with a woman, it is an abomination.

—LEVITICUS 18:22

On the eighth day the flesh of his skin shall be circumcised.

—LEVITICUS 12:3

The aspect of Judaism I found most difficult to understand during my study for conversion was the relationship posited between the body and the soul. Indeed, I was so imbued with the dualism of Christianity, believing that the body is a casing for the soul, a container that will be shed on the Day of Judgment and Resurrection, that even when I left behind a belief in the Resurrection of Jesus Christ, I found it hard to abandon the soul-body hierarchy.

My misapprehension of the relationship between body and soul within Judaism also led me at first to think in terms of spirituality versus corporeality rather than in terms of the more Jewishly accurate categories of purity and holiness versus pollution. I did not realize until a year after converting that biblical Judaism, some lines of rabbinic Judaism, and important medieval Jewish philosophers do not recognize the dualism of the earlier Hellenistic Greeks and Christians. Not grasping this distinction had led me to all sorts of misunderstandings of text and of practice.

Judaism conceives of holiness and the body very differently than does Christianity—or for that matter, than do most people living in a secular culture like ours imbued with body makeovers, cyberbodies, technobodies, bodybuilding, and the Genome Project. Judaism understands the body differently—as secreting fluids that can defile (menstrual blood or wasted semen, for example) and as suffering from diseases that can pollute (psoriasis, leprosy, boils, or disabilities that disqualify a person from approaching the ark). Laws about physical pollution in Judaism were originally connected to the mishkan (the Tabernacle) and the Temple cult. So, for instance, lepers could not stay in the camp around the mishkan, and priests suffering from boils could not serve in the Temple until their bodies were "unpolluted." Only the most holy and most clean could serve or remain close to God and be near the presence of God on earth. Yet this is not a matter of hygiene but of holiness.

Until I completed a course in rabbinic Judaism, I had not realized that *spirituality* as a word and concept is not at the heart of Judaism (except in Jewish mysticism). The key concept, rather, is holiness. But what, I then wondered, does holiness mean? And how, if at all, is it related to bodies, clean or unclean? Judaism demands holiness of each person, not just of religious leaders, such as the priests serving the Temple cult or the learned teachers, the rabbis. God's goal with His covenant was to embrace a kingdom of priests and a holy nation (Exodus 19:6), and that included each person. Moreover, the Pentateuch specifically commands each individual to strive for holiness: "God spoke to Moses saying: Speak to the entire assembly of the Children of Israel and say to them: You shall be holy, for holy am I, God, your God" (Leviticus 19:2). All are charged equally to emulate the Creator; it is thus axiomatic that every Jew holds the potential for realizing holiness.

But what does being holy really mean? Or for that matter, I wondered, what would the potential of holiness be? Literally, Kedushah (holiness) means separation or isolation—the notion of being set apart from that which is not holy. It is significant that the first epigraph to this chapter links separation with holiness and pollution. In Torah, God is set apart, dangerous to approach. Thus, in the Temple cult those places, things, and practices associated with God must be treated with great care; they are set apart. This includes food eaten by special rules (kashrut). Moreover, there are gradations of holiness, depending on how close one is to God: for instance, some angelic beings are superior to others, and the inner shrine of the Tabernacle housing the Shekhinah (the indwelling presence of God on earth) is holier than what is outside of it. Finally, it can mean Kiddush HaShem, or martyrdom for the sake of God—elevating the name of God by sacrificing one's life for Him. It is significant that a minyan (group of ten Jews) is needed to say the Kedushah, the prayer that sanctifies God's name. Holiness is not achieved privately but through public performance.

Importantly, holiness is connected to ethics and morals. In this regard it means a turning away from the physical, material world and a turning toward God. Torah aims to guide not only individuals striving toward a state of holiness but the holy nation Israel, a holy society whose social fabric, being constituted through holiness, makes certain kinds of behavior commanded and other kinds of behavior not only impermissible but unthinkable.

We are charged to be sensitive to the situation of the disabled, the aged, the widow, the stranger, the laborer. We are to be kind in the treatment of animals. Our laws are concerned not only with action but with intention. Leviticus 19:15–18 (Parasha Kedoshim, a key section for the holiness code) spells this out with regard to different kinds of relationships and different, but related, actions: "You shall not render an unfair decision: do not favor the poor or show deference to the rich; judge your neighbor fairly. Do not deal basely with your fellows. Do not profit by the blood of your neighbor. I am the Lord. You shall not hate your kinsman in your heart. Reprove your neighbor, but incur no guilt because of him. You shall not take vengeance or bear a grudge against your kinsfolk. Love your neighbor as yourself. I am the Lord."[1] In this area, Torah is concerned as much with feelings and intentions as with actions, because the price of anger or hostility is so often violence. Thus, one test for the presence of holiness is to look at the purpose of any action: Judaism understands that the same action can be holy or unholy depending on the time, place, or purpose. Finally, holiness is connected in some Torah passages to the land of Canaan. Practices that occur elsewhere, such as idolatry, are not to be tolerated in Israel, since a Jewish community is expected to be a model for others and a Jewish state is expected to be different from others. What we do individually matters not only to society but to the nation and the world, and even to the universe.

Holiness is often misunderstood as hygiene because of the stress in Torah on physical decay or damage or disease (tuma). For instance, chapters 13 and 24 of Leviticus deal with skin eruptions. The term *tzara'at* is commonly translated as "leprosy," but a number of diseases or irritations are included in this untranslatable word. A fungus on a house is an equivalent form of impurity, which illustrates that we are not talking about human physical hygiene. To neutralize the disease, however, separation of the person from the camp is required, and a sacrificial rite is performed. In the case of a house, in Leviticus the affliction is remedied through scraping and replastering and sacrifice; otherwise, it is destroyed. In all cases, the solution seems to be physical separation from defilement and a striving toward the potential for purity. In less severe cases of defilement, rituals of purification, such as those in mikvahs (ritual bathing pools), were routinely practiced by priests in the Temple cult as well as by congregants.

For the ancient Jewish people, the sexual organs held the possibility both for life and for defilement. Death was the source of the greatest pollution. Thus, holiness includes the avoidance of anything in which the life force has vanished, such as not touching a corpse.[2]

The sexual act could itself be defiling, and it is significant that the Israelites were commanded to refrain from sexual intercourse for several days before receiving the revelation at Mount Sinai. They were expected to be in the purest state possible. Moses, it is reported, abstained from sexuality for the rest of his life. Semen and menstrual blood are both treated as putting a couple into a state of defilement. Niddah, that which is to be shunned, refers to the impurity of a menstruating woman. We thus find rules for separation between husband and wife—abstinence—for seven days after the end of a period and for the wife's immersion in the mikvah before a resumption of sexual intercourse.

Major commentators differ on how narrowly or broadly to interpret the commandment to holiness. Aware of the importance of the topic of sexuality in connection with the holiness code, Rashi holds that the commandment to be holy refers to the laws of chastity, but his critics, such as Nachmanides, challenge such a narrow view. Nachmanides holds that this "purity" is associated throughout the Talmud with the pious, called Perushim (abstemious, saintly), and that holiness also includes abstinence in the area of personal and social conduct—in short, in every area of life.

In addition to trying to understand further what holiness may mean, any student of purity, pollution, and the body must have a rudimentary understanding of Judaism's beliefs about body and soul. These beliefs are somewhat confusing, since they have changed slightly over time. The Bible sees the body as entirely equal to the soul; indeed, their relationship is such a non-issue that there are no elaborated views on it. A man or a woman is considered a unified living being, a nefesh. That term is also used of emotions or feelings. The Bible draws on neshamah (breath) as a synonym for the living being and ruah (spirit) as that power coming from outside the body that causes life.

Biblical Judaism does not make value judgments about the body. Thus, if the body is polluted by a discharge, this does not mean the person herself or himself is bad or evil. It means *only* that the body is in a state of nonholiness and unable to approach the possibility, at that time, of purity. To understand those chapters of Leviticus that deal with pollution and disease, it is critical that we put aside notions of value judgment.[3] A diseased body is not bad; it is polluted and needs to be set apart from the community until healed or repurified.

For the rabbis of the Talmud, however, who were influenced by the idea of a life hereafter, the soul is separable from the body, because it departs during sleep to gain refreshment (*Genesis Rabbah* 14.9) and it leaves the body at death to be joined again at resurrection (Sanhedrin 90b–91a). This view is consonant with that expressed in Leviticus Rabbah 34.3 that because the soul is a guest in the body on earth, the body must be respected.

However, a new emphasis on messianism in the rabbinic period does not adequately emphasize that even in the early rabbinic period, when Christian and Jewish attitudes toward the body were not definitively distinct, most of the Jews of Palestine and Babylonia differed from Hellenized and Christianized Jewish formations in their orientations toward sexuality and the body. As Daniel Boyarin puts it, "Rabbinic Judaism invested significance in the body which in other formations was invested in the soul. That is, for rabbinic Jews, the human being was defined as a body—animated to be sure by a soul—while for Hellenistic Jews (such as Philo) and (at least many Greek-speaking) Christians (such as Paul) the essence of a human being is a soul housed in a body."[4]

It would be incorrect and overly simplistic to imagine that the body was in some way repellent to Christians but not to Jews. Although some dualists represented the body negatively, some represented it positively. Some nondualists saw the body, especially the female body, as a source of anxiety and disgust, and some did not. As I suggested previously, rabbinic Judaism is not monolithic in its attitudes. Indeed, it is often most interesting for its debates and for the cultural disagreements and power struggles it both authorizes and represents.

Moreover, as Boyarin suggests, the complex struggle between rabbinic Judaism and Hellenistic contenders over issues related to the body located itself in various halakhic and social areas, including gender, sexuality, marriage practices, genealogy, and ethnicity (in the rite of circumcision), and in entire areas that did not directly involve the body but were connected to issues of tradition, desire, and holiness, namely, reading practices of the Bible.

The Christian mode of Platonic allegory is based in a dualistic notion that complements the dualism of body and soul. In this system of interpretation, meaning is a disembodied element prior to incarnation in language, which then is the outer casing of an inner substance or soul of a text. The Jewish hermeneutical mode, midrash, by contrast, eschews such a dualism of inner and outer. The Jewish hermeneutic is reflected even in ritual practices and interpretive modes; it is a signature aspect of Judaism. As a convert trying to rethink body and soul, I came to realize that if I didn't "get" it, there would be a lot I would never understand.

To sort out the Jewish view on the body, to understand holiness better, and to continue my critique of certain aspects of Judaism, this chapter isolates several issues related to the body through a consideration of topics central to Judaism: mikvah, childbirth, disease and pollution, homosexuality, circumcision, and, finally, opposing views of holiness and the body offered by two Jewish medieval writers, Bachya Ibn Pakuda in his eleventh-century work *The Duties of the Heart* and Maimonides in his *Mishneh Torah* of the twelfth century. This central debate within Judaism about the body was never really decided one way or another.

Immersion in the mikvah (ritual bathing pool) for purification is required for a conversion to either Conservative or Orthodox Judaism. On the morning of March 19, 1999, conversion day, I prepared early for the mikvah by washing my body and hair (which I had already washed the night before). A friend and I would meet my Conservative bet din, composed of three rabbis, at a brand-new mikvah in Pennsylvania. I removed my wedding ring for the first time since I had been married and dressed in something easy to slip off and on. I packed a bag of towels, my forms, and other essentials. I was excited.

A friend had gone to an Orthodox mikvah for her conversion immersing and was disappointed by her reception. Hers was rushed and rigid. But my rabbi had given me a different choice. A body of natural water would also be legally acceptable. He offered me a private cove on the Atlantic Ocean or a mikvah housed in a Reform synagogue led by a woman rabbi. Because of the month, March, I rather reluctantly chose the mikvah. Still, given that I would go to a pool within a synagogue, I was anticipating a relaxed visit at which I could focus on spiritual matters. I purposefully made the forty-minute drive to the mikvah by myself in order to have a chance to meditate. I found myself nervous about the oral examination in Judaism to follow, even though I was well prepared.

And I realized en route that I knew very little about a mikvah. Indeed, I was not prepared for the mikvah at all. In retrospect, I realized, I knew shockingly little about this incredible ritual. The morning after, by a strange coincidence, I came to realize just how little.

I was under the very mistaken impression that the issue was one of cleansing and that I was dirty and morally filthy for having been a non-Jew. The Jewish religion wanted me pure, I thought, as if this were the physical version of renouncing all other faiths. In other words, I was under the impression that a mikvah visit is a judgment visit as well as a depolluting one. I had not known enough to ask my rabbi to educate me on this issue. I didn't know the questions to ask. Moreover, I was embarrassed to discuss mikvah with him.[5] In addition, the mikvah had neglected to send me information about water and immersion symbolism within the Jewish tradition, information that routinely accompanied the letter confirming an appointment. I might have grasped more had the insert been present. Finally, no woman I consulted, except an older Orthodox friend, had been to a mikvah more than once. Most had gone before marriage, and it seemed that nobody had anything really good to say about a mikvah or the experience, whether related to conversion or to rituals of family purity, since nobody, after all, had ever gone back.

There was, as I would discover later on, a larger silence about mikvah among Conservative women than among the Orthodox. Some interesting parallels to my own experience turned up during a live web chat held on the Jewish Theological Seminary learning site with guests Judith Hauptman, professor of Talmud at JTS, and Shari Rothfarb, the installation artist of the 1999 mikvah installation "Water Rites" at the Jewish Museum, New York.

For example, Rothfarb described mikvah as a topic "enshrouded in modesty." It is rarely discussed. Most women who go for family purity issues are Orthodox; even they tend to go in the evening to ensure even more privacy and modesty. Purity rituals are apparently not widely practiced among Conservative Jews. Hauptman noted that while the Conservative movement officially views mikvah as part of its rituals, most Conservative Jews do not observe Shabbat or kashrut or the rules of family purity; she added, however, that women rabbis and new interest in spirituality have reopened this issue. She later remarked that Rothfarb's installation, which includes the film *Ocean Avenue*, gives mikvah a more positive presentation than it gets in Talmud. In ancient times, she argued, men were repulsed by women's menstruation because they associated blood with death. A negative association with mikvah may be a projection of a patriarchally influenced view of woman involving fear and loathing.[6]

A writer of articles on mikvah, who has had trouble getting her work published, commented in the online chat that in her lectures to Conservative Jews, including Sisterhoods, she had found that many had not even heard of the laws of mikvah. Nothing was being taught about mikvah in the curriculum, and she added that many women rabbis she had spoken to were opposed to it. A man who participated in the chat observed that mikvah is a mysterious ritual about which he knew little, while another praised it for its role in his marriage.[7] Clearly, experiences differ, and my own conversations may not be representative, but I have been surprised that among the observant Conservative women I know who do observe Shabbat and kashrut, mikvah is irrelevant.

My young son and I happened upon "Water Rites" in 1999 on our first visit to the Jewish Museum, a trip we took after my conversion. I did not come upon this chat about the installation in the JTS archives until later. My own response to the installation was strongly positive. The film, which also interested my son, includes a mother-and-daughter debate about mikvah. In addition, the installation conveys a sense of the antiquity of mikvah through photographs and offers the effect of primal light, reflection, and water in the central area of the exhibit. The dark of the film room and the light of the other parts of the exhibit represented for me the holiness of both the nighttime and the daytime mikvah experience.

Despite my ignorance about mikvah prior to my conversion, I knew that it was important to me. I had heard that conversions were sometimes done in bathtubs or swimming pools if a mikvah was not available. Those options were unacceptable to me. Even though I did not understand the meaning of the mikvah, I wanted a Conservative supervising rabbi who would insist on halakhic law being fulfilled not only in spirit but to the letter: a regulation mikvah or a natural body of water. In fact, I had chosen my rabbi in the first place in part owing to his requirements about the mikvah, in spite of the fact that I didn't know much about its meaning.

The Reform mikvah was hospitable on conversion day, and I immediately felt at ease there. An attendant turned on the natural water flow of rainwater. My friend and I took our places inside the mikvah, and the rabbis of the bet din took up their post on the other side of a slatted door. I dipped under water entirely three times and said the blessings. But in spite of the positive setting, the warm water, the magical light, the playing of light on water, the support of my friend, I just couldn't get into the right frame of mind. I hurried to be done.

The next morning, my first full day as a Jew, I rose early. I stole downstairs for a few moments alone as a brand-new Jewish woman and delayed my breakfast, quickly fed the cats, but left the newspaper outside for the time being. I curled up in a living room chair with a book a friend had given me at my conversion, *Four Centuries of Jewish Women's Spirituality*, and let it fall open anywhere.[8] It fell open at page 324, the end of a special mikvah ceremony written by a woman for a woman who had been raped. The first footnote explained mikvah. Only then did I realize, with some shock, what I had lost by not understanding it the day before.

> Mikvah has many meanings in Hebrew. It is a confluence of water, a reservoir, a pool, or a ritual bath. Mikvah is also understood to be a source of hope and trust, another name for God. The mikvah ceremony refers to the ritual of immersion in such places for purposes of ritual purification. According to halakhah, Jewish law, the ritual of immersion is required for conversion to Judaism, but it is most commonly associated with "laws of family purity." Within monogamous heterosexual Jewish marriages, "as menstruation begins, a married couple halts all erotic activities. A minimum of five days are considered menstrual, then seven 'clean' days are observed with the same restrictions. After nightfall of the seventh day, the woman bathes herself . . . and immerses herself in a special pool built to exacting specifications."[9]

Mikvah is part of the traditional Conservative and Orthodox conversion process; when I converted, mikvah was optional in the Reform movement. It affirms the transformations that have been achieved by the convert through formal study and through her or his agreement to take on the yoke of Israel.

The night of my conversion, at the home of my Orthodox friends where we were having a celebratory dinner, my host asked me where I felt the presence of God on that day: "At the mikvah?" I shook my head no. "At the bet din?" I said, "No, it was at the ark while reciting the Sh'ma." But part of me was troubled by my answer, intuitively feeling it could first have been at the mikvah, a meeting place of primal origin.

As I learned the next morning while reading, my ignorance had cost me a great deal emotionally and spiritually. I missed the powerful connection to my Jewish foremothers—the many generations of women who went to mikvahs in such far-off or such near-by places as Lodz, Poland; Toledo, Spain; Mainz, Germany; and Brooklyn, New York. I misunderstood the nondualism of body and soul and did not realize that a value judgment was not being put on me that morning. I did not understand that I was naked totally so that the waters could flow in and out of each orifice and every part of my body and being. I did not grasp that natural water means sustenance, care, and life. Most grievously, I did not know what the Talmud tells us (which I should have figured out for myself)—that the ultimate source of all water is the river flowing from Eden and that the rainwater in the mikvah linked me to a primal spiritual state of unity. Rabbi Sue Ann Wasserman, who wrote the mikvah ceremony for and with her friend Laura Levitt, documented in *Four Centuries*, describes mikvah as fundamentally about human encounters with the power of the holy.

I loved the mikvah so much more when I understood where I had been, what had happened to me, and why. I yearned to return, and I took a trip back with my friend Ilene on the Jewish anniversary of my conversion, again going in the daytime. On this visit, when I emerged into the dressing room from the pool area, I looked in the mirror, imagining I would simply wait for the first thoughts. This time they weren't *hurry, clean, almost Jewish* or *bet din exam next,* but *woman, happy, whole.* Each visit after that, one on the anniversary of my conversion and one right before the next Yom Kippur, brought me an even deeper sense of peace and fulfillment.

In January 2000 my then nine-year-old son journeyed with us and a bet din to the same mikvah for the second part of his conversion. I was in the waiting room and did not share in his experience directly. Still, his joy in the mikvah was so great, I am told, that he didn't want to get out. One could argue that little boys generally like warm water, and mine clearly liked going underwater. But how am I to interpret his own expressed desire to revisit the mikvah on *his* anniversary? Was it to be like his mother? Did he just like the mikvah pool? Or does his soul sense that something about the ritual is incomparable?

A year later we made the trip to the mikvah between his conversion anniversary and mine, so we celebrated them together. My husband came along to serve as the "buddy" to each of us. Now the mikvah is a family ritual in a new sense of the term. We are writing for ourselves the holiness laws. Today mikvah brings us all together and reminds us of who we are at the same time that it purifies and renews us.

I took my epigraphs for this chapter from Leviticus, the location in Torah of the priestly code of holiness. In Leviticus 6–15 the overarching concern is tuma vetahara, ritual impurity and purity, largely as connected to the priestly service to God, including animal sacrifice, and to maintaining the purity of the Tabernacle, or mishkan. God directly addresses Aaron, the high priest: "And you shall distinguish between the sacred and the common and between the impure and the pure. And you shall teach the Israelites all the laws which God spoke to them through Moses" (10:10–11). To understand the location of the human body in discussions of purity and impurity, we have to understand more about the relationships between death, birth, sexuality, and purity.

The section on which I wish to focus briefly is the parasha called Tazria, Leviticus 12–13, which opens with a much-debated section on childbirth: it is significant that the child at birth immediately brings defilement upon its mother.

God spoke to Moses saying: Speak to the Children of Israel, saying: When a woman conceives and gives birth to a male, she shall be contaminated for a seven-day period, as during the days of her separation infirmity shall she be contaminated. On the eighth day, the flesh of his foreskin shall be circumcised. For thirty-three days she shall remain in blood of purity; she may not touch anything sacred and she may not enter the Sanctuary, until the completion of her days of purity. If she gives birth to a female, she shall be contaminated for two weeks, as during her separation; and for sixty-six days shall she remain in the blood of purity. (Leviticus 12:1–5)

This passage raises a number of problems for a modern reader, particularly a feminist reader. Why does the woman remain in a state of defilement longer for a girl child than for a boy child? Some commentators suggest that the b'rit milah (circumcision) is such a strong covenantal gesture on the part of parents that in some way it begins to atone for whatever sins the woman has committed while pregnant. Having no such opportunity for atonement with a girl child, the mother must remain separate longer. Other commentators suggest that in birthing a girl the woman is doubly removed from the state of being able to birth life (two wombs are not in the process of conception—one is bleeding from giving birth and the other is brand-new). I don't know. It remains a contested and difficult passage.

Moreover, why would pollution be connected to birth at all? Normally we associate defilement with death, decay, and dissolution; within Judaism specifically tuma (impurity) is related to dead animals and human corpses. Wasted semen or seed, whether through masturbation or through homosexuality, is also considered a loss of life because it does not issue forth in life.[10] Thus, in rabbinic Judaism, so committed to procreation, wasted seed is a form of defilement.

Rabbi Judah Halevi argues that tumot that express loss of the life force or fertility or the creative force account for all forms of tuma, except the one chosen to open the list, childbirth. Perhaps the key is the loss of the fetus by the mother's body—the separation of the mother from her created being. Possibly the key is the loss of the potential to give birth once birth has just occurred. Possibly, then, Torah is acknowledging the importance of this loss and marking the mother in recognizing the importance of changing boundaries. However we interpret this section, we could hypothesize that the new mother, tied to her biological function for nine months, is now asked to recognize the relationship of biology to holiness by observing a period of tuma. This period is related in Leviticus 12:2 to a period such as that of menstruation (akin to a loss of male seed in that it is a loss of an opportunity for fertility). Only after this period of time and separateness is she again allowed access to the sacred with sacrificial offerings.

One reason put forth is that although the creation of human life is the most important phenomenon, it is never enough, for life must always be put in the service of God. This is true for both mother and child. The offerings and rituals presented in this chapter of Torah, including the b'rit milah for the boy child, represent the privilege of birth and the raising of a child to a life of holiness.

Many religions contain paradoxical notions of the defiling character of creative powers, as David Biale reminds us. Thus, the power to defile may not be located only with a "negative force," such as death, but may also inhere in a "vital one," such as life.[11] In other words, impurity is part of normal biological processes in biblical culture that have everything to do with boundaries and proper times and places.[12]

Later rabbinic sources are sometimes ambivalent about the body and sometimes neutral about it. Generally, however, Talmud and midrash show that it is desire, not the body per se, that troubles the rabbis. Both Boyarin and Biale substantiate this view. Moreover, Ephraim Urbach, in his monumental text *The Sages*, brings a multitude of examples to argue the case that despite any elements of dualistic anthropology to be found in the rabbinic sages, the antithesis between the body and spirit in rabbinic dicta is far "less drastic" than in Hellenistic and Stoic-Platonic writings.[13]

Urbach quotes the saying of Rabbi Akiva, who lived in the fourth generation of Tannaim: "Reflect on three things, and you will not come within the power of sin: know whence you have come, and whither you are going, and before whom you are destined to give account and reck-

oning. Whence you have come: from a putrefying drop; whither you are
going: to a place of dust, worms and maggots; and before whom you are
destined to give account and reckoning: before the Supreme King of
kings, the Holy One, blessed be He." As Urbach notes, the rabbi does
not mention body and soul but speaks of the whole man who stands for
judgment. He is not speaking of an afterlife, but of a reckoning at death.
The outcome of the accounting depends on a man's deeds when he was
body and spirit, whereas the reason for the accounting is to discover
whether or not his soul will return to God. The alternative, offered by
Rabbi Avdimi of Haifa in a commentary on Ecclesiastes, seems to be that
the soul will be burned in front of the man. The purity of the soul, then,
is neither automatic nor immutable but results from the life lived on
earth.[14]

For the rabbis it seems that the struggle for control of sexual impulses—and thus also the attainment of greater holiness—becomes a conflict
not between body and soul but between aspects of the will.[15] As David
Biale and Boyarin indicate, this view also is supported by the heavy rabbinic emphasis on the importance of marriage as a mechanism for con-
trolling sexuality, by highly detailed writings about sexual practices
between man and wife, and by their view of a lust to read Torah as an
appropriate channeling of sexual desire.

The priestly code of holiness and the rabbinic attitudes toward the body
and sexuality cause me great anguish when they are still applied to our
lives today, especially to women and homosexuals. But as I indicated earlier, I am able to deal with family purity issues by focusing on the union
of the physical and the spiritual in an act of holiness. The mikvah puts
me in touch with Edenic creation. There I am able to put aside problematic assumptions about a negative or dirty female body, even those I
may have internalized from my culture and from certain texts within
Jewish tradition, because I don't believe in them.

I cannot remain as sanguine, however, about the biblical naming of
male homosexuality as an abomination and about the negative rabbinic
literature on the subject. For the intolerance still displayed toward
homosexuals within Judaism today is unacceptable and unjustifiable, as

the great film *Trembling Before God* illustrates. The traditional position of Judaism on homosexuality has no place in our lives anymore.

What first troubled me about Judaism, in fact, was not its positions on women but the general resistance on the part of contemporary patriarchal Conservative and Orthodox Judaism to engage fully with issues of sexual orientation. Religious laws are strict concerning male homosexuality: It is an abomination—to'evah. For a man to lie with another man is a sexual transgression, according to Leviticus 18 and 20, one as serious as adultery or incest, because the act involves the wasting of seed, or life. Lesbians are considered wrongdoers but not defilers, because in their sexual practice there is no wasted seed.

I should explain briefly why I consider sexual orientation a central issue that institutionalized religion should address by altering laws and mind-sets. Sexuality, marriage, and community—all central issues to Judaism—are historical constructs. They develop in historical contexts, and they change over time, as Michel Foucault, Thomas Lacquer, and countless other sociologists and historians of sexuality and the family have shown. But we need not turn to academics to find this out. The shift from polygamy to monogamy within Ashkenazic Judaism itself in the Middle Ages is just such an example. Moreover, on some issues, as rabbinic and contemporary history show us, the rabbis found ways to change laws, adapt them, or widen rights to bring Jewish practices in touch with the contemporary moment or the ordination of women within the Conservative movement, for example. Issues of sexuality, however, which have everything to do in Judaism with procreation, with community, and with holiness, apparently cannot be addressed except in the face of great resistance. On the question of the status of homosexuality, the Conservative Committee on Jewish Law and Standards of the 1990s continued, uncourageously as far as I am concerned, to accept both left- and right-wing statements. As Rabbi Lionel Moses articulates it: "Tradition continues to have a veto."[16] It is time to reopen the debate about the status of homosexuality.

Because I have close Jewish gay friends of both sexes who all left Judaism as soon as they could, I questioned learned, observant Jews about the attitudes toward homosexuality. I discovered that in my circles, which were supposedly enlightened, there was enormous ignorance about homosexuality, Jewish rules about it, and attitudes toward it. Most of the college-aged heterosexual Jewish college students to whom I spoke, even those who were adamant about social justice, did not know the Conservative or Orthodox platforms on homosexuality and were pretty shocked when I informed them. The response of adults out of college was almost identical.

Where I found informed or personal knowledge about gay and lesbian homosexuality, halakhah barred any untroubled acceptance. And where I found intelligent, thoughtful responses, I often found anguish in Jewish hearts. I have run across a general unwillingness—in both large and small groups—to discuss this *as a central issue* about which anything could be or should be changed within the religion. This response has infuriated me as much as Jewish anti-Semitism.

In the quest for a just society and in partnership with God for tikkun olam (repair of the world), I follow the lesbian radical feminist call to reunderstand and reframe Jewish law on sexuality. Thus, I support Judith Plaskow's 1991 call in *Standing Again at Sinai* for a revaluation of the traditional Jewish rejection of homosexuality. Both Jewish law and Leviticus concede that male homosexuality may be a predisposition but nonetheless view it as a choice. Because of the element of choice, homosexuals are counseled to stop practicing. Moreover, traditional Jewish law maintains that one can denounce the "sin" of such a choice while still loving the sinner. I learned that Conservative Jews at rabbinic conventions have supported civil equality for homosexuals and have stated that openly gay Jews may join congregations, camps, youth groups, and schools, but this is only one step in the right direction. Openly gay Jews are not welcomed as rabbinical students by the Jewish Theological Seminary. Rabbis who are gay often must stay in the closet. This is life denial of a kind more damaging than wasted seed.

Strong opposition to homosexuality from within the religion, which feeds into and is further shaped by the general social prejudice against same-sex love and sexual practice, is thus located around important Jewish rituals and institutions such as marriage and the rabbinate. Men violating religious laws openly may not be included in these institutions.

Even a ceremony of commitment may be considered a mockery of Jewish law. The heterosexual rabbis who support gay rabbis and who perform ceremonies of commitment or gay marriages are found mostly within the Reform and Reconstructionist movements.

Conservative Judaism views Torah as a cultural document whose interpretation can respond to changing historical conditions rather than one that is viewed through an Orthodox lens as the permanent and unalterable word of God. Yet there is ambiguity in this stated principle of the conservative platform: "Halakha is . . . what the Jewish community understands God's will to be."[17] This can imply that halakha are fixed as the "will of God" or it can mean that interpretation of the authority of Torah, as a human document, rests in the human community, representing our understanding and interpretation of God's will. Thus, it seems to me, our interpretation of Torah also represents our understanding of God. In certain areas the Conservative movement has been very slow to adapt laws to our historical situation and to come to new understandings of God.

The central issue is the statement in Jewish law that there is only one path to holiness through sexual relations: heterosexual marriage. This law fosters the survival of the nation through procreation and the hoped-for holiness of the nation. The radical feminist position argues, by contrast, that there are various paths to holiness through sexual relations, various kinds of families, various ways to procreate and adopt, and different ways for a nation to be holy and to support communal values and experience. How, I ask, can we embrace a halakhah that does not allow the affirmation of every Jew, wherever sexuality and holiness are united within herself or himself. I cannot agree with Conservative and Orthodox positions regarding homosexuality—that is, I do not see homosexuality as a sin or as a predisposition related to choice (except the choice not to follow one's predisposition and thus to remain celibate). I don't see one's sexual orientation as entirely a willed subjective or self-indulgent act, but precisely as a form of life energy. I cannot accept Jewish law on the subject.

As Plaskow argues, for many the connection between sexuality and spiritual energy lies most richly with those of the same sex. Why, then, should these Jews have to hide or suppress this connection or pretend they lead heterosexual lives or give up an entire dimension of their embodied beings?

Of all the commandments in Judaism, the b'rit milah, the covenant of circumcision, is the one most observed today. Even secular Jews who do not observe Judaism in any other way tend to have their sons circumcised. Circumcision is a physical, outward sign of Jewish identity and a mark against assimilation. In the United States the majority of males are circumcised in hospitals anyway, so one could argue that circumcision is an aspect of assimilation, but there is much more to the Jewish ceremony than the surgical cutting of foreskin. In fact, a hospital circumcision by a physician does not count in the Conservative and Orthodox movements as religiously legitimate. According to religious tradition, if a regulation circumcision is not performed, the child will have no place in the world to come, may die childless or prematurely, and automatically loses his attachment on earth to the Jewish people.

Like many Jewish mitzvot or commandments, this one is sometimes incorrectly regarded as related to hygiene or health. However, any medical benefits from circumcision, such as a reduction in the risk of certain cancers, are irrelevant to the b'rit milah. Circumcision is a commitment made by parents to a bond between father, mother, son, and God. It is a challenge precisely because there is no logical reason for it. Indeed, it opposes human reason, it seems bizarre and barbaric, and it requires our own efforts to effect. If it were not an act of such magnitude, requiring faith and our decisions and effort, says Rashi, the lack of a foreskin would prove meaningless.

B'rit milah is what we do as our part of a relationship. God's part, as stated in Torah, is to make the Jewish people fruitful, make a nation of us, establish kingship so that the Jewish people will be able to suppress idolatry and serve as the model of a holy nation, and award the Land of Israel to the Jews. The commandment is found first in Genesis 17, where it is enjoined upon Abraham as his half of this holy arrangement:

God said to Abraham, "And as for you, you shall keep My covenant—you and your offspring after you throughout their generations. This is

My covenant which you shall keep between Me and you and your offspring after you: Every male among you shall be circumcised. You shall
circumcise the flesh of your foreskin and that shall be the sign of the
covenant between Me and you. At the age of eight days every male
among you shall be circumcised, throughout your generations—he
that is born in the household or purchased with your money shall surely be circumcised. Thus, My covenant shall be in your flesh for an
everlasting covenant. An uncircumcised male the flesh of whose foreskin shall not be circumcised—that soul shall be cut off from its people; he has invalidated My covenant."

Circumcision is performed on the eighth day of the child's life by a
mohel, a pious, observant Jew, often a rabbi, trained in halakhah and in
the particular surgery. If a child is born without a foreskin or if a child
was previously circumcised without religious intent, a symbolic circumcision may be performed. Called hatafah dam b'rit, this ritual requires
drawing a drop of blood of the covenant.

Shortly after my own conversion, I began to debate whether or not
to have our son convert at the age of nine or just before his bar mitzvah at thirteen. At first, knowing nothing in particular about b'rit
milah, I tried to get out of it. No apologies; I didn't want the knife, or
equivalent, on my son's genitals. He'd been circumcised on his second
day of life in the hospital by a Jewish obstetrician. That, I thought, was
good enough. And I might have persisted in my willful ignorance and
obstinacy had I not thought to check on the bar mitzvah situation for
him first. I went to one of the leaders of my minyan and asked whether
my son could celebrate his bar mitzvah in that congregation. I was asking for a Conservative minyan to perform a Reform bar mitzvah, and
the answer was no. To have a bar mitzvah among the friends in the
minyan that had so welcomed us, our son would also have to undergo
a complete conversion ritual, including hatafah dam b'rit. This was a
major dilemma.

On the one hand, I felt there was no way out. It made no sense to be
Conservative Jews but to have our son in the Reform movement. The
main point of my own conversion had been to bind us closer as a family

unit. Our son's half-brothers and half-sister were Conservative Jews too. It would have to be done. But when? Should his father and mother merely announce it to him or should he be given the choice close to bar mitzvah age as part of his responsibility at reaching that milestone? If we did not go forward now, we would be considered parentally, religiously negligent. If we did go forward, we were making the choice for him. Was this a medical issue, a psychological issue, or a religious issue?

For us it was a time of utter confusion. I was being strongly lobbied against this rite by some friends, and we were very subtly encouraged by others who said it was an absolute necessity. Realizing that we wanted a Conservative affiliation (and what it represented) for our son, no matter at what age, we decided to go forward with the ceremony early in the new secular year. This would give us a bit of time to assemble a bet din of his choice and to find a mohel. And it would give us all time to get used to the idea.

We wanted to give our son some say in this matter, so we suggested that he choose the members of his bet din from a list of observant men whom we all knew well. He selected the men who would participate on the basis of their relationship to young male children, choosing observant fathers of sons thirteen or under in age whom he had seen in loving interaction with their boys and whom he liked. He knew exactly what he wanted and was happy with his choices. Our rabbi located a mohel for us. All the anxiety and concern of the day was clearly mine. As the mother, I was as troubled as I would have been had he been eight days old and ready for full circumcision. I was biologically troubled—concerned about the body of my child being hurt, feeling my own body going under the knife, ready to take the knife in his place.

Since I was not permitted to be present for the ceremony, I fled to the second floor and closed the door of our bedroom and buried my head, waiting for a scream of pain. But none came. After a while I got curious and walked downstairs, only to be greeted in the hall by my son, who was joking and smiling. He was delighted, even jubilant, and excited about proceeding to the mikvah. Everyone asked me later, how did it go? I had nothing to report but the totally joyous completion of half of the covenantal agreement.

Yet four months later, when we attended the Orthodox b'rit milah of my son's infant nephew, the child of his half-sister, who was given only some wine for a painkiller, I really understood why the birth grandmothers stood in the back holding hands tightly and why the parents shed tears. Circumcision requires a faith and love of tradition that overrides all other human feelings and reasoning; holding such faith and acting on it is very emotional. It hurts deeply to put one's child under the knife. No matter how trusting one may be of the mohel, one always fears a slip, because every circumcision is different, as any mohel will tell you. No matter how experienced the mohel, and no matter how quick the procedure, it seems endless.

Circumcision is a major test of willpower, faith, and tradition. I don't know what it feels like for a Jew-by-birth mother, but for a convert mother this aspect of Judaism was a trial. I was able to feel more joyous at the infant's circumcision than at my son's hatafah, but only, I'm convinced, because we were in the presence of an eight-day-old baby being inaugurated into the covenant. Everyone present was still joyful about his birth. We were thrilled for the young couple. But in my case, remembering my biological ties to my own son, I also empathized entirely with the mother and father. I was happy, I admit, not to be in a position of having to give the infant over.

Choosing circumcision, if I can even say one entirely "chooses" it, reminds me of Milton's comments in his brilliant political treatise *Areopagitica* on the necessity to test the good. Although the treatise argues against restricting freedom of the press and has nothing overt to do with my subject matter, it is one of Milton's best-known works for its rhetoric and for the elegance of its argument. The specific context of the passage I have in mind concerns the Christian wayfarer and the inexplicable mixture of good and evil in life. Yet Milton's articulation of untested versus tested virtue remains important for me as an articulation of the trial of performing any very difficult religious act:

> I cannot praise a fugitive and cloistered virtue, unexercised and unbreath'd, that never sallies out and sees her adversary, but slinks out of the race where that immortal garland is run for, not without dust

and heat. . . . That which purifies us is trial. . . . That virtue which is
but a youngling in the contemplation of evil . . . is but a blank virtue,
not a pure; her whiteness is but an excremental whiteness.

I am not claiming that it is a virtue to circumcise—it is a commandment,
not a virtue. Nor am I indicating that one must face the "evil" of death
or cutting via circumcision in order to become a good Jew. Rather, I am
suggesting that I was scared, weak, and conflicted on this issue. I am con-
fiding that, in many cases, it is emotionally no easier for a young couple
with an infant boy to follow tradition than for an older couple with a
young boy. It is not necessarily easier for a Jew by birth than for a convert. Following mitzvot is not meant to be easy on anybody. And it isn't.

A small number of Jews are tremendously opposed to b'rit milah. They
object to the pain of the procedure, its medical superfluousness, the
infant's lack of choice, the genital mutilation, and the sexism of the ritual.
Defenders of the b'rit milah counter with any number of arguments.

Among these aspects of the ritual, the ones that bothered me most
were the pain—which I've explained—and the sexism. The b'rit milah is
a male bonding ritual in which the mother who bore the son has
absolutely no part. There is no such covenantal ceremony for girls.
Hence today Jews have a custom of Simhat bat ceremonies (the joy of
welcoming a girl into the covenant). I finally had to accept Judaism's sexism in this area, with all the obvious and unresolved conflicts. I felt that
the religion is still largely patriarchal, that establishing covenant through
male flesh is certainly antimatriarchal, but that if I chose to avoid b'rit
milah, I would be choosing to avoid Judaism. This did not mean I
couldn't fight for reviews of halakhah in areas that bothered me, but it
did mean that if I was going to join a religion, I had to acknowledge the
centrality of this command.

Other avenues were definitely open. A good friend suggested that I
write my own ceremony and that we do a symbolic hatafah. The problem was that this would not have been acceptable to my worship group
or the Conservative denomination of Judaism, and my son would therefore not be a Conservative Jew. I also confess that for a while during my
obstinate phase I wondered how many "Conservative" men never had a

b'rit milah ceremony, only a hospital circumcision, and therefore weren't "really" Jewish. Who's to know? But I reflected rather quickly that my son was to know, we were to know, and my rabbi and minyan were to know, since I'd already raised the question. And most of all, God was to know. Would I lie to my son, my friends, and my God? It was a very charged situation for me, and I thought about it for a long time.

In the end I was persuaded by my love of Judaism that circumcision was necessary; inner emotions, not reasons, persuaded me. Rabbi Samson Raphael Hirsch explains that a commandment consists of two parts—the physical act and its underlying moral or spiritual dimension. Neither aspect is complete without the other. In other words, I found my own way to the point quoted earlier by Rashi: closeness to God had to come about by my own efforts.

The Jewish emphasis on the body is present in much of the literature, not only that of the biblical or rabbinic periods but also that of the medieval period. Bachya Ibn Pakuda and Moses Maimonides are just two of the thinkers who have much to say and to recommend about the care of the body and its relationship to holiness. In fact, one may argue that their approaches are very nearly opposite and therefore worth juxtaposing because both views are authentically Jewish. While Ibn Pakuda argues for abstinence in a variety of contexts, linking it finally to a form of selflessness, Maimonides argues for achieving holiness by making sacred acts out of the fulfillment of physical desires.

The concept of holiness that is often put forward, by Christians as well as by Jews, is that of abstention from things that are forbidden. Jewish examples include excessive consumption of food or drink, any consumption of forbidden (unkosher) foods, and illicit sexuality. However, in Ibn Pakuda's hands, the idea of abstinence is not merely a refraining from pleasurable physical activities that may cause harm to the body and, by extension, harm to others. For Ibn Pakuda, abstinence is a tool of introspection intimately related to internal duties of the heart. In his eleventh-century treatise *The Duties of the Heart*, he distinguishes between physical mitzvot, or "revealed obligations," and duties of the heart, or "concealed obligations."[18] Searching in Torah and the Prophets for material, Ibn Pakuda was not satisfied with what he found, so he set about remedying this systematically, by writing a text about the nature of our concealed obligations and how to fulfill them.

Ibn Pakuda understands man to be a conflicted creature with "many opposing elements, traits, and motives" ("The Gate of Repentance," introduction). His greatest concern is to help us overcome the conflicts and divisions of our beings and thereby become better able to appreciate the cardinal belief of Judaism, the Oneness of God. We need abstinence, he argues, because one of the greatest deterrents to a love of God is an excessive love of the worldly.

There are, he suggests, different types and degrees of abstinence, but he cites the Jewish nation as elected to practice abstinence more than other nations. Extremely noble and selfless people, he says, are too unworldly for their own good, while the Torah-sanctioned form of abstinence is more acceptably moderate, and the civil form too limited. Everyone needs abstinence in order to live a balanced life of law, manners, and politeness but also as a foundation of self-discipline. We do not necessarily have to diet or exercise constantly, but we do need to practice forms of realistic self-denial. Exceptional abstinence (asceticism) is called for, he advises, only when Jews begin to spiral into pleasures that lead to bad habits, bad decisions, misjudgments, humiliation of others, and self-degradation.

Yet how does Ibn Pakuda avoid proffering a philosophy of self-denial? And how do we know when to stop pleasure? The more we cultivate pleasures for their own sake, the more we stray by allying ourselves with our evil impulse, he argues. The more the world is attractive to us, the more attractive its power becomes. When he details Torah-based abstinence, Ibn Pakuda differentiates among the kinds that influence our relations with others, those that affect our bodies, and those that affect our inner being. The common denominator is that we must avoid anything that might lead to rebellion against God or neglect of His commandments. If we can practice such abstinence, we will satisfy the needs of the body and soul "in both worlds" ("The Gate of Abstinence," introduction).[19] Thus, abstaining from forbidden things, such as excesses of food or illicit sexuality, is not the only definition of holiness here. Ibn Pakuda importantly widens the notion of abstention as an act of avoidance to include a reining in of emotions—for him the holy Jew is compassionate, polite, even-tempered, mindful, open to others, and not always putting his own needs first.

Moses Maimonides offers a different approach to the body and holiness, one in line with his adaptation of the ethical teachings of Aristotle and the doctrine of the golden mean, which views morality as taking a middle way between extremes. In *Mishneh Torah*, Maimonides advocates moderation in all matters. He notes the virtues of prudence, self-respect, and modesty, examples of the golden mean. Unlike Ibn Pakuda, therefore, he sees no virtue in excessive abstinence. Extremism can be remedied only by a movement in the opposite direction. Since Maimonides frowns on excess, he also frowns on abstinence.

It is useful to understand how Greek culture handled the body in order to grasp the fundamental difference between Ibn Pakuda and Maimonides. In Greek culture, which dominated Jewish life during the Hellenistic period, the beauty and sanctification of the human body were highly esteemed. To illustrate this point, we need think not only of Greek sculpture and the Olympic Games but also of the heavy emphasis on the body in the poetry of Homer, the plays of Sophocles, or the philosophy of Aristotle and Plato. In Greek society, holiness was achieved when the body was both celebrated and satisfied.

The Jews accepted the Greek view of holiness no more wholeheartedly than they accepted a Christian view of the body as bestial and the soul as angelic. Rather, Judaism promoted the idea that since man is made up of an integrated body and soul, each part has needs that must be fulfilled. Denying the body is problematic, but so is fulfilling bodily needs too much. Judaism resolved this dilemma by suggesting that the needs of the body should be satisfied in moderation and only for a holy purpose.

Thus, to go back to the point about intent, action, and holiness, if one uses physical enjoyment to honor God, the act is holy. Two examples pertain to Shabbat: sexual expression with one's mate on Friday night and the drinking of wine for Kiddush. Taken to excess, done without proper motives, or done at the wrong times, neither act would be holy.

Yet the body's desire for sex and for wine are totally natural. Therefore, Judaism sets aside a special time for these basic bodily needs and pleasures to be fulfilled. Likewise, the amount of time we humans spend on buying, preparing, and consuming food is enormous compared to the habits of other species. Yet Judaism elevates eating to a holy act by offering us the laws of kashrut and by connecting the holidays with special foods.

Maimonides in his *Laws Relating to Moral Dispositions and to Ethical Conduct* goes so far as to offer strict guidelines for when we should eat and drink, how much, where, and what. For instance: "Food should be taken to repletion; during a meal, about one-third less should be eaten than the quantity that would give a feeling of satiety, and only a little water should be drunk—and that mixed with wine." Equally rigorous laws are offered for hygiene, being bled medically, drinking, sexual intercourse, and the relationship of dress to the body, but all the laws are put into the context of "he who regulates his life" so that "his soul may be upright, in a condition to know God."[20]

The sanctification of daily acts and the use of the body in moderation offers us one Jewish view of holiness and the body. Ibn Pakuda links a greater degree of holiness to greater abstention from the two main physical drives: hunger and sexuality. I'm not sure that these positions are quite so irreconcilable as they may seem. Both Ibn Pakuda and Maimonides plead for moderation. Both advise living life in the service of God. Moreover, it is clear that whatever the official literature of legal codes advised about bodily practices during the biblical, rabbinic, and medieval periods, they may have embodied the ideals of a certain class (patriarchs, priests, rabbis, philosophers) but these ideals were not necessarily the norms or the universal practice of the larger society. One can argue the reverse, that precisely because bodily practices were not always sanctified to God's service or to strengthening a harmonized soul, such ideals and rules were necessary—just as the commandment to circumcise is necessary—to remind Jews that their bodies do not merely belong to them for any purpose they please.

Still, what the literature shows me is that as time went on, from biblical times, through the rabbinic period, through the Middle Ages and after, distinctly different approaches were taken to the issues of holiness, pollution, and the body. Moreover, as sexuality and desire came to be discussed more often and grew more problematic during the rabbinic period—perhaps in large part because of the pressures of differing traditions such as Hellenism or Christianity—different ideologies clashed constantly.

A historical view of the family, the body, the holy, sexualities, and sexual practices is, I believe, not only necessary but essential. Such grounding helps us understand the origins, permutations, and conflicts around these issues. It will not solve the larger problems of faith or the necessity felt by some Jews to be strictly observant or the urgency felt by others to revise and adapt rituals and rules. Important issues concerning sexual orientation, particularly those such as the exclusion of open homosexuals from the Conservative rabbinate and the resistance to officiating at homosexual unions, must continue to be thoughtfully talked over and decided by individuals, families, congregations, and governing bodies of wings of the religion. Ignorance and avoidance, willed or otherwise, can no longer serve as excuses for intolerance.

PASSAGE 4

The Akedah, the Binding of Isaac

Thoughts on Vayera, Genesis 22:1–24

*And it was after these things that God tested Avraham and
He said to him, "Avraham," and he responded, "Here I am."
And He said, "Take your son, your favored one, Isaac, whom
you love, and go to the land of Moriah, and offer him there as
burnt offering on one of the heights that I will point out to
you."*

—GENESIS 22.1–2

*Thinking about Abraham is another matter, however; then I
am shattered. . . . One approaches him with a horror religio-
sus, as Israel approached Mount Sinai.*

—SØREN KIERKEGAARD, *FEAR AND TREMBLING*, 1843

The paradoxes and puzzles of Abraham's binding of Isaac, the Akedah,
continue to haunt generation after generation. This part of Genesis
engenders so many questions in fact that books have been written on it
alone. One of the central texts of the religion and a story we hear read at
Rosh Hashanah services each new year, the Akedah illustrates Abraham's
desire to serve God without reward and regardless of the personal cost.
For me the Akedah has always been problematic. Sorting through the

many commentaries, I have had to come to my own understanding of
Abraham's actions and words and of why it is such a paradigmatic narrative for Judaism.

Commentators have plumbed every aspect of the events of the Akedah
and nearly every phrase of the telling. They have searched out the
silences, the gaps, and the absences. They wonder how God could command Abraham to do something so objectionable—and immoral by
God's own laws. They ask how Abraham could fall silent and act without
protest. Could the silences mean objection as well as devotion, they wonder? Or is his silence an outward illustration of unquestioning love and
faithfulness? They have offered ideas about Sarah's thoughts and about
Abraham's reasons for not telling her he was taking Isaac away; they have
asked why Isaac apparently does not descend the mountain and where he
might be at the end of the narrative. Has he run away from a father who
was about to slay him? Has he been whisked away by the Angel of God?
Commentators have searched for a hero in the tale—is it Abraham, who
is loving and obedient? Is it Isaac, who asks "Father?" but does not object
and proceeds united in heart with his father? Is it the ram, which gets
sacrificed instead? Is there no hero? Are we outside such genres as
tragedy or epic—is this a tale of the absurd?

Moreover, this event is often explained in terms of what comes before
and after it in the Abraham story and in the Pentateuch in general. Many
commentators view the Akedah as the last of a series of tests or trials of
Abraham, interpreting its opening "Achar ha-devarim ha'eleh" as "Some
time afterward" or "And it was after these things [that] God put Abraham
to the test." Writers on this episode have connected it with verbal or sit-
uational parallels from prior moments in the portrayal of Abraham's life.
For example, they have linked the binding to the story of Ishmael and
Hagar, to Abraham's hospitality to the three angels, and to Abraham's
circumcision. In the Talmud, we are offered a particular meaning for the
opening. According to Sanhedrin 89b, Satan dreams the Akedah and
God is forced to place unthinkable demands on his beloved Abraham. In
this view, mentioned by Rashi and a staple of midrash, Satan cruelly and
demonically instigates the testing.[1]

Not only does the Akedah serve to bind Genesis stories, but it is also
used to connect major aspects of the religious tradition. One of the

Tannaim, 40–80 C.E., Rabbi Hanina ben Dosa, goes so far as to suggest that every part of the ram in the story, the substitute sacrifice, has been used in Jewish history and ritual: "That ram, not a part of it went to waste: its tendons became the ten strings of the harp that David used to play on; its skin became the leather girdle around the loins of Elijah; as to its horns, with the left one the Holy One, blessed be He, sounded the alarum at Mount Sinai; and with the right one, which is larger than the left, He will in the future sound the alarum at the Ingathering of the Exiles in the Age to Come."[2] He pointedly shows how the Akedah seeds and feeds other major narratives and the foundational beliefs of Judaism, including the giving of the Ten Commandments.

Yet however we parse the details, we are still left with the troubling issue of sacrificing a son. God has forbidden human sacrifice, thus setting apart Judaism from other ancient religions. This fact is taken for granted. Yet what are we to make of his commanding Abraham to take his best beloved son up Mount Moriah? And how are we to interpret Abraham's reply—"Hineni" ("Here I am"), spoken without any great protest? Would listeners not assume that this test is in fact a foregone conclusion?

Still, many commentators discuss the Akedah in terms of choice. On the one hand, Abraham has no choice. As Nachmanides reminds us in his treatise on reward and punishment, *Sha'ar Hagmul,* God tests only those whom he believes will succeed. Abravanel, who sees the test as one promoting the welfare of the world, tells us that the word for test, *nissah,* means "elevated," like a banner flying above a ship or an army.[3] Thus, the phrase "God tested Abraham" could be rendered "God exalted Abraham" or "God raised him high, test after test." According to this interpretation, after the binding of Isaac, God does not address Abraham again, because Abraham has reached a height above which he can go no further. Abraham's worthiness draws this supreme test to him.

On the other hand, Abraham's choice is critical. All may be foreordained, but free will is still given. Nachmanides explains that the term for "trial" or "test," *nissah,* implies that we are viewing the situation from the point of view of the man in question, rather than from God's point of view. He argues that man has free will to act or not act. For Nachmanides, this is a test in which there is a right choice and a wrong one, but still a choice. The value of the choice lies not necessarily in the resulting action but in its intention.

Some argue that Abraham's zeal was excessive and that his choice was incorrect. For these thinkers Abraham is a monomaniacal religious zealot. God would never have condoned the sacrifice of a human being or the destruction of a family bond to sanctify His name. Abraham, this argument goes, acted foolishly (and not faithfully) in thinking for a moment that he was supposed to take Isaac. From this point of view the Akedah is a warning about a negative trait in Abraham. It shows that obedience can go too far. It tells the story of a man who was too quick to be dutiful, who did not in fact exercise enough reason or caution. Abraham's love for God was blind and thus not to be trusted as a model, except as a dubious kind of religious fundamentalism. The end of the story, according to this view, does not name Isaac because Abraham's love of God has so overwhelmed and displaced earthly love that the son is either referred to as one of the group of retainers or he disappears.

For Nachmanides, however, Abraham makes the correct choice, and it is not a rash one but utterly faithful and reasoned. The verse "On the third day Abraham raised his eyes and saw the place from afar" illustrates not only the time that had elapsed in which Abraham could have changed his mind but also a certain spiritual distance from the mountain, even when at its base. In *The Fundamentals of Judaism, Sefer Ha-ikkarim,* Yosef Albo also comments on the issue of time and reason. He points out that Abraham was not obliged by duty and was fully conscious of what he was doing—thus he acted from absolute freedom of choice, prompted neither by overwhelming emotion nor by externals.[4] It is significant that when God appeared previously and received Abraham's devotion, rewards were given: the promise of children, the covenant, a sacred land, and the promise of Jewish survival. For this trial there is nothing held out but potential loss. Thus, many writers insist that the only thing prompting Abraham was love of God. Maimonides, in writing on repentance, makes a similar judgment on Abraham while carving out a role for all Jews:

> The one who serves God out of love, occupies himself with the study of the law and the fulfillment of its commandments walks in the paths

of wisdom, impelled by no external motive whatsoever; moved neither by fear of calamity nor by the desire to obtain material benefits. Such a man does what is truly right because it is truly right and ultimately happiness comes to him as a result of his conduct. This standard is indeed a very high one; not every sage attained to it. It was the standard of the patriarch Abraham, whom God called His lover because he served only out of love.[5]

If we agree with this interpretation, we might also note that descent is often connected with sin, and it is possible that we do not see Isaac "descend" Mount Moriah because he is not to be tainted by being associated with anything negative. Therefore, it is not that he is left out of the scene, or absent, but that the narrative spares him any reduction of worthiness.

Whether we believe that Abraham had a choice or not, it seems clear that God does not test Abraham to prove anything to Himself. He tests Abraham to improve something. Commentators differ over what that something might be. Some think that God improves Abraham's soul and spirit. In testing Abraham, God brings forth spiritual potential that never would have emerged without this kind of real-life situation. Abraham has sacrificed before in the sense that he has given up close ties in order to preserve his closeness to God. But this test translates sacrifice into its literal meaning in a most challenging trial. Since it is difficult to see spiritual improvements in Abraham, however, and impossible to know what he was thinking or how he reacted to what he had done, the question is not about his elevation perhaps but about the elevation through him (merit of the ancestors) of those who will follow him in the religion.

A wider view asks, not how the Akedah trial brings out Abraham's spiritual depths, but what difference the Akedah makes in the bigger picture, the world of what would become the Jewish religion. How does the Akedah secure closeness to God not only for his greatly loved patriarch but for all the Jews? In this interpretation, God is concerned with improving the place and the rituals in which we will worship Him. If we regard the Akedah from this more comprehensive view, we may see that it initiated two important religious changes. The first is that it established the space of God on earth, "YHVH Yireh" (22.14). According to tradition, Mount Moriah is the same hill upon which Solomon built the Temple (2 Chronicles 3:1). Second, the ram was substituted for a human sacrifice. As Rabbi Hirsch suggests, this substitution inaugurated sacrifice to God. The daily Temple offerings were a national continuation of the Akedah.[6] Others have suggested that a third belief of Judaism finds its sources in this episode. In rabbinic midrash concerning the near-slaying of Isaac and his subsequent release, we find a connection between human beings and the resurrection of the dead. Rabbi Yehuda suggests in *Pirkei d'Rabbi Eliezer*, for example, that Isaac's soul flew out of his body when the knife touched his neck, but that it was restored when the divine voice intervened.

Another view asks what difference the Akedah makes, not to Abraham or to the Jewish religion, but to us as individuals in our relationship to God, by its example. For it could be interpreted as a negative example. It may be a story that sets up human sacrifice only to reject that option entirely. In other words, Abraham may be both critiqued and praised at the same time through his actions. As a test of spiritual depths and commitment, the Akedah offers all of us a chance to evaluate a particularly difficult life trial in terms of our spiritual worth, our values, and God's laws. But it also provides an opportunity for us to evaluate our lives in relationship to trials that have not yet taken place. One of the most insistent questions of the Akedah for most people seems to be premised on potential identification: "What would I have done in the same situation?" In this sense the Akedah forces a self-examination.

The rabbis interpreted the Akedah in light of a special relationship to the Days of Awe, and it is worthwhile examining what that relationship might be in the context of its centrality to the religion. This passage of Genesis is read on the second day of Rosh Hashanah. Many of the prayers of the Highest Holy Days, including Yom Kippur, refer to Abraham's devout action. We are charged to "remember the Covenant with Abraham and the Binding of Isaac and return the captivity of the tents of Jacob, and save us for the sake of Thy name." Tradition tells us that there is a double reason we are counseled to recall Isaac's binding: The Akedah took place on Rosh Hashanah, and Sarah had miraculously conceived her only son Isaac on Rosh Hashanah. Thus, the Akedah is read on that day in order to inspire us to follow the models of righteousness established by our matriarch and patriarch, but also to remind us of our dependence on God and on the devotion that is owed to Him.

It is worth considering the themes of Rosh Hashanah more deeply. On that day Jews start the process of teshuvah, turning back to God. This part of the process is called hirhur teshuvah, the "awakening" of teshuvah. The new year, Rosh Hashanah, initiates the Days of Awe, when we reestablish intimacy with God and when he approaches closest to us. On this day we are commanded to hear the shofar blasts for a particular purpose. Like many other mitzvot, this one combines an objective act with a subjective intention. The shofar is blown on Rosh Hashanah to a special end, as an awakening from a slumber. We are advised to examine our lives, that is, in terms of the extent to which our actions of the past year have alienated us from God or brought us close to God. Most often, when we look within, we find ourselves in great need of renewed closeness to God.

The mood on Rosh Hashanah is thus terrifying, and yet it includes an element of joy and hope. With the books of life and death lying open and God preparing to judge us for another year, we become aware of our need to repent and to feel awe. At the same time, however, we praise God in our liturgy as the King of Glory. The first set of shofar blasts pierces the silence to inspire fear and duty, the second set to inspire anticipation. The Akedah is especially relevant to this day because it describes man's relationship to God in terms of fear, with its concomitant sense of awe and readiness to act for the sake of heaven. But Rosh Hashanah also expresses a level of spiritual joy as we enter the period of Atonement and hope for God's mercy as well as His judgment.

I wonder if the Akedah is so straightforward, however, as any one of these commentators' views alone maintain. It seems extraordinarily complex to me even in its biblical version, without the layering of midrash, Talmud, and modern commentary or other biblical stories. It seems significant, for example, that "Hineni" ("Here I am") is uttered three times. God calls to Abraham, and Abraham answers, "Hineni"; Isaac calls to Abraham, and he answers, "Hineni"; the Angel of God calls to Abraham, and he calls, "Hineni." The separate callings to Abraham may not only reflect the consistency of Abraham's answer but also represent an internal but unspoken conflict between the Divine and the human within Abraham himself, even if that conflict is not played out in his actions. Difficulty and overcoming reluctance is at the heart of the story. So too Isaac is not purely innocent and faithful but also may be seen as wondering and doubtful when he turns to Abraham asking, "Father?" Whether one sees Isaac as naive depends on how one interprets that question and with what inflection: As "Where are we going?" (questioning); as "Exactly what are we doing without a sacrifice?" (challenging); or perhaps as "In taking me here, are you being a father to me?" (fearfully). I interpret Isaac's question multiply, as straddling serious doubt and utter faith and sliding on the spectrum between them. Moreover, God in the story is neither wholly demanding nor wholly merciful, but both—a God inspiring both fear and love, a God of law and mercy. Perhaps the story is not totally positive or totally negative, not totally exhalting or totally critiquing Abraham, but purposefully mixed. In this sense, and transcending the particular characters, the Akedah may be about both the terribly difficult human condition and kinds and degrees of faith, expressed variously: human to human, human to angel, human to God.

Chapter Five

FACE TO FACE:
THE FATE OF THE OTHER

⁂

*Jewish life and thought is not merely a reconciliation of these
two [the soaring power of prophecy and the careful performing
of the mitzvot with precise attention to detail]; it lives in the
rhythmic fluctuation between them as the only possible course
of holiness.*

—ADIN STEINSALTZ, *THE THIRTEEN PETALLED ROSE*, 1980

*The face with which the Other turns to me is not reabsorbed
in a representation of the face. To hear his destitution which
cries out for justice is not to represent an image to oneself, but
is to posit oneself as responsible, both as more and as less than
the being that presents itself in the face.*

—EMMANUEL LEVINAS, *TOTALITY AND INFINITY:
AN ESSAY ON EXTERIORITY*, 1969

Adin Steinsaltz identifies the course of Jewish holiness as living in
a space between two central commitments: attending to the
word of God both in Torah and in daily action (performing
mitzvot, sacred commandments). Whereas Steinsaltz considers the poles
of Jewish commitments and how we move between them, my concerns
encompass the space and relationship between two persons as well. A
model of how an individual relates to the other taken from Emmanuel
Levinas informs my discussion in this chapter.

Early in my conversion training I was struck by the emphasis in
Judaism not only on study but also on actions and on one's relationship

to what is outside the self, including other people: other Jews, the stranger, non-Jews. I found the different kinds of relationships at the heart of the religion to be one of the most compelling aspects of Judaism for me. Immediately, I began participating in a program that provided casseroles anonymously for a soup kitchen, delivered by other volunteers from the local synagogue to a community half an hour away. As time went on I found other outlets for giving and for relating to others, such as starting a book fund and welcoming friends to my home for the Sabbath. But I still felt that I was not really coming to grips with this issue of self, selflessness, and action. The giving seemed thoughtful, but it became routine. The serving of food in my home was important, because it was a personal act of sharing. Still, I had a lot to learn about relationship within Judaism.

My premise is that Jewish spiritual life, as a practice, a belief system, and an ethics, has little to do with interiority and more to do with exteriority—*the opening up of one's self* to alterity, to otherness, to difference, to action, and to pluralism. One could argue that Judaism is fundamentally about relationship (God's to Israel) as codified in the covenant. Here I explore the two poles of Jewish spiritual life, as articulated by Steinsaltz, and mark out with the words panim ("face") or panim el panim ("presence" or "face to face") the various key types of relationship that drew me so powerfully to the religion.

There were different kinds of relationships I experienced most meaningfully in my conversion study: (1) prophecy, between God and Moses; (2) hermeneutics, between the reader and a Jewish text, another reader of the text, or the textual tradition; (3) halakhah, in terms of the mitzvot of how the Jew relates to a dying or sick Jew; (4) moral philosophy, in the ways a Jew relates to any other person on a daily basis and in terms of Emmanuel Levinas's concept of the relationship of an I to the other as obligation and interruption; and (5) political philosophy, in the relationship of a Jew to Jews and non-Jews in a just community or state or nation. Although I separate these kinds of relationships for purposes of heuristic exploration, I am aware that they overlap and also inform and support each other.

As I view the poles of commitment isolated by Steinsaltz, I hear in his words a call to balance the religious and the ethical; worship, work, and home; Torah reading and Torah doing; the spiritual and the practical; aspirations to the ideal and the hard work of reality; the general and the particular. Hardly opposites, these sets of commitments imbue each other with meaning and offer overlapping avenues to holiness. However, Steinsaltz's invocation of a space "between" poles is critical too, both as an image and as an ideal. Levinas also speaks of a space "between" myself and the *face* of the other. It is the space of fluctuation, the space between two sides of an encounter, the space of the presence of God.

Judaism demands a double perspective. Leaning too much toward one side can temporarily deny the call and responsibility of the other side. Thus, in self-absorption, one's self blots out the otherness of the other, whereas in excessive responsibility to the other, one can find oneself in a state of self-denial. Likewise, one could devote one's self too much at one extreme to texts or at the other extreme to action in the community. Is it really enough to study Torah but never perform anonymous charity or attend to the sick and dying or help out a widow? Consider the reverse. One donates clothes to the poor, instructs children in Hebrew, sends medicine to Jews in Central America, and visits sick Jews but has minimal contact with Torah and skips Shabbat services.

These dual commitments face each other. Our responsibility is best expressed, I believe, in the quest for a balance. God speaks to us and we approach closest to Him, literally and figuratively, from the space between. The concept of two equal sides and a space between them, a place from which issues something greater than either side, has been the key image governing my conversion.

It seems to be a reworking of the divisions I felt as a child. The most terrifying dream I ever had recurred a number of times over several years, starting when I was about nine years old. There were two identical balls on a string. All night long the balls went back and forth, never touching, never meeting. It was a dream of perpetual frustration and discomfort: I wanted the ends to meet, but they never did. Of course, the balls could have represented many things, any duality within which I lived, and plenty more: sides of a conflict, aspects of selfhood, parents, divided loyalties, growth issues. What a great anxiety dream—it covers so much that almost anything about it could be argued. I wanted synthesis in this dream and never got it. Now I realize that synthesis does not always have to occur, that the space between is important too.

I want to use the idea of "face" (panim) and "face to face" (panim el panim) to explore a set of issues that came to mean a great deal to me in the years of preparing for conversion and in my first year as a Jew. Above all others, this word and this phrase represented for me exactly the tensions and rhythms and space about which Steinsaltz speaks and the responsibility toward the other of which Levinas speaks. Panim and panim el panim are for me major aspects of the soul of Judaism.

If I ring changes on this word and phrase, I am doing so in the spirit of Moses Maimonides, the great Spanish medieval commentator. It was Maimonides who showed us the multiple meanings of so many words and ideas from Torah in his brilliant and abstruse *The Guide of the Perplexed*. I will return in due course to his statements about the words *panim* and *panim el panim*, which he treats in book I, chapter 37, of *The Guide*.

Because my first encounter with the phrase *panim el panim* is lost, I can't say for certain where I read it. But I do remember that the first context in which I noticed *panim el panim* concerned the seating arrangement between teacher and student, face to face, like reading partners, with no hierarchical distinction between them. It is a democratic arrangement when the teacher can hear and see the students and they can see and hear the teacher. This arrangement, as I read it, is not about gaining access to learning but about learning within a relationship not governed by power relations, one mandating equality and openness and mutual respect. Just as the teacher can teach the student, so the student can teach the teacher. Such placement and such accountability increase the fullness of learning and teaching. This concept of "face to face" journeyed with me through my conversion training and grew in meanings and significance.

The most notable occurrences of the phrase "face to face" in the Pentateuch are in connection with Moses. That magnificent phrase beautifully sums up the uniquely intimate spiritual relationship between God and his best, chosen prophet. During the course of my first year as a Jew,

I volunteered to give the dvar Torah (offer comments and lead a discussion) on Shabbat Yitro, the Sabbath when the weekly Torah reading speaks of the covenant at Sinai and the giving of the Ten Commandments. But in volunteering, I misremembered what the parasha was about. I recalled it *not* as the one about the Ten Commandments that opens with Jethro the Midian priest and father-in-law of Moses, but as the one that charges Israel with becoming a "holy nation."

It was therefore with some shock that I discovered this was, of course, the Sinai parasha. Having then accommodated myself to the fact that I was supposed to speak on what for many would be the most important moment in Exodus and the most important parasha in the Pentateuch, I comforted myself further with another misremembering—I remembered the phrase *panim el panim* as being central to the Sinai experience. I remembered that at the great moment of revelation, God came to Moses "face to face," out of fire—meaning "in the presence of" (that is, not a literal facing or a literal face)—and I decided that I could unravel this phrase in the remarks of my dvar Torah. I had my theme. However, after a word search in Pentateuch, I soon discovered that the phrase was not in the parasha at all: *face* was there, but not *face to face*. What I thought must of necessity be present was, in fact, absent. So, necessity being the mother of invention, I decided to look closely at where the phrase did turn up in the Pentateuch, to report my misremembering, and to speculate in my dvar Torah about why it was not in Yitro.

I discovered that the phrase is usually used for a one-to-one relationship, but that at the heart of the revelation at Sinai a communal spirit predominates. It is true that Exodus 19:2, which says that the Jewish people camped at Mount Sinai, offers a singular verb for *camped*, but that is to indicate that they were all of one heart, not to single out individuals. In fact, as Gunther Plaut tells us in his Torah commentary, the revelation is unique "in that it takes place before a whole people, who then act upon what they have seen and heard."[1] The revelation at Sinai is expressed in a particular figure of speech, synaesthesia, a confusion of senses: The people hear sights and see sounds. So frightened are they by this experience of direct communication with God, so sensorily confused and awestruck, that they fall back and ask Moses to be their intermediary.

Still, a midrash comments that if even one person of the six hundred thousand present at Sinai had been absent, the Jewish people could not have received the Torah.

A later account in Deuteronomy of the experience of communication at Sinai, however, does use *panim el panim* to describe what occurred between God's words coming out of a cloud and the people's reception of them. My notion, which could be quite wrong, is that parasha Yitro in Exodus avoids this phrase since up to this time it has been used to stress a special relationship of the Divine to a key Jewish figure. Yet the Sinai experience must be read as a communal event and as God's intervention into the history and life of a people. Understanding it only as a private revelation to Moses would be a serious misreading.

Several times in Exodus and Deuteronomy the word *panim* and the phrase *panim el panim* portrays the close relationship between God and Moses. It also appears in the account of Jacob's meeting with the angel: Jacob meets the Divine "face to face" and survives. Exodus 33 details the renewal of the covenant after the episode with the Golden Calf, and there we find mention of a Tent of Meeting. This is assumed to be Moses' own tent that he took out of the camp because God had withdrawn from the camp. It becomes a place of meeting between Moses and God. Here, as elsewhere, their communication is characterized as "face to face": "The Lord would speak to Moses face to face, as one human speaks to another." Torah stresses relationship—not that Moses is divine but that God relates to his humanity.

Later, in Numbers 12:6–8, God defines more specifically the uniqueness of His relationship with Moses and uses a term even more intimate than "face to face." Aaron and Miriam speak against Moses, their brother, and assert that their own prophetic powers are as important as his; they declare that Moses is not the only one to whom God speaks. But, decrying their boasting, God differentiates between kinds of prophecy: "Here these My words: 'When a prophet of the Lord rises among you, I make Myself known to him in a vision, I speak with him in a dream. Not so with My servant, Moses; he is trusted throughout my household. With him I speak mouth to mouth *peh el peh* plainly and not in riddles, and he beholds the likeness of the Lord. How then did you not shrink from speaking against My servant Moses?"

Significantly, at the very close of the Pentateuch the phrase "face to face" is singled out as a testament and tribute to Moses' uniqueness: "Never again did there arise in Israel a prophet like Moses—whom the Lord singled out, face to face." It is noteworthy too that in contrast to the early patriarchs who turned to God, Moses was "singled out" by God for a special mission and for His special favor. We never hear the phrase "the God of Moses" as we do "the God of Abraham, Isaac, and Jacob," for Moses is the man of God, the man singled out by God as the most worthy of generations to fulfill the redemption on earth of the Jewish people. God appears to the first patriarchs and His presence hovers over their tents, but His spiritual relationship with them is not as close or as intense as His relationship with Moses. One could also argue that the spiritual relationship of God to man builds over time, through years of human adversity and humbling, and reaches its climax with Moses.

Following Maimonides in his comments on *panim* in *The Guide of the Perplexed* (chapter 37), I take the use of *panim el panim* in this context as describing a spiritual relationship of deep, intuitive apprehension.[2] The words *face to face*, therefore, do not refer to a literal seeing. In fact, God's own words to Moses in the parasha Ki Tisa (Exodus 33:19–23) indicate the nonvisual, the nonrepresentational: "And He answered, 'I will make all My goodness pass before you, and I will proclaim before you the name Lord, and the grace that I grant and the compassion that I show. But,' He said, 'you cannot see My face, for man may not see Me and live.'" God stations Moses in the cleft of a rock and shields him with His hand until he passes by. "Then I will take My hand away and you will see My back; but My face must not be seen."[3] This statement resonates with God's commandments to the Jews never to make representations of divine beings unless He orders them to do so.

In his listing of the uses of the word *panim*, Maimonides offers a notion of direct encounter: being a presence to another presence without an intermediary, such as an angel. Likewise, Maimonides (citing Deuteronomy 4:12, "Ye heard the voice of Words, but ye saw no figure, only a voice") asserts that *panim el panim* can mean "this kind of speaking and hearing as being 'face to face'" and not a figure presence at all.[4] When he glosses "My face shall not be seen" (Exodus 33:23), he suggests that God means: "The true reality of My existence as it veritably is cannot be grasped." Thus *panim*, as understood by Maimonides, carries various overlapping and singular meanings: presence, face, nearness, word, and the reality of the spiritual presence as it cannot be fathomed but is nevertheless felt to be.

In developing my thoughts on *panim*, it is relevant to segue a bit to the very special Jewish mode of engaging with a text. Certainly, every reader and writer, I believe, enters an unspoken dialogue with those readers and writers who came before. Indeed, our very conventions of reading are conditioned by our cultural moment and by those who have come before us. But the form of engagement with texts that I have come to know as distinctively Jewish is dialogic to the hundredth degree! I came to embrace this process over the course of my ever-deepening studies.

Indeed, various examples of rabbinic writing even refer to interpretations of oral and written Torah as aspects, or faces, *panim*. Various interpretations, when *panim el panim*, stand in a multiply dialogic relationship, as in so much Jewish thought and debate. Each comments on the others, raises questions, provokes answers, all in the service of revitalizing our tradition through our readings of them. I will refer to *panim* in this sense as I discuss what I see as the role of the reader who confronts midrash (oral Torah, commentary on Torah).

Jews are in a dialogue with the past that is itself in a dialogue with many other pasts. Judaism fosters a certain form of sacred text engagement through the study of midrash, which is central to all Jewish religious writing up to the modern period. In fact, Jewish renewal movements and feminist movements feature workshops and courses in modern midrash, so the form is alive and well, if different from ancient midrash.

Midrash is a kind of literature and a type of interpretive activity. There is no one preeminent book that stands for all the rest. Rather, there are collections of midrashim, and they come in two different types: haggadic (concerned with law and behavior) and aggadic (nonlegal, imaginative). Thus, midrashim were used both to derive points of law from Torah and to offer stories and parables.[5] These impulses blend into each other, however, and midrashim can rarely be described as entirely pure examples. The ancient midrashim were written between 400 and 1200 C.E., though originally these texts were communicated orally, as sermons or teachings. In a larger sense, it is helpful to think about the very nature of Jewish textual interpretation as an endless series of "face-to-face" encounters of one text with another or of one reader or audience with another in an ongoing debate of interpretation.

Midrash was probably written to respond to certain sociocultural issues. But it also reflects the simple love of Torah—the profound pleasure that comes from learning Torah and using passages to comment on other passages. For example, *Genesis Rabbah*, a midrash on Genesis, responds to the rise of Christianity, with its emphasis on Jesus and angelology. Seeking to refute Christian and Gnostic sects, the midrashic commentary on creation stresses that God worked alone in His endeavors to create the world. The only entity at His side was Torah, which He had made as well.

Yet midrash also responds to the style of the Pentateuch, which is a selectively silent form of writing. As Erich Auerbach showed many years ago in *Mimesis*, his classic book on narrative, the Hebrew Bible does not offer motivations, feelings, or many character traits. It does not always offer motives for events. There are major omissions of transition, of place description, of detail. There are jumps from one scene to another. And this accounts for only the most narrative of the books, Genesis and Exodus. What we find in many other places are lists of laws or of names or prohibitions presented in an order that often seems to make no obvious sense at all, interwoven with shorter narrative moments. Auerbach called the Hebrew Bible "laconic." He was probably not the first to say so, and certainly contemporary critics after him have made similar claims regarding the nature of the Pentateuch, calling it "frictional and trace ridden" (Geoffrey Hartmann) and "gap-filled" (Barry Holtz, James Kugel, and Steven Fraade). Thus, although written Torah is often read as if it were a classic realist novel—with a narrative drive of cause and effect, with a plot, with interpretable "characters," and with a hierarchy of meanings and discourses provided by a central narrator—it is hardly so tightly woven.

Gary Porton makes a key historical and philological point about midrash: The link between the roots *drs* (to search out) and *mdrs* (midrash) in the rabbinic period "designates the process by which one interprets, explains, corrects or expounds the text *as well as* the interpretation, explanation, correction of exposition itself."[6] Midrash, then, is both a process of interpreting (a hermeneutics) and interpretation itself (a set of meanings). It both draws on sections of Torah and brings them to bear on a verse or verses. It is a set of multiple meanings and theological principles and statements let loose to circulate. Not just the content but the very act of interpreting is religious.

What could this mean? Midrash, from the verbal root "to study or search out," is itself a searching attitude toward Scripture, an extreme form of close textual study featuring endless encounters of one passage with others, of one proof text with a scriptural base text, of one interpretation with another. Midrash roots out; it picks apart each word, each detail. It looks for problems in the text and poses questions to the text. It reads until it finds a knot, or what critics call a bump, in the smooth text of Scripture. And if midrash does not find such a problem, it will create one. Posing a question may simply be a pretext for an extended examination of a religious issue. The midrashic relationship to Scripture is therefore more than a mode of reading and interpretation. It is the foundation of religious relationship: past to present, knot to knot, meaning to knot, question to answer, question to question.

Steven Fraade offers one of the most interesting models of midrashic textual engagement as religious activity: Midrash is multiply dialogic as a series of encounters and interfacings. I draw on Fraade to gloss my sense of how Jewish thinking works, both religious and textual thinking. But in no way would I suggest that this take on midrash is the exclusive one. Many studies—more than ten significant ones in the last twenty years alone—have been devoted to midrash. There are thus many differing definitions of it, many angles, various ideas about why it came into existence, and numerous explanations of how it works on readers. Some critics emphasize content, some the process of text–proof text, some the worldview, some the relationship to the community of speakers or readers, some the presence of midrashic activity already within the Pentateuch itself, some the function, some the political aim, some the literary features of its forms, some its epistemology, and some the relationships of its varied styles.

Fraade's introduction to his book on the midrash Sifre Deuteronomy, *From Tradition to Commentary*, is notable, however, because it draws on contemporary literary theory to offer a model of textual engagement.[7] Fraade refers specifically to the notion of textual performativity from speech act theory (originally from J. L. Austin, *How to Do Things with Words*). Although Fraade's discussion is complex and wide-ranging (for example, he opens with an important historical comparison of Sifre with the Dead Sea Scrolls and Philo's *Commentaries*), he is most interesting for my purposes when he begins to describe how this example of midrash—and by extension other midrashim—works on the reading community. His theory attempts to heal what he sees as a critical split between hermeneuticists, who ignore sociohistorical context, and historicists, who ignore the hermeneutical grounding of a text's performance. Thus, he argues that rabbinic commentary—and not only this midrash of Sifre but also other midrashim that work in similar ways—engages the audience in understanding itself socioreligiously and transforming itself. It does so by conducting a double dialogue: first, new meaning is produced by the historically located commentary in relation to the text (a portion of the Pentateuch), and second, additional meaning is produced by historically located readers who read the commentary on/with the text.

Fraade thus theorizes different interfaces of meaning production. Ancient scriptural commentaries, he states, are more than "constative conduits of meaning"; they also transformatively bring two worlds toward each other—that of the text and that of its students—without merging them. These worlds "confront each other through the double-dialogue of commentary." Fraade then refines the notion of dialogue, which he argues is not that of two voices. Rather, the term *dialogue* denotes for him the "dynamic, interrelational ways in which commentary creates and communicates meaning" (p. 14). As modern critical theory illustrates, meaning is not inherent in the text, waiting to be pulled out, nor is it produced solely by a commentary or by readers reading such a commentary. Rather, meaning is located in the spaces between.

Fraade's analysis is not always entirely clear. His text equivocates on the number of interfaces—sometimes two, sometimes three, sometimes two that are actually opposite sides of the same coin. He adds redactors later in his argument—for example, as yet another face to take into account. So we do not have just Scripture, a single commentator, and readers who put the midrash in final form. There is also a redactor of commentators.

In working their way through the text, the rabbinic disciples, Fraade argues, are like a "sieve" that sorts and weighs the teachings and multiple interpretations gathered in midrash "as they pass through" (p. 18) the disciples. In this "oral circulatory system" (p. 19) of study, debate, learning, and teaching, many heterogeneous traditions and opinions are collected and contained, but they are not rigidly hierarchized in this particular literary structure. Although some interpretations are clearly privileged over others—for example, that Israel is a chosen nation, or that God worked alone in creation—the rabbinic creators of midrash do not seek only to instruct in *correct* (that is, dogmatically correct) interpretation of Scripture. Most interesting to me, and most important about Jewish textual engagement, they also seek to teach a *way* of Torah debate that is itself of sacred and historical importance.[8]

The weighing and sifting, the testing of interpretations, and the discussion and debate constitute precisely the exploration of the spaces between assertions of points of view on a spectrum of possible meanings. Asking questions of the text to fill gaps, asking questions of questions, probing why something is offered or left out of Torah—the very style of midrash is the backbone of Jewish thinking and religion. Take the great rabbinic pair of the Talmud: Hillel faces Shammai, not only because one must hold a majority view and one a minority view, not because one is right and one is less right or more wrong, but also because the discussion and the details on interpretation are important in their own right. What happens in dialogue matters; out of the dialogue between Hillel and Shammai arose the two main schools of interpretation.

From face-to-face reading partnerships to dialogue and questioning as the major Jewish intellectual activity, to reaching consensus through debate on certain religious beliefs, to the presence(s) of the past elicited by our readings, the study of Jewish Scripture and tradition itself illustrates endless variations of panim el panim. At the one end of the spec-

trum that Steinsaltz offers us—the sacred Scripture and prophecy end—
there is also a double facing that is endlessly dialogic between text and
readings.

In the last months before conversion, *panim* and *panim el panim* began to
assume for me the wider meaning they hold for the twentieth-century
French philosopher Emmanuel Levinas, who was influenced by Franz
Rosenzweig: an ethical attendance on the other. This emphasis takes us
to the other pole of Jewish commitment referred to by Steinsaltz in the
first epigraph to this chapter—away from God's relationship to his chief
prophet, away from Torah written and oral, and into the realm of action
in daily life. I think back to Maimonides' notion of *panim* as showing
regard for and offering one's presence to those in need. I also think, however, of a relationship modeled in the innermost sanctum of the Holy of
Holies, that of the cherubim.

In researching widely before writing my biblical commentary on
Tamar from 2 Samuel during the summer of my conversion study, I was
struck by a phrase in Exodus 25, "parasha Terumah," in a passage that
describes the Holy of Holies and the ark. There the two golden angels—
the cherubim, who are part of the ark cover—"confront each other" (literally, "their faces shall be turned toward the other"). They sit atop the
ark face to face, panim el panim. This cover is taken by rabbinic commentators to be the throne of God on earth and the place where the
Shekhinah (the feminine indwelling presence of God) resides. Further,
God says His voice will emanate from *the space* between these two figures. It is from between two, face to face, that the voice of God comes.
For me, even though they are never seen by the populace, and by the
high priest only on Yom Kippur through a veil of incense, they model a
type of relationship to which we can aspire.

Maimonides isolates a further meaning of *panim* that is very important
to me for this discussion. He points out the frequent usage of the word
panim to mean "showing regard to or for the poor." It is my strong sense
that the relationship modeled by panim el panim between God and
Moses is *not* to be taken solely as one of intimate relationship and
prophecy between a special man and God, although that is clearly a

prime meaning. Moreover, panim el panim between the cherubim is not to be taken solely as one of holy intimacy and service to God, though that is clearly another prime meaning. Such a relationship, I believe, is precisely a model for how we are to treat our fellow human beings, poor or not. We are all needy in many ways; we are all at times unfortunate; we all at times suffer and feel deep pain. Providence, then, in its sense of divine care but also in its sense of meeting the needs of another, is joined in this equivocal phrase *panim el panim* in the sense of regard, aspect, providing one's presence, an unfathomable but felt sense of beingness. One can still be equal, one to another, but also be in need of attendance by another.

An anecdote reportedly told by the twentieth-century German philosopher and religious thinker Martin Buber may be relevant here. I have read this story in two different versions, but the main points are the same.[9] In both versions, a troubled young man, a student, came to see Buber at a time when the philosopher was busy (writing an article or a book, in one version; just emerging from an ecstatic meditation, in the other). Because he was busy, Buber paid no attention to the stranger and sent him away. Soon thereafter the young man committed suicide, and Buber felt some responsibility. He had not been attending to the needs of the other person; he had not attended *at all* to the other person.

Buber's later work treated God as the "Eternal Thou" realized in every true and real encounter between one person and another. God gives meaning, says Buber, to each personal encounter, each instance of attendance on another. Though I do not agree with Buber's assertion in this later work that God can be experienced only through other persons—I believe that there are various committed ways to experience God—I do agree that this is one very powerful avenue. I understand Buber's remarks as being relevant to the discussion of panim el panim, not only because of his views on the encounter of the "I and Thou" but also because of his view of God as presence. In a true encounter, argues Buber, God reveals himself as presence through the reciprocal human interaction.

I differ with Buber, since I follow Levinas on the relationship between the "I" and the other. I suppose that I would also add mysticism to the idea of encounter, since I believe that there is a spark of divinity in each one of us. My own take is that in a true encounter, panim el panim, the "I" responds to the face of the other and in so doing calls forth the divine spark in the self and the other. Because of that level of attendance and the move out of subjectivity into intersubjectivity, that the "I" and the "thou" can feel the presence of God in the space between. But whereas Buber insists on a flow between the "I and Thou," I do not believe that there *has* to be reciprocity in relationship or that the "I" should expect return.

In following Levinas, I see the other's face as summoning forth my responsibility to him or her, regardless of return. This is the moment of connection, an act of attending to the other that is transpersonal and ethical. Certainly, if we make a practice of ignoring real others, of looking at them or through them but not attending to them, of disregarding their calls upon us—and I am filled with failures of this type all the time—we participate in extinguishing holiness and shutting out God's presence.

One of the most important sacred commandments in Judaism is known as bikkur holim, visiting the sick. One sits beside a loved one, a friend, or even a stranger who is ill or dying, even if there is nothing to do—one provides "presence." We come face to face with each other, with suffering, and with death. This sacred responsibility, required of congregational rabbis, is also an opportunity for each one of us to attend to the other. It is one of the highest mitzvot and one of the most important for all of us to perform.

Why, we might wonder, does this mitzvah assume such weight? Why is Jewish law so particular about treating a person at the edge of death (a gosses) with the same respect as a living person? Even if the dying person is unconscious, there is still the need to be with her or him in person, face to face. For one thing, as Anita Diamant reminds us in her book on Jewish death, burial, and mourning rituals, *Saying Kaddish*, the dying person remains a full member of the prayer community until dead. If conscious and aware, this person can still be counted for a minyan, can still serve as a witness, and can even sit on a bet din (p. 34). The Talmud, as quoted by Diamant, insists: "A dying person is to be considered a living person in all matters of the world" (Mishnah, Masehet Semahot, chapter 1). Legally, we are attending to an equal member of our community. There are reasons for this mitzvah, then, that are both personal (to relieve the sick) and communal (the community's responsibility to the community as well as to the individual). Moreover, coming face to face with suffering and death humanizes us, the living. It puts our lives into dramatic perspective. Going to the deathbed forces us to face our own mortality and thus reminds us to live fully.

Diamant further explains that a legal, ethical fence is set up around the person who is ill to ensure that she or he not be treated as a "corpse-in-waiting." It is forbidden to start mourning until death actually occurs. It is forbidden to talk about the person as if she or he were not present. It is forbidden to talk about a dying person in the past tense. Diamant also tells us of things we *can* do. These I find terribly significant: we can listen; we can follow the lead of the dying; we can accept the kind of death that allows the person to be who she or he is in death, as in life, unconditionally; we can speak about our feelings; we can apologize for misunderstandings between ourselves and the dying person and forgive that person for any unkindnesses done to us; we can read aloud or pray or chant; we can touch (so important to the sick); we can reassure the dying person that the living will be all right; and we can make sure that we care for ourselves as well.[10]

As I pondered these matters and issues of suffering in particular, I remembered that the Jewish tradition mandates that we consider each day as if it were our last day on earth. Doing so, we find ourselves being kinder both to our friends and neighbors and to strangers, as well as more complete in our execution of mitzvot. We must be ready for the reckoning of God. In a sense, we must live as though we have a terminal illness, as though we are always dying.

What I have not understood about Judaism, and what still puzzles me, is why these two mandates—attending to the dying and considering each day as though it were our own death day—are never joined in another ethical precept: to attend to the other as if it were his or her death day as well. What would it be like if I approached everyone I saw in a single day with the thought, not just that it might be my death day, but that it might be the other person's last day on earth? Maybe we would let go of the things we so often keep to ourselves, maybe we would praise more, console more, just plain listen better, attend more. Maybe we would seize the opportunity to do exactly the things that Diamant recommends at a deathbed: forgive, accept unconditionally, apologize, share our deep feelings, touch.

I asked my supervisor a year to the week after I became a Jew: Why is there no such precept? Did I miss it somewhere? No, I didn't miss it, he said. He could not locate such a precept anywhere. He suggested there might be a different ontological premise behind each of the ideas: Assuming it is one's last day on earth belongs to the individual consciousness of death; attending to the dying concerns the community. I grasped his words, but I felt that perhaps the ancient rabbis and modern commentators had missed a moment for debate here.

I realize that this is a scary and strange idea: Who would really want to think this way very much of the time? We often wait to confront mortality only when death suddenly strikes a parent, a child, even ourselves. Our friends tell us that breast cancer or a stroke or AIDS or the aging of a parent into senility served as a wake-up call for them. Most of us prefer a very long break between such moments in our lives. Sometimes, even with wake-up calls, we do not look at ourselves for a long time. For instance, David Ariel, the president of the Cleveland College of Jewish Studies, recounts in his book *Spiritual Judaism* the story of how he came to terms with a cancer diagnosis and surgery.[11] For two years, he says, he was unable to discuss it with anyone but his wife. This may be an extreme case—or maybe not so extreme at all. The response of denial or postponement or fear—to illness, to disability, to aging, or to the diseases of those we love—is characteristic of most of us.

During my study my mother required her third operation in a decade. This surgery was not as serious as the others, but any operation is serious for a woman in her eighties. This episode gave me yet another chance to ride the roller coaster of illness and suffering up close and personal. I've spent so much time locating or confirming good doctors and nurses for my family and myself over the years that I consider it my greatest shopping effort. Even if we are fortunate enough to have good, caring doctors, however, and are convinced they are doing all they can for us, hospitals are very scary to most of us: surgery floors and intensive-care units are terrifying, and wards are understaffed even in stellar hospitals and nursing homes, especially on weekends and at night. I've worked in a nursing home for terminally ill women on the 7:00 A.M. to 3:00 P.M. shift, and I've visited several good hospitals in different states and done the fetching and calling of doctors or prescriptions for medications or bedpans myself. I deeply respect the people in the profession; one of my stepsons is a doctor, and one of my cousins is a nurse. But pain and painkillers can make patients unrecognizable to those who know them, and surgeons often do not explain enough when patients do not know the questions to ask. The nurses working shifts and the doctors on call or covering for a weekend range from overworked and indifferent to extremely attentive and in between, but you hardly ever know whom you're getting.

When we finally face these times and situations—whether with a parent, another loved one, a child, or ourselves—and examine our mortality, we begin to understand the real meaning of community. A Jew does not let another Jew die alone. I look at my Jewishness now, daily, in this context—life as a mortal illness—and I wonder what it adds up to. If chosenness means anything in a world that distorts the meaning of that concept in so many ways, it should mean a chosenness to attend to the other, not only at death but also in life. Why should a Jew allow anyone to live uncared for, unasked after, lonely, unattended to?

After conversion and through a particular experience of suffering, repentance, and forgiveness, I came to see an even wider meaning for panim el panim. I also began to understand the absolute necessity for moral intersubjectivity on deeper levels and on a wider scale than I had ever understood before. Perhaps I could call this relationship that of the individual to the (good of the) community, both in its single and its multiple membership. I would also characterize this relationship as transpersonal, transcending the individual, yet still very much dependent on individual forms of presence. Then I began to wonder how we could achieve a just society and how relationships with others could ensure such a state.

During the first months after my conversion it happened that I went through a period of suffering. A colleague and I wounded and pained

each other, not once but several times over a few months. The colleague
and I were both Jews, and I knew I had to handle this conflict as a Jew.
There was plenty of time left in the year before Yom Kippur, however,
so I didn't have to rush to atonement. I was disinclined to think in terms
of the calendar as a deadline anyway. Meanwhile, I wasn't sure what I had
done wrong, and I didn't really know what to do. I knew very little about
forgiveness or repentance, and I hadn't suffered or caused suffering this
serious in many years. At the same time, I understood that I was being,
to some degree, scared and defensive.

Repentance, suffering, and forgiveness bear different aspects. The
aspect I knew most intimately was owning up to a misdeed, because my
father had taught me a lesson at age eight in a way that left an impression that remains with me to this day. One day I was playing barber outside with about five other children from the neighborhood. We'd sta-
tioned each other—some were haircutters, some were getting haircuts.
One of the children had brought scissors. We dared each other to use
them, and when nobody else would, I did. I trimmed a child's bangs.
Naturally, I did a lousy job. When my father asked me that evening if I
had done this, I lied. I didn't want to feel guilty or wrong or be punished.
My father left the room so that I could think about it, then returned to
confront me again, saying that other children had seen me do it and that
the child's mother was insistent. There was no way out anymore. He had
me get dressed to go out again, and then he marched me right over to
the mother of the child whose hair I had cut. With all five of her children looking on, I was forced to admit that I had done it, that I had lied
about it, and that I was sorry. This experience made an indelible impression on me. I realized that, on some level, I had humiliated the child, my
father, my family name, and myself, and this was not a good thing.

Still, a child's wrong is not equivalent to an adult's wrong. And a clear
act of physical harm and overt lying, compounded by dishonoring one's
parents, can be easier to manage than a series of confused and complex
misunderstandings that end in hurtful words, misconstrdctions, and deep
inner pain. For a few months during this crisis with my colleague, I felt
I had been wronged but was not sure exactly what I had done wrong or
whether I had done wrong at all. Neither of us had intended to hurt the

other, and even when it had begun, I was thinking about how to be a responsible Jew. A lot was at stake in this first year of my new identity; I didn't want to blow it. No matter what I had or had not intended or thought I had or had not done, the effect of my actions had been to cause pain and anguish equivalent to what I had received.

I consulted a learned Jew about texts concerning forgiveness. He suggested I read Rabbi Joseph Dov Soloveitchik's *On Repentance*. I was baffled—I wanted texts on forgiveness, not repentance. They went together, he said, so I skimmed sections of those texts and came to see that it was immaterial whether I erred unwittingly or willfully. Jeremiah was right: The human heart is devious. It became clear that I might never, in fact, know the extent of my wrong, where it began or ended, or whose wrong was greater or smaller. In fact, I couldn't get to remorse and shame or real forgiveness of the other person or myself until I understood that I did not know the truth of what happened between us and that, in the end, it did not matter who was wrong or right, or who was more wrong, because I had erred in some way. Not to admit it and examine it further was to go to sleep in my pajamas with my teddy bear as a lying child. I'm not even sure what held me back from deep self-examination, whether it was assumed ignorance, indifference, fear, or pride. But it took me three months to work this through satisfactorily. Now I see that I was slow and late and cowardly. I'm not quite convinced that I atoned enough, though my time came again on the Day of Atonement.

When my colleague first admitted wrong and asked my forgiveness, it was very easy to grant it automatically and with some honest kindness and goodwill, even with some panache. But, as I discovered later, when negative feelings returned, it was not really so easy to feel or grant forgiveness. Nor was it easy for me to ask for it, in return, in a way that was not also perfunctory. Working out the complex emotions took much longer. But I discovered what is probably quite obvious—I could feel real forgiveness only after I also admitted my own errors, asked for forgiveness in a deep and meaningful way, and accepted it. I had to open myself fully and be as vulnerable as I could be.

Finally, I had no choice but to open up, because the negative thoughts I harbored about my colleague and about the deteriorated situation between us began to eat at me. I saw a very literal, physical image and experienced a terrible physical feeling at the time—I was being picked over by birds, like carrion. I am not exaggerating when I say that every day that went by I felt myself dying more. Through the breakdown of this relationship and my inability to repair it, I realized the absence of God. It was agonizing, and I couldn't stand it anymore.

The feeling of sin, Soloveitchik says, is not a moral experience but an anti-aesthetic one.[12] He refers to it as an illness. That was my experience. There came a point where I woke early every morning at dawn in a stupor. I understood almost nothing except that I had reached a moral turning point of some kind. I felt guilt about being a Jew and not knowing how to make atonement or repair the relationship.

How does one get out of a state of suffering? I asked another friend: What can I read about Jewish suffering besides Job? What else is there? She suggested Harold Kushner's *When Bad Things Happen to Good People*, thinking it might have a bibliography. The book didn't address the problem I faced, but it was very interesting and showed me that I was focused in the wrong place. In fact, Kushner's own experience of losing a child and his other stories of far deeper suffering than mine only led me to ask more questions.

I then did something radical and new (for me). I logged onto the web and e-mailed my questions to a rabbi. What do I read on the Jewish response to suffering? Where do I even begin? The ten-page reply started with sources from Torah from which certain concepts could be derived.[13] This section concluded by teaching me that the Talmud focuses on suffering (in the tale of how Rabbi Elisha Ben Abuya became a nonbeliever) because it is suffering that can lead someone to lose a belief in God. The rabbi then provided eight ground rules about Judaism; one of them was to look at suffering as an "opportunity for growth." It made a lot of sense to look upon the pain and hurt between my colleague and myself as a test and an opportunity for change in myself, and I tried to start thinking of the situation this way. But nothing happened immediately.

Until a week later. Lying in bed in one of those half-stupors at dawn, the word *forgive* repeated itself over and over in my head. I buried my head in my pillows. But it felt as if a meditation focus point had finally come to me. This was the moment of turning that I had forged for myself, so I listened.

Maimonides, in his Laws of Repentance in the *Mishneh Torah*, discusses two types of repentance, the first being what Soloveitchik calls sin sickness—repentance emerging from an emotional shock. Physical revulsion to wrongdoing is so strong that doing it again will never be an option. Soloveitchik explains that not everyone, however, gets to repentance through emotional suffering. Some people achieve the same end through understanding. A strong will and intellect, impelled by a resolution to change and make a better future, can prevent this kind of sinner from repeating error. In my case, I ran the gamut, proceeding from intellect and will, with understanding and mental resolution, and when that didn't work, going on to the emotional upheaval of feeling physically the self-destruction of error and guilt. That did work.

The process of forgiveness involved finally reopening the wounds of the past months and re-experiencing them. Most important perhaps was going over the whole thing together with my colleague. Having rather successfully avoided each other for a long time, we stopped, faced each other, saw each other's pain, and decided to help each other. We narrated the past in our different versions so that we could accept but also change the circumstances and conditions in which we had related badly. We needed to move on. To accomplish this transformation of the past, we had to walk together into fear, dread, traumatic mutual wounding, and acceptance of each other as flawed. It was a period of mourning as we tried to accept the past as something to be used, not blocked out. We realized that we would have to choose either to get reacquainted or to let go of each other. This process elicited the bounties of repentance and teshuvah and did bring us relief.

Facing each other (literally, figuratively, morally, ethically, emotionally) allowed us to become closer than we had been before our difficulties.

What I have described so far is mainly from my point of view and about myself, but there was another meaning present in *forgive* besides giving up a resentment, making excuses, or pardoning a wrong. The word kept resonating for me, and I saw that another meaning is to grant relief, as in relieving someone from payment of a debt. Because I realized the intensity of my own pain, the other's pain was before my eyes as something in my power to relieve. I felt the force of the word *give* in *forgive* as an opportunity to set my colleague free. But that would not happen with merely a passive acceptance of an apology and a letting go of my pride and of the past. It would happen when we each signaled a willingness to work on improving our relationship and to make a new beginning.

I had never experienced anything like this process before in my life. It was pretty clear to me that I had made myself do it because I was a Jew. I felt obliged to forgive and repent as a matter of human dignity, to preserve not only the dignity of my colleague but also my own. It also seemed the right thing to do. I had no expectation of success and no idea of the rewards that would flow back. Indeed, I was shocked at their abundance. Not only did physical, mental, and moral relief ensue, but I also gained fresh access to my colleague's sweetness and sense of responsibility and justice, qualities that had merely been clouded over by my own fear, anger, hatred, shame, remorse, and self-criticism. In feeling the full presence of the other, and the obligation to do so, I was able to have positive feelings that displaced the negative ones and made healing and renewal possible. Within a few weeks my negative feelings about this episode were gone, and with my new positive feelings, I could heed another commandment and demand: the requirement to love. Without making an effort to love my colleague—my neighbor and my equal—I would be missing the essence of Torah, and the hope of redemption, of making our world a better place, would once again go unrealized.

I tell this particular story with no sense of pride at the process or the outcome, which was positive. I'm not even quite sure how it happened, which may be all to the good. I can appreciate the mystery. Certainly, I pay tribute to my colleague. We are all so different in how we go about such matters and in what we can do; circumstances differ profoundly as well. I'm thankful that my colleague wanted to heal as much as I did and wanted to help me, because neither of us could have done it alone.

The Passover seder includes symbols of suffering, the greens in salt water, to suggest the possibility of growth and rebirth even in the middle of pain. The Exodus story is very clear that the way out of the narrow straits is to take bitterness and pain and fear into ourselves, experience and digest them, then let them be transformed. This process makes us free. The personal story I've just told is about wrongs, suffering, and atonement between two individuals. The resolution of our difficulties had a ripple effect in my life, as all such successful resolutions can. The experience has made it easier for me to avoid such conflicts in the future by oiling the rusty hinges of the doors to my vulnerability and in all ways strengthening my emotional courage.

How could such encounters and resolutions be related to social justice writ large? The philosopher who most directly addresses attendance to the other is Emmanuel Levinas, who speaks in terms of the "face" and of the "face-to-face" presence of the self and the other.

I first heard of Levinas some years ago when a friend, Bob Gibbs, wrote a book about Levinas and Rosenzweig. At that time, however, I found both thinkers fairly inaccessible. I read some of Bob's book and was sympathetic to it, but having had no training in Judaism and very little in philosophy, I found it almost impenetrable. Still, I rediscovered Levinas somewhere, somehow, and after this second encounter he made more sense. I returned to his work again after my study of repentance and forgiveness. Today it is his work that recounts the shattering of the subjective in the face of the alterity of the other that is of interest to me. In any of its permutations—or "waves," as Jacques Derrida has called it—the philosophy of Levinas is fundamentally about relationship, just as Judaism is fundamentally about relationship.[14] If Judaism is concerned with the relationship of God and man in a covenant, Levinas's philosophy is concerned with the relationship of man and man. Through intersubjective relationship the trace of God is felt. Torah states that the voice and presence of God come from between the cherubim, face to face equally on the ark. Levinas does not retain a theological vocabulary, however, and so does not go so far. It would be more accurate to say that for Levinas the human face-to-face encounter marks the absence, not the presence, of God, but it is a special absence—the absence of that which has left a residue behind.

Levinas states that through relationship or the encounter of the solitary subject with the other, face to face, religion—meaning charity, responsibility, and justice—is born. For my purposes, then, Levinas draws out an ethics at the heart of Jewish religion, though for me it is not its equivalent. He stresses the human encounter as absolutely essential.

I cannot offer here the history of Levinasian thought, which is both incremental and multifaceted, nor would I be capable of doing so. In particular, I cannot deal fairly with his subsequent critique of his early utilization of the language of ontology. I cannot trace his position in the history of Western philosophy or his relationship to Martin Heidegger or to other modern philosophers. Nor can I adequately comment on his position within phenomenology. What struck me forcefully, however, when I was studying for conversion and trying to work out issues of repentance and forgiveness was that the meaning of ethics for Levinas depends on the relationship that one has with the *face* of the other.

As with Torah, as with Maimonides, Levinas means not the literal, fixed, pictorial face, but rather face as "presence" and "a regard for." Ethics for Levinas challenges self-sufficiency. It is the interruption of the solipsistic self by another. He describes this interruption in different words: an obligation, an imperative, a responsibility, an imposition. But the interruption comes about only in an encounter with the *face* of the other ("*le visage d'Autrui*").[15] Levinas uses the face to articulate that which interrupts self-absorption and reorients the "for-itself" to "for-the-other."

Importantly, this interruption is not intentional. The ethical relation with the other is not something I decide to do, nor is it a matter of my generosity. Rather, the face of the other *breaks in* on my solipsism (the coherent self of Western philosophy). The interruption does not lead necessarily to relationship, as in Buber's theory of I and Thou. Levinas sees ethics, as Bob Gibbs points out, as "requiring concern without hope of ongoing relation" (190). Ethics is not sentiment, then, nor is it a desire for relationship that returns equally what is given; panim el panim may not inaugurate any kind of continued meetings. It commences as an asymmetrical relationship. The experience of the other and the obligation to that person is a demand placed by social existence on each individual—no more, no less.

In a face-to-face encounter, the mobility of the other's face as a signifying system prior to language commands me, in vulnerability. The other's gaze imposes on me responsibility to the other, but the gaze of the other does not impose on the other equal responsibility for me. I must act whether the other feels a command to responsibility or not.

At the same time, however, Levinas deconstructs this subject, this "I." The relationship with the other, he argues, puts the "I" into question: It is no longer coincident with itself. The ordinary tendency of the solipsistic self is to deny alterity, to "murder" the other, to put off the other, to shut out the other, but this is precisely what the encounter prevents. Thus, the encounter also destabilizes power and authority, even as it destabilizes subjectivity.

Although the interruption is not connected to sentiment or intention, the responsibility Levinas locates in the space of the encounter between the "I" and the other is equivalent to love of one's neighbor. But this is a particular kind of love: "Love without Eros, charity, love in which the ethical aspect dominates the passionate aspect, love without concupiscence. I don't very much like the word love, which is worn-out and debased. Let us speak instead of the taking upon oneself the fate of the other."[16] It is possible that Levinas recalls Rosenzweig's interpretation of the command to love thy neighbor. I do not love my neighbor for his own sake, "but because he happens to be nighest" to me. So the neighbor for Rosenzweig is both unique but also representative of any other, where the other does not have to be a person, but could be, say, a sacred text.[17]

What is the significance of this encounter? The encounter is a singling out of solipsism for transcendence and a connection with something larger. This is why Levinas often cites the important phrase from the Pentateuch used at critical moments by Abraham, Jacob, and Moses—for example, in response to God, "Hineni," "Me voici," "Here I am." It means "Here I am *for* the other, in the presence of the other, before that which is, in fact, wholly other to me and possessed by the other." To be human, according to Levinas, is to be open to the alterity of the other. It is not to subsume the other to sameness, but to accord the other difference, a non-indifference.

Levinas is not much interested in theology. He is careful to say that God does not reveal Himself, His face, except in His "trace," and that to approach Him we must approach others who are in the trace.[18] But as I read Levinas (and this is where I take liberties), this relationship of the "I" and the other is premised on the relationship modeled by God and Moses. In another sense, it bears a resemblance to the Hebrew nation's relationship to God at Sinai. There the people as individuals and as a group were stunned out of their self-absorption and offered a relationship to God. Their ordinary perceptions were interrupted so violently that they fell back and begged Moses to intercede again for them instead. I am suggesting that hineni, panim, responsibility, revelation, and redemption are bound up together.

The relationship between Moses and God is a foundational one. Special, unique, and remarkable as it is, it sets a standard on the divine-human level to which we should all aspire on the human-human level. Likewise, I believe, the relationship of the cherubim on the ark is about much more than two gold angels facing each other. The many faces of Torah and the dialogue and debate of the rabbis in their midrashic commentary and Talmudic discussions give us the text-based version of this relationship that interrupts solipsism or single points of view.

Each of the panim relationships I have tried to characterize shatters the subject of being. *Being for* is not the same as *being with* or *being together*. If all our relationships were one-way relationships, of course, we would accumulate many obligations in the sense that Levinas construes them. But he well knows that we do not live in a world of nonreciprocity. Nor could we care for ourselves at all if we did everything for the other and got nothing in return. This is where ethics turns to politics and to issues of justice. For there are never only two persons in our daily encounters or in our lives but also a third, who is representative of our discourse with all others and of a wider sociality and the social world.

The ethical one-way street, as Simon Critchley puts it, must bear the weight of two-way traffic. For a third, by his or her presence, will set limits to responsibility or obligation and raises the question of justice.

Justice is the moment, shortly after recognition, when I become the other's equal, one of a community that can demand rights as well as perform duties. In my words, though not in those of Levinas, this is the moment when *face* changes to *face to face*, panim el panim, in the human realm, the moment when ethics becomes politics, when I and the other become a "we," co-citizens in a common polis, yet remaining within the trace of ethics and divinity.[19] This is also the moment when I can question and judge the actions of the other.

Even if, following Levinas, I divide a moment of encounter, panim (ethics), from a moment of the introduction of the third (justice), ethics and justice are nevertheless intimately related. We are not just on a continuum of one-to-one encounter but also live among many other citizens every day in communities, societies, countries, and globally.

A just community is impossible, however, without the relationship of the "I" facing the other. Justice will not work unless we take upon ourselves ongoing responsibility for what Levinas calls "the fate of the other." He writes: "Justice only remains justice in a society where there is no distinction between those close and those far off (*entre proches et lointains*), but in which there also remains the impossibility of passing by the closest (*du plus proche*); where the equality of all is borne by my inequality, by the surplus of my duties over my rights."[20] Levinas goes so far as to test the legitimacy or illegitimacy of the state in terms of whether the interpersonal relationship with the face is possible. If not, the state is totalitarian.[21] If we cannot give the other priority by substituting ourselves for every person—not just every Jew but every person— there is little hope for a just society.

Their Faces Shall Be One Toward the Other

Thoughts on Terumah,
Exodus 25:1–27:19

It says (25:8), "Let them make Me a sanctuary that I may dwell among (or within) them"—in them, the people, not in it, the sanctuary. Each person is to build Him a Tabernacle in his [and her] own heart for God to dwell in.

—MALBIM
(MEIR YEHUDA LEIBUSH BEN YEHIEL MICHEL, 1809–1880),
"HATORAH VEHAMITZVAH," 1874–1880

The section of Exodus referred to as Terumah is the first of six chapters at the end of the book that describes the Tabernacle that Israel is asked to build, as well as the holy vessels and service that belong within it. On Mount Sinai, Moses is presented by God with something like a blueprint, a pattern (tavnit). He learns the details of the building plans, the style and fabrics of the garments and the curtains, how the ark shall be made, the nature and construction of the table, and much more. Terumah ends with a reminder to keep the Sabbath.

Commentators have wrestled with the question of why the construction of the sanctuary is introduced at such length at this point in Torah. They have also wondered why it is featured directly after the theophany and the code of the covenant. Perhaps it is out of order? Midrashim maintain that Moses was commanded to build the Tabernacle only after the people had worshiped the Golden Calf. So perhaps Ki Tisa (the Golden Calf episode) should come before Terumah. Or does Torah present it out of order in order expressly to show that God has the antidote ready for a moral illness even before it breaks out? Maimonides disagrees. The Tabernacle series, he holds, is hardly an afterthought, a cure for a disease, an atonement for a sin of idolatry, or a way of channeling man's materialistic leanings. Rather, he argues, God had the Tabernacle in mind from the beginning and it was always designed to strengthen the intimacy between God and His people.

Still, to some the elaboration of the planning and building of the Tabernacle appears anticlimactic and, in light of later sections such as Pekudei (Exodus 39 and 40), overly repetitive. Gunther Plaut reminds us that ancient Near Eastern typologies demand that a deity be enthroned in a house of his own and that the repetition is necessary. Others argue along the same lines that if these chapters were not here we might justifiably wonder where they were or whether they had been lost. Others stress the importance of the Tabernacle as the symbol of Israel's link with an indwelling God during its wanderings. Yet others take the descriptions to be fictitious, nothing more than old traditions patched together to provide an account of the "origins" of the Temple cult. Some register discrepancies between the meanings of Tabernacle and Tent of Meeting. Other scholars read the descriptions symbolically instead of historically or metaphorically and tease out meaning from every detail: the numbering, the cloths, the specifications for producing each vessel. Still others connect this section with Genesis—rightly, I think. The creation of the Tabernacle and its belongings, they contend, is the human version of God's creation of the world. As God labored for man and beast, so man now labors for God by creating something for Him in turn. It is therefore significant in this reading that six sections of Terumah talk about creation and the seventh concerns Shabbat, the day on which God rested from creating the world.

It is Franz Rosenzweig's interpretation of this section, however, that is closest to my own spiritual understanding of it. For him the building of the Tabernacle is the climax of the Pentateuch: Terumah, that is, stands as the most important point of the most important book. Why does Rosenzweig so privilege this section? Because it is here that the listener/reader in some sense enters the Holy of Holies. In this moment of profound holiness, one comes closer to God on earth than at any other moment in Pentateuch, except for our apprehension at Sinai. We as readers enter the otherwise forbidden inner sanctum via our imagination. As happens when we rise on tiptoe in the Kedushah prayer, this parasha affords us closeness. In its emphasis on both relationship and holiness, we see the realization of a celestial pattern on earth, the Israelites' education into a relationship of giving and taking in spiritual intimacy, and a wider application of relationships—to God, to Torah, and to each other.

At this point in Exodus we have heard the liberation narrative. The Israelites are provided with sustenance. The social and legal spheres are regulated. Commandments and codes are given. But the cult—its rites, practices, symbols, institutions, and personnel—is not organized. So this section begins that organization. It does so with a glance back at the parasha Yitro (the Sinai section) and continues to flesh out the notion of a "kingdom of priests and a holy nation," not only materially but spiritually.

Overall, I think, this parasha continues to chart a changing relationship to God after Sinai. There is a midrash concerning the frailty of the Hebrew people, who were so conditioned to slavery and to a culture of idolatry that they could not readily grasp an abstract monotheism. The Tabernacle opens up a connection to the invisible God. It is given by Him as a form, and its unity and architectonic wholeness is stressed, reminding us of God's unity and perfection. The Tabernacle is the material, numinous symbol of His immanence. Although only the selected may hear His voice, the Tabernacle is nonetheless a visible symbol of His care for all the people, a symbol of immense significance. As the people move away from Sinai spatially, they need a way to stay close emotionally and spiritually. Just as the ark is overlaid with gold inside and out, so the Tabernacle gives outward expression to inner religious concepts. Conversely, it is structured by degrees of interiority and holiness.

Recall here that the Tabernacle is not for God but—by His request—for the people, that they may be close to Him. It is a concession to their needs. God does not need a home or a building or a monument, and the people's Tabernacle is not a stone monument to a pharaoh. Rather, theirs is a portable structure that travels with them, honoring holy time and not just holy space. The people are engaged here in a requested but voluntary act of creation. It is also significant that the Tabernacle was erected on the first of the month—to initiate a new phase in the life of the community of Israel.

In Exodus 25:2–3 we might dwell on the word terumah (gift), which appears three times, and the verbs tikhu and veyikhu (take), which appear three times but are used in two different senses: to give and to receive. The verb phrases mean "Bring me offerings," "Take for me offerings from everyone," and "Take from them offerings for me" in the senses of "Give me gifts" and "Receive gifts from them for me." The verbs work together, and the single verb *take* harbors both meanings, as if it contained a relationship within it. There is a connection, even a continuum, the verses seem to say, between a giver and a receiver. Buried here is a notion that we receive what we give, and that when we give, the bounty we receive back is magnified. There is no intentionality here to receive when we give. Rather, there is a fluid relation in which we builders and givers and readers gain both meaning and identity in relationship to God through building and giving and reading. This has nothing to do with making a forced payment, cutting a deal, repaying, or bartering. Terumah emphasizes that everyone "whose heart moves him" (25:2) is welcome to give.

The highlight of this parasha for me, however, lies in 25:17–22, which offers us a celestial pattern of relationship as a model to be reproduced between ourselves on earth. This section describes the cover of the ark, fashioned of angels at each end, which is referred to elsewhere in sacred writings as the "footstool of God":

You shall make a cover of pure gold, two and a half cubits long and a cubit and a half wide. Make two cherubim of gold—make them of hammered work—at the two ends of the cover. Make one cherub at one end and the other cherub at the other end; of one piece with the cover shall you make the cherubim at its two ends. The cherubim shall have their wings spread out above, shielding the cover with their wings. They shall confront each other, the faces of the cherubim being turned towards the cover. Place the cover on top of the ark, after depositing inside the ark the Pact which I will give you. There I will meet with you, and I will impart to you from above the cover, from between the two cherubim that are on top of the ark of the Pact—all that I will command you concerning the Israelite people.

The ark is the most important article for the Tabernacle, and it comes first in a long list of holy items. Some commentators worry about the cherubim as idols. The angels, in fact, were left out of the Second Temple entirely. Maybe they are cultish? Gold images? Figures to worship? Still, there is no suggestion at all that they are idols. In fact, they are made-up creatures, fabrications with multivalent meanings. And their pattern is reproduced in some of the cloth for the Tabernacle. But what is their purpose here?

It appears that the angels, which are not free-standing figures separate from the cover, convey matters of a world of spirit central to the religion. The rabbinic sages, referring to Genesis, Ezekiel, and other sites in the Hebrew Bible for support, suggest two main functions for the angels: they symbolize the throne of God, their wings being a footstool for the Shekhinah, and they are guardians, here of the law of the covenant. Each angel is positioned, they suggest, over one of the two tablets within the ark.

The angels remind us of the world of spirit, but I think they do much more. I am intrigued especially by their faces and the space between them. Confronting each other, their faces are directed one toward the other, and yet their faces and eyes are also angled downward toward the law. Thus, they turn toward each other, but they do not gaze at each other. Nor do they look up at God: their eyes are modest. From between them, says God, I will meet you and impart to you. The Hebrew here is in the passive voice—"There I will be met, there I will be known by you." We have the sense of "known at a fixed time." The meaning seems to me not so much that we will meet there but that the divine voice will be met, from between them, by you.

Why are there two angels, not three or four or five? As suggested, perhaps each is intended to guard one tablet. But there is more. Since only God is one, then all else is multiple, and two is the first multiple. Thus, this seems to me to be a celestial model of how multiples may relate— two because they are in relation. Note that although they are described as a pair, and although we presume they are exactly alike, they are never described as being identical. There are various ways of interpreting their twosomeness. One may represent our relationship to God and one to humanity—even as the Ten Commandments are sometimes said to divide that way. They have faces, panim, and they may represent, as I think they do, human relations. The sages propose that they may represent male and female, teacher and student, two children, two men. In any construction we make, we need to see them, I think, as depending on each other and as accountable to each other.

One conclusion we might come to about these cherubim is that holiness is not just a mystical relationship reserved for the high priest entering a Tabernacle or for angels on the ark cover. Rather, it involves a celestial pattern that is available to us too when we relate to each other. It is to be attained on earth with the trace of God's voice between. It can be attained, suggests Terumah to me, through a relationship to the law and Torah, and it can also be attained in and through our attendance on the other before us. But preferably through both simultaneously.

Chapter Six

In Pieces: Facing Germany

What counts, when one attempts to elaborate an experience, is
less what one understands than what one doesn't understand.
—JACQUES LACAN, LES ECRITS TECHNIQUES DE FREUD, 1966

Sure, the signs and the documentation and the films help us to
understand. But the concentration camp as memorial site?
Landscape, seascape—there should be a word like timescape to
indicate the nature of a place in time, that is, at a certain
time, neither before nor after.
—RUTH KLUGER,
STILL ALIVE: A HOLOCAUST GIRLHOOD REMEMBERED, 2001

A rabbi to whom I spoke years earlier about conversion suggested
that commitment must involve deep engagement with the type
of persecution represented by the Holocaust. "If there's a second Holocaust, you go with the Jews," he said pointedly. That stopped
me in my tracks. I stared back. Conversion was clearly not going to be as
simple as I had thought. Did I really want to join the Jews? Once an
observant member of the religion, there would be no way out but dis-
avowal or death. Just how strong was this faith of mine? What exactly
was being asked of me? The connection of identity to persecution and to
anti-Semitism frightened me. I backed away.

For some years I continued to ponder the rabbi's words. He had asked
too much of me, I thought. In truth it was easier to complain about such
standards than to admit I simply wasn't ready to convert. He had challenged me, and I failed to meet the challenge. But his words persisted,

insisted, even. And after I became a Jew they remained with me as a moral obligation to the dead and the living.

The evil of the Holocaust has been for me the element of the Jewish historical and theological experience that is most difficult to face and to understand. My relationship to it changed, however, during my first year as a Jew; my ignorance gave way to some knowledge, and I went from fending it off to taking it in. Realizing I had to go, I traveled to Germany in the summer of 2000; I wanted to go but had to force myself nonetheless. My nervousness approached dread as my departure day drew near. Fearful of what I would see and have to accept in myself, I was plagued by second thoughts and had a lot of trouble remaining positive when friends wished me a great trip.

As it happened, England and a professional conference would be my final stop before coming home, so I went to Germany with what I can only describe as highly mixed feelings and with the goal of leaving for England. I thought deeply at this time about what German Jews suffered in their desire to get by the passport officials, reach England or another safe haven, and feel some degree of relief.

I realize that it is difficult to believe that a twenty-first-century, forty-nine-year-old tourist and convert, happy as a clam with her morning muesli, easy life, and comfy accommodations at home and abroad, could identify at all with German Jews trying to escape the Nazis. More to the point, I am aware that even a superficial likening of my fears to those of German Jews living under the third Reich is an obscenity.

Clearly my anxieties bore no relationship to the deep, desperate traumas felt by Jews and other victims in the war.[1] My reactions, which had nothing whatsoever to do with staying alive, could only be virtual, approximate, identificatory, even if they were real. The realities brought into collision were quite different; the huge gap between historical moments and personal situations did not escape me. I was in search of my humanity, but I was no victim at all.

The gulf between the world of the Holocaust and the world of today threw into bold relief for me how those of us unaffected directly by World War II share the burden of failure. We cannot understand except through empathy, yet even reaching out with compassionate feelings of identification will never be enough to grasp what happened to the victims, displaced persons, refugees, and survivors. Empathy is particularly inadequate in the face of genocide.

My post-Holocaust anxieties stemmed from my quest to deepen an identity by choosing to face the worst and, I hoped, by learning to live a better life. My fears came from choice and aftermath, not from a condemned existence. The victims of the Holocaust did not have the luxury of choosing or abandoning identification, they did not have the option of dwelling on emotions beyond those needed for day-to-day survival or, in some cases, for the relief afforded by death. I don't know whether my own feelings were more right than wrong, or whether my trip was a stupid self-indulgent, private mission or a contemporary American drama of wanting to understand and failing—or both. Still, the rift within me only deepened over the course of the visit to Germany. No stories or pictures can replace an actual visit.

I traveled not just as a tourist and friend of German Catholics but as a Jewish convert and wife of a man whose family lost everything except each other in their escape from the Nazis. These are the different, competing selves I brought to Germany: tourist, friend, former Christian, Jew-by-choice, and wife of a survivor. My stay was overwhelming and filled with highly contradictory feelings and bits of information, with multiple points of view, including my own varied reactions, and with history's insistent black, white, and red intrusions into my present. I became a Jew torn in pieces.[2]

The past was often with me in Germany, though it was a highly mediated past. Especially during the first days of my visit I was haunted, suddenly and almost arbitrarily, by images from photographs, old documentaries, newspapers, and paintings wherever I was—on trains, on buses, on walks—of the rise of the Nazis and of the suffering they wrought. These visions appeared before great art and at the buildings of concentration camps, when speaking German or hearing it, in lovely gardens, or when clapping appreciatively among well-dressed Germans at a Spanish flamenco ballet at the Munich State Theater. In short, images of the Holocaust appeared anywhere, at any time. I struggled with echoes of a past I felt I should *get beyond*, and at the same time I was shattered emotionally by this encounter with a suffering that was finally meaningless, in ways both speakable and unspeakable, tellable and untellable.[3]

For me, the paradox of Germany only grew: the beauty and refinement, the sophistication and culture, the war memories and the barbarity, and the pro and anti-Semitism of today. I was stimulated by the lofty beauty of the Alps and the pleasures of Hamburg, Berlin, Munich, and my dear German friends. I was confused about the present situation of Russian Jews, who continue to arrive in large numbers, many having only the most tentative or tenuous ties to Judaism. The continued presence of anti-Semitism, including five attacks or desecrations—in Neuengamme, Düsseldorf, Bamberg, Rockenhausen, and Dielkirchen—in the two weeks after I left Germany, troubled me deeply. At the same time, I agreed with Germans that the Holocaust should not be part of some political agenda to blame them forever. Certainly I applauded the attempts by the younger generation to remember the past and to show no tolerance for racism in the twenty-first century. Concurrently, I noted German ambivalence about an open-door policy of support for Jewish immigrants, an arrangement found nowhere else in Europe.

Nothing was straightforward or simple. I had hoped to visit the Jüdisches Museum in Berlin, but found that no displays could be viewed until the completion of its interior, which had been postponed a year to September 2001. I went to Germany with insights into the incredible political complexities surrounding the building, even its filing system. Could they use "J," for instance, or would that painfully recall "*Jude*"? This was only one of the many small and large questions for the organizers, as reported by W. Michael Blumenthal, the museum's American chief executive, in a lecture I heard at Princeton in the spring of 2000.[4] But I came back with an even greater sense of the difficulties in modern Germany concerning memorials in particular and the Holocaust in general.

Holocaust memorials in Berlin were seriously delayed. At one point the Jüdisches Museum had a building without an exhibit, an exhibit without a building, and a vacant lot for an even more delayed public memorial. The museum plan had been approved in 1989, the building and grounds, designed brilliantly by architect Daniel Libeskind, were completed in 1997, and the public was let in for a look in 1999. Still, the museum had not opened when I went in 2000, though it has since then and I have now seen it. The "Topography of Terror" exhibition, another Holocaust cultural project, then had no permanent building. Further, a tedious debate continued raging over the Holocaust memorial (a field of columns), which was to be built near the Brandenburg Gate. "The Jewish-German question is so delicate and hot that any person who takes on these projects is going to be burned in some way, but perhaps more so a German," commented Wenzel Jacob, director of the Federal Museum of Art in Bonn.[5] Moreover, cultural projects and their delays don't begin to tell the story, as there is hardly any part of German national life in the major cities that is not somehow touched by the memory of the Third Reich, as Roger Cohen of the *New York Times* has made clear in his reporting. W. Michael Blumenthal explains that the Germans must be given credit for what they are doing to come to terms with the Holocaust. The problem, as he notes, is that many "are doing it for the Jews, not for themselves."[6]

So these are a few of the contrasts of civilization and barbarity, order and chaos. *Forget and forgive*, I say to myself. *Remember and witness*, I counter. *But my country has bombed this country!* I think. I'm divided by my convert status, on the one hand, and my identification with my husband, a Jew-by-birth who fled. How do I belong here? Where do I belong here, if I belong at all? I remain hopeful about the German assumption of national responsibility for what happened to the Jews and profoundly despairing over the concentration and labor camps, mass graves, distorted death numbers, memorials, and bombed synagogues that I saw. Much about the visit was positive, but I wonder if I can return.

Many theories have been put forward to explain what the Holocaust scholar Lawrence Langer has called "the aversion to crisis faculty" that kept potential victims, civilian bystanders, and the Western nations in a state of denial, ignorant disregard or willful downplaying of, or indifference to the plight of the Jews, other political prisoners, homosexuals, the disabled, gypsies, and others.[7] I don't know the answer myself. "Aversion to the Holocaust" was my own state of mind for years. It is morally untenable.

My difficulty with facing and processing the Holocaust has been long-standing. Like many non-Jewish or Jewish teens, I had been intrigued by Anne Frank's diary, devoured Leon Uris's novel *Exodus*, and browsed in Holocaust materials in the library. As I look back on this early period of my life, I see now that what attracted me was the thrill of hiding from Nazis, the threat of imminent discovery, and the adventures of Zionism, with their own romantic and idealistic tinge.

It is with embarrassment that I realize that the Second World War fascinated me and I had no awareness of the ethnic and racial cleansing policies of that time. When I was a little girl, my father, who was a veteran, routinely attended Army Reserve meetings; my uncle had died on active duty in the Navy; my aunt's first husband had been in the Marines. The family military connections made it natural for me to think about patriotism, the defense of democracy in the face of totalitarianism, serving one's country, killing the enemy, dying on active duty. But these connections did not predispose me to dwell on European civilians, the Jews, other persecuted minorities, labor and death camps, or genocide. Nor do I remember any discussion of these aspects of the war in school or at home. My high school history survey did not get beyond World War I, and in college I happened not to study modern European history beyond that of the nineteenth century.

So it is perhaps no surprise that when I wrote a doctoral dissertation on the poetry of the Second World War, treating the survival of the lyrical impulse during traumatic historical events, I once again ignored the Holocaust entirely, as if it had never happened. Flashback to 1980: My future husband is asking me, "So what is your favorite poem of this period you're working on?" "'Vergissmeinicht' by Keith Douglas," I say quickly. "It's arguably the best poem by the best British war poet after Siegfried Sassoon and Wilfred Owen." I happily explain how the poem weaves romance with realism, letting the reader settle with neither easily, but ultimately points to commonalities between a German and an English soldier, one dead, one alive, both lovers and killers. "It's a great poem," I say. "Touching. Haunting." It does not explore the differences between them. Neither do I.

For years afterward my husband tried unsuccessfully to engage me with books, stories, newspaper articles, television shows, and films about the Holocaust. He'd leave the newspaper open to articles, he'd request that I read stories—underground stories, Swiss-bank stories, memorial or museum stories, stories about cemetery desecrations, murders of Jews, reunions of relatives. He'd share autobiography or fiction: Wiesel, Ozick, Levi, Fink, constructed from the heart of the ashes. Obituaries. I paid no attention. I was equally uninterested in hearing about contemporary anti-Semitic attacks around the world. "It's all so morbid," I'd respond.

It is not that I ever questioned the historicity of the Holocaust or the unthinkable brutalities it rained down on millions of Jews and non-Jews.[8] I simply did not want its huge ugliness continually intruding on our domestic life. There were still other reasons for my resistance, reasons I did not understand, concerning the extent to which I was open to being moved—even shaken—by what obsessed my husband. Displacement and loss had shaped his childhood identity and still marked his life. His survival guaranteed him a lifetime of remembering loss, even as he somehow transmuted it into gain, following the example of both of his parents. After years of pressing materials on me, he gave up, resigned that I could never feel this pain with him.

I dwell on my responses as a teenager, graduate student, and young wife because I believe them to be typical, sadly, of many educated, well-meaning Jews and non-Jews who prefer not to be disturbed. As the Russian poet Joseph Brodsky has observed about mass murder: "Western man, by and large, is the most natural man, and he cherishes his mental comfort. It is almost impossible for him to admit disturbing evidence."[9] For most of my life I have been invested in not allowing myself to get too near to depravity and horror. Like most people, I have preferred the familiar and comforting; I have grabbed the freedom to refuse to deal with human-generated ugliness or a reality without ethics. My self-protection seems to me based in distaste but also in fear that I did not have the resources to cope with my own inhumanity. In retrospect, I can better understand my predeparture tears and the sources of the dread. After fifty years of keeping evil at bay, I had decided to open up.

What happened as I became a Jew? During my conversion training I exhibited a similar mix of fascination with this historical period and an inability to face the horror. When I arrived at the Holocaust tutorial with my rabbi, he said, "So, what did you read? What films did you watch? What shall we discuss?" "I read oral testimonies of survivors," I said. The rest tumbled out: "And war history, genocide material, theological responses, and psychoanalytic trauma theory. I saw *Schindler's List*, *The Last Days*, *Nazis*, *Holocaust Survivors*, and *Shoah*." "And?" he said. I felt overcome. Not as if I would break down. But numb. I felt that nothing I could say mattered. I had hit a wall where my reasoning, analysis, and wordpower didn't work anymore. "It's too much. I don't have questions or comments. I don't know what to say." The regular processing routines didn't work. I went home. My rabbi accepted my silence that evening. Perhaps I could not.

By the time I reached conversion day, I believed I understood the rudiments of the difficult history of the Jews. Victimized and marginalized, they had been maligned in many places over many centuries and by various groups, including the most devout, who drove them out of their homes, tried to convert them, or tortured and killed them in the name of Jesus Christ or God. Some of my understanding was general, but some of it was also particularized as I learned about the Spanish Inquisition, the expulsion of the Jews from England during Catholic rule, and displaced families elsewhere in the world. I realized, as well, that a pattern does not account for individual instances and that the Jews are no more to be idealized than any other group—that the Jews are made up of individuals.

But I could not grasp the enormity of the Holocaust, and I could not understand how a civilized and Enlightenment-influenced nation such as Germany had allowed, fostered, ignored, and sometimes took pleasure in such an atrocity. I wanted to see concentration camps, German cities, bombed synagogues, homes, families. In some sense I wanted to connect places and names and faces and landscapes with my own feelings. But mostly I wished to mourn. And then to move beyond mourning, to get on with the task of living humanely in the aftermath.

In the summer of 2000, I could have gone to Israel but decided that making that connection—through origins or through present political history or through sacred land—could wait. Instead, I spent two weeks visiting Hamburg, Berlin, and Munich. I went to Germany to claim my membership in the Jewish community unified by its history of exclusion, suffering, and genocide. Perhaps I also went to face my own obliteration of the Jews.

I did confront entrenched myths and tried to replace them with realities rather than more myths. Like so many others at a young age, I had uncritically absorbed not only the myth of victim par excellence fostered by the Anne Frank material but also other mythic views about the victims, perpetrators, resistance fighters, victimizers, and bystanders.[10] For instance, I preferred stories of courage and freedom to the sheer facts and realities of death figures and brutality. I preferred tales of Danish boat rescues, French resistance, and German officials who looked the other way to protect Jews and their sacred places. I romanced morality into extraordinary heroism, which it is not, and used it to mute the suffering of victims, a suffering so acute and denigrating and enormous that it cannot be spoken adequately or grasped entirely by the human imagination. And it shouldn't be.

Moreover, for some years, insofar as I considered the Holocaust at all, I thought that nobody at the time really knew what was going on under the Third Reich, including the leaders of other nations and the average German. As I learned, of course, there were plenty of signs, for anyone paying attention, before and after the institution of camps: the rise of nationalisms in Europe; the publication of anti-Semitic essays and books on the "Jewish question"; Hitler's failed revolution attempt in 1923 and his reduced prison sentence; the Nazis' electoral successes in 1933 (6.5 million votes, making them the second-largest political party); President von Hindenburg's coalition with Hitler, which led to Hitler's becoming chancellor; the book burning; the closing of Jewish businesses; the elimination of Jews from public life and universities; the closing of yeshivas; the boycott on Jewish shops; the detentions; the ghettos; the Nuremberg

Laws; the outlawing of intermarriage; the closing of the professions to Jews; the yellow star; the roundup of Jews with Polish citizenship; Kristallnacht; and much more. But was anyone paying attention? Did we foresee Hitler's "final solution"? It is so much easier to see patterns in retrospect. Many German Jews themselves downplayed the negative and waited too long to flee, assuming always that things had reached their nadir. Realizing that no country would open its doors to the Jews beyond their minute immigration quotas, Hitler understood they could now be disposed of for good. This betrayal of the Jews by the "Allied" countries and even by many American Jews is one of the greatest immoral acts of the Holocaust. As for me, embracing political naïveté, I simply did not want to believe that economic or military interests would totally, and for many complicated reasons, override any moral action to prevent the systematic elimination of millions of people.

It has been documented that world leaders Churchill and Roosevelt knew details of what was occurring in the concentration camps and ghettos and chose not to intervene in any meaningful way.[11] The Shoah was, as Dominick La Capra correctly designates it, a "relatively open secret."[12] A few examples and voices will serve as representative of countless more. The first reports on Dachau, the original concentration camp (1933), were published abroad in worker newspapers in Moscow and in the *Manchester Guardian* in 1934; they described corporal punishment, outrageous living conditions, torture, and ill treatment leading to death.[13] By 1938, after Kristallnacht in November, David H. Buffam, the U.S. consul in Leipzig, could write: "The most hideous phase of the so-called 'spontaneous' action has been the wholesale arrest and transportation to the concentration camps of male German Jews between the ages of sixteen and sixty."[14] The most hideous phase was just the first phase.

One of the more dramatic instances of "other" priorities was the story of the *St. Louis*, a luxury liner that sailed from Hamburg on May 13, 1939, with 937 passengers, more than 900 of them Jews, seeking asylum in Cuba, where they hoped to wait until the United States called their quota numbers. But they did not know that their immigration landing permits, issued by a corrupt director of immigration, had already been invalidated by the Cuban government. Nor did they know that it was the

United States that had blocked their landing in Cuba because the American government did not want them too close to its shores.

The ship was forced to turn back to Europe. Pleading with world leaders, Morris Troper, the European director for the Joint Distribution Committee, was finally able to secure havens for the passengers in France, England, Holland, and Belgium. They were scattered to children's homes, private homes, refugee camps, and quarantine stations. In the end, the Nazis occupied the countries where they had found refuge, and many died in the death camps.[15]

The obituary of Jan Karski, a Polish underground officer, pointedly reminds us that he received negative responses from his Polish diplomatic superiors, from Britain's Anthony Eden, and from President Roosevelt when he reported a crisis. Karski's risk-taking secret visits informing them of the annihilation of the Polish Jews of the Warsaw Ghetto and begging for intervention met with no response. As he put it: "Almost every individual was sympathetic to my reports concerning the Jews. But when I reported to the leaders of governments, they discarded their conscience, their personal feeling." He explains their response as seemingly valid but morally indifferent: "Nothing could interfere with the military crushing of the Third Reich. The Jews had no country, no government. They were fighting, but they had no identity."[16] How fiercely theories of nationalism on both sides worked against the Jews, but how important they would be during and after the war for the establishment of the State of Israel.

Not only did I hold myths about the public knowledge of what was going on, but I knew nothing about the extent of brutality in the German armed forces. I believed the legend propagated about the decency of the German army, which reputedly kept its distance from Hitler. I thought only Nazi leaders, the Gestapo officers, and the SS men and women, such as those who served on extermination squads or camp details, acted brutally. That notion has been largely overturned on the basis of first-hand evidence. The International Military Tribunal that met in Nuremberg after the war did not declare the Wehrmacht (the armed forces of the German army, navy, and air force) a criminal organization, although judges did order individuals suspected of crimes brought before

courts and severely punished. As we now know, the crimes of the
Wehrmacht were vast.

In *The German Army and Genocide: Crimes Against War Prisoners, Jews,
and Other Civilians in the East, 1939–1944,* the Hamburg Institute for
Social Research and Omer Bartov explode this myth of the honorable
German soldier. Documents and hundreds of photographs drawn from
archives across Europe were first shown in a controversial exhibition in
Germany, "The Germany Army and Genocide," and toured the country
after opening in Hamburg in 1995.[17] The book reveals average German
soldiers of the Wehrmacht beating, hanging, and bayoneting harmless
civilians during operations on the eastern front in Serbia, White Russia,
and the Ukraine. It reveals that the occupation of Poland was a deliberate experiment in a war of annihilation against peoples, not armies,
informed by a "politics of ethnic cleansing, colonization, and enslave-
ment."[18] Jews, prisoners of war, and civilian groups were eliminated as
mercilessly as the dead of Nanking, Vietnam, Bosnia, Rwanda, Kosovo,
Somalia, and so many other sites of slaughter. There is a clear moral distinction between fighting a war in order to win and torturing civilians in
the process. That distinction has rarely been upheld during wartime, but
it seems to have been ignored more easily in the twentieth century and
has apparently become habitual, whether the soldiers are wielding
weapons of mass destruction or machetes.

Of course, because the German press and the Nazi political machine
engaged in a systematic propaganda effort of denial, fabrication, and
cover-ups, as do all wartime governments, the truth of torture was sometimes difficult to establish. The details and phrasings of this propaganda
system are made quite clear in the Dachau concentration camp exhibit of
documents, although the complete phrasing on all secret documents,
such as "for internal use only," is still not available to the non-German-
speaking public, as my German friend pointed out to me while translat-
ing.

Visits to the concentration camps of Hamburg-Neuengamme,
Bergen-Belsen, and Dachau showed me firsthand just how huge and effi-
cient the killing machine was. Sachsenhausen, Buchenwald, Auschwitz,
Treblinka—I had read and seen pictures of major camps in Germany and

outside its borders, but I had not realized that the major concentration and labor camps had satellite camps. As exhibits at Bergen-Belsen and Dachau dramatically illustrate, inch after inch of the map of Germany was dotted with them. Take one instance: From 1942 the concentration camp Hamburg-Neuengamme itself spawned *eighty* slave labor satellite camps where prisoners worked for the war economy in the armaments industry, in cleanup brigades for bombed cities and towns, and as construction workers in the new industrial complexes. By 1944, forty thousand people, nearly one-third of them women, worked in these eighty camps.

The killing machine was enormous, and so were the killing fields, so enormous that neither victim nor bystander could have escaped it. People disappeared all the time or surged into public places unprotected on their way to ghettos, labor camps, holding camps, distribution centers, reception camps, concentration camps, or prison ships. So many names for death. It is inconceivable that German and then Austrian and Polish citizens did not know, although this point of view still persists within those countries among some of the older generation. On the contrary, they were brainwashed and bullied into accepting the murder of Jews and other peoples as being for the "good" of the Reich. And many feared for their own lives.

In a typical narrative, told to me by a German friend, two little Jewish girls disappeared from her aunt's neighborhood during the war. "Where did you think they went?" asked my friend. "Oh, we thought they went on holiday." "But what about the fact that they never returned?" "We thought they moved away." "Without their parents?" "Well, of course, we thought they moved in with other people." "Why would they do such a thing?" No answer. Hence the problem—moral indifference and a kernel of truth, enough to stifle any questioning or self-questioning.

The fact is that thousands of Germans, of all backgrounds, were also displaced by the war. The German family holding this very dialogue was split apart and forced to settle in different places in Bavaria. Moreover, within the family some served Hitler, some resisted, and some were conscripted against their will. This hardly excuses the replies. Nor do I remotely suggest that this family's experience was comparable to the genocide of Jewish families. But the layering of self-deception is complicated.

There is still a resistance to factual accuracy among some Germans, however, about those who disappeared. On the day my German friend and I journeyed by bus and foot to Neuengamme, it was closed, as it is every Monday. Nevertheless, my friend, not to be deterred, sought out the offices and explained how far I had come. A kind young man opened the memorial building for us. "No problem," he said. "I'm glad to do this for you." He directed us on how to walk around the grounds (which feature a brick factory, a shooting range, former buildings, now a prison, called Detention Center XII, and other locations), while apologizing to us several times that he could not open the exhibit.

He unlocked the doors he could unlock. The memorial building/document center is two stories high; the bottom floor houses offices and records, including the death registers from the prison camp sick bay. The Reich's penchant for hierarchy and order was evident here. Each inmate who died in the camp was recorded with prison number, name, date of birth and death, and hour and cause of death. Most were in their thirties and forties. Some were executed, and some committed suicide. Some were shot dead for provoked "escape attempts." In other causes of death cited—"cardiac insufficiency," "pulmonary oedema," "heart debility"—one reads: starvation, brutality, random shooting. Upstairs the red walls are hung with long white scrolls. Each contains the names of the dead, by date. Lists and lists of names of human beings with families, people who once harbored hopes, dreams, and goals. They were men and women, gypsies, Russian prisoners of war, political prisoners, and approximately thirteen thousand Jews. We walk, stunned, whispering occasionally, reading all those names, more than twenty nationalities represented. The young man waited downstairs.

Outside at the entry to the rest of the camp the young man turned and stopped us. "I want to be sure you see this and understand it," he said. He wanted me to hear in English and my friend in German the story of the camp memorial stone. So he told it twice. "This marker," he explained, "gives the name of the camp, its dates, and the numbers of the dead. When the sign was carved, the figures on the finished stone were incorrect. Digits were omitted, leaving out thousands of the dead. Upon asking the stonecutters how such a mistake could have occurred, the committee for the concentration camp memorial was told that 'so many people could not have died there.'" He paused to watch our faces. He was a gentle young man, and one of the only Jews I had seen in Germany. "Instead of letting the error be masked by the carving of a new stone," he said, "the committee demanded that small stones be carved with the correct figures and affixed on top of the original." He looked at the corrections, looked at us, then walked back to the offices.

The memorial stone serves to remind us today not only of the atrocities committed from 1938 to 1945 but of the forgetfulness, disbelief, and wishful thinking that occurred four decades later. So where does "knowledge" begin and end?

In the peaceful fields across the river that served the brick factory, cows grazed among brilliantly colored wildflowers. It was gray, calm, hinting at rain on the way. On the other side of us, in the distance, prisoners of the contemporary Detention Center XII played ball on an exercise ground. My German friend and I walked along a well-worn path by the river, alone, in silence. For us, the earth was still permeated with the smell of death.

On the tenth day of my stay, having seen three concentration camps, two bombed synagogues, three art museums, and elaborate gardens, and having toured major cities by bus, by train, and on foot, I made a pilgrimage to my husband's first home on Max-Joseph-Strasse in Munich, near one of the two synagogues destroyed during Kristallnacht. The scars of destruction and reconstruction that I had seen in Berlin were not in evidence here. Nor were there any poor, homeless, or jobless in sight. Munich, rebuilt according to strict building codes, remains a city of lovely vistas, colorful houses, Jugendstil style, neoclassical buildings, palaces, majestic fountains, parks, and flower gardens. My friend had driven me by the house on an initial tour of the city, but I wanted to return to take more pictures of it and get a better sense of its location in relation to other areas of the city. It was the most personal connection I had to the Holocaust.

Hardly anything remains today of Munich's Jewish history, which was once significant. The first Jews settled in Munich in the twelfth century, but their presence there was never easy. As Billie Ann Lopez and Peter Hirsch report, in 1285, for instance, "180 Jews were burned to death inside their synagogue. Persecution in the face of the Black Death forced many to flee in 1348–49, and Jews who returned repeatedly encountered expulsion or death. Finally expelled between 1440 and 1450, Jews were not officially allowed to return to Bavaria until late in the eighteenth century."[19] Their numbers then increased steadily during the nineteenth and into the early twentieth century.

After World War I, anti-Semitism in Bavaria raged again. "During the Third Reich era," Lopez and Hirsch report, "4,500 Munich Jews were deported and few survived. Although today Munich has one of the largest Jewish communities in Germany, little remains to explain what precisely has been lost" (p. 191). Only graves. There are two Jewish cemeteries—one from the nineteenth century and one from the twentieth. The small Jewish museum (just two rooms) advertised in major guidebooks had vanished when I looked for it at Maximilianstrasse 36. Upon my return home, I heard from my friend that it had been moved and that a large Jewish museum was being planned for Munich.

Grass grows where synagogues once stood and communities flourished. "There are memorials to the synagogues destroyed in 1938 on Herzog-Max-Strasse and on Herzog-Rudolf-Strasse. The main synagogue had already been demolished to make room for a Nazi parking lot. The Orthodox synagogue was destroyed during Kristallnacht. The synagogue of the eastern European Jews at Reichenbachstrasse, built in 1931, was ransacked but not burned in 1938 because of its close proximity to other buildings. Restored, it serves today as Munich's main synagogue" (p. 191).

Responding to anti-Semitic attacks in various parts of Germany in the weeks after my visit, the German foreign minister, Joschka Fischer, remarked that Germany had been too silent about the recent rightist violence against Jews. Deregulating the German economy, not hate crimes, has been at the top of the government agenda, though the leaders are beginning to grasp the ideological and real relationships between the economy, violence, and the country's reputation. They attempted to address anti-Semitism again at the millennium.

In the wake of the Third Reich, and as Germany enters a new century, the call has gone out for an ethic of "Zivilcourage" (personal courage rooted in morality), lest the rebuilding of the country's reputation over fifty years be in vain.[20] It is apparently time to buttress this personal value. Uwe-Karsten Heye, spokesman for Chancellor Gerhard Schroeder, announced a new publicity campaign designed to encourage Zivilcourage, "Show Your Face," an initiative in which famous sports stars and celebrities will exhort the nation to stop racism, xenophobia, and anti-Semitism. Will this campaign do any good? It is hard to say. Reactionary groups have been broadening their appeal across the entire country, and my Bavarian friends report a genuine nervousness about the NPD (Nationalpartei Deutschlands) and the DVU (Deutsche Volksunion), not to mention their apprehension about right-wing political developments in neighboring Austria and uncertainty as the leader of Switzerland steps down.

Little in Munich today is Jewish. My encounter with the old house that my husband had misremembered as an Italianate villa with a goldfish pond was therefore very important to me. I had not realized just how important until the morning I set off to find it on my own. Taking a route from Schwabing through the university area, I headed to the center of the city, and when I arrived at the street, the Karolinenplatz Obelisk at one end and Maximiliansplatz at the other end, I recognized it immediately. The house was large, elegant, beautiful. My husband's parents had rented the ground floor of this prestigious-looking six-story building, now home to government offices. It was not a villa, nor did it have a goldfish pond, but it was certainly of neoclassical Tuscan style, white and amber colored, with clean lines, stone carvings, and a magnificent portico. The ground-floor French window frames looked like mahogany and ran ceiling to floor all around the house, letting in so much air and light that small shutters were needed on the inside for privacy and shade. The house had surprised me when we drove past it in the van, but now its size and grandeur stunned me.

As I stood in this place I thought a good deal about my husband's parents, whom I never knew, and the situation they faced as Jews in Bavaria and Austria during the early 1930s. Reflecting back on this pilgrimage to a house, I felt I had adopted or even stolen my husband's early life and that of his parents, because I had no past in European Jewry. And yet I identified so strongly with them. As I searched for my Jewish identity in Munich, the only shred of meaning I could find was this home to which my husband had been brought as a newborn infant. In 1934, when my husband was three, his father's Jewish engineering firm had moved the family from this house in Munich to ill-fated Vienna, assuming incorrectly that it would be safer. In 1939, after various attempts to leave Austria, the family fled through Italy to Bolivia.

The story of my husband's flight reminds me of other people's narratives that I have read, especially one related by Michael Winerip called "Dear Cousin Max."[21] As I walked around the house, I began to imagine the letters that must have passed between my husband's parents and their relatives and between his father, a civil engineer heading a German business, and the Dutch-Jewish engineering firm that tried repeatedly to secure the family passage out of Vienna. Standing in front of the first house where my husband lived, I remembered a narrative told in letters of a far less fortunate engineer and his family.

In 1938 Max Schohl, a fifty-four-year-old chemical engineer, faced the same dilemma as my father-in-law. Like his counterpart, he had fought in the German Army during World War I and had also earned medals for his bravery. He, his wife, and their two daughters lived in a large home in Flörsheim, near Frankfurt, where he operated a dye factory. An expert in metallurgy, he tried for years to get out of Germany.

Desperate to save his family, he wrote to his American relatives for help, pleading for money and for political interventions to get them immigration permits. Only one cousin, Julius Hess, a salesman in West Virginia, did not brush him off. Schohl's heartrending letters became more and more insistent. The time lags between his letters became mysterious and frightening. Just as a job and admission for the Schohls to England was secured, Germany invaded Poland and Britain declared war on Germany. All outstanding permits to England were revoked. Schohl then tried to get to Chile. The family sent money to Holland to secure the permits, but by then the war had spread and the mail severely disrupted; by the time the money was received and confirmed, Chile was also closed. The next possibility was Paraguay, and after that Brazil.

The letters also tell the tale of a good, childless American Jewish cousin raising thousands of dollars he didn't have himself in order to help a German relative he had never met. They tell in broken English a story that must be explained elliptically at best to get by censors. They tell of the increasing poverty and despair on both sides of this exchange. It is a story that was repeated in so many families, individually, differently, yet we can barely comprehend it: losing all ties to one's job, one's business, one's colleagues and friends, one's place of worship, one's schools and social halls; denied one's bank accounts; denied privileges and equal rights; denied self-respect; forced to write in code or in languages not well mastered to try to convey the severity of the situation—hoping those letters would reach their destination.

In the end, we learn, the Schohls emigrated to Yugoslavia. That country fell to the Nazis in 1941, and the Schohls lived in poverty. No letters reached Julius Hess once the United States was at war. Max Schohl, who had barely survived Kristallnacht and Buchenwald, was killed at Auschwitz in 1943. His wife and eldest daughter survived the war and returned to Flörsheim after it was over. His eldest daughter converted to Roman Catholicism; his youngest daughter joined Julius Hess in America and settled there.

Standing in Munich, I found the Schohls' story interweaving with that of my husband's family. Only extraordinary luck saved the one man, whereas the other perished. I now understand, for the first time, the shape of luck—pure arbitrariness. Schohl's daily struggle to save his family recalls my father-in-law's attempts to get permits for three persons. He had gotten his family out of Germany, and he would leave Vienna only if he again obtained three immigration permits. The diligent Jewish Dutch engineering firm with which he had contacts offered him a job in India, but with only one visa, none for his wife and child. Then Ceylon. One visa. More letters. Then Cyprus. One visa. More letters. Peru, one visa, as time and armies moved along relentlessly. He held out. Miraculously, three permits finally materialized for La Paz, Bolivia.

Earlier in my trip, during my last evening in Hamburg, my German host, a friend of my husband's who was also raised in Bolivia, showed me videos taped from a German television travel show of Oruro, La Paz, and Lake Titicaca. One featured the carnival for which Oruro is world-famous. My husband lived in La Paz and then Oruro, Bolivia, from age eight to twenty—not amid the Alps but amid the Andes, not surrounded by the colorful, southern beauties of Munich, so like Italy, but surrounded by the even more southern blank and colorless altiplano, dotted with llamas and scrub. I was immensely grateful to our friend for sharing those videos. But five days later I stood at my husband's point of origin, in Munich. I was stunned by the harsh visual contrasts and internalized for the first time the loss of a European way of life and what it meant. I felt as if I were not only living another's life but also surviving it in a backward time warp.

While obsessively photographing every angle, every door, the front portico of the house from up close and from side streets, I somehow understood that bringing home pictures of a house was crazy, since there was really nothing to bring home. I had come that day, without even knowing it, seeking the traces of a family, an event, a time. I am what James Young, in his book on Holocaust memorials, calls a "memory tourist."[22] Yet for me there was nothing but the absence of a trace. A friendly German official inside the front door permitted me to walk around the marble hallway, but that couldn't muffle the loss. There was nothing at all left there, in the house, the city, in Bavaria, to hold on to. What had I expected?

I walked away toward Maximiliansplatz to see what was on the other side of this place that was once home to my husband. I passed a small park on the right with a statue of Goethe and gazed on the left at the wonderful Maximiliansplatz fountain. My mind wouldn't give up searching for some hook in an older reality. I imagined 1931 and my husband as an infant in a pram, being walked by his German nanny to one of these green havens. We still have some of those tiny black-and-white pram photos, only two inches square, but what was in the background and where were they taken? I wracked my brain to recall details of the photos. Did he ever enter this park? See this fountain? Look up at his magnificent house to pots of flowers hanging from the sixth-floor balcony, as I did now?

My strange, almost surreal experience does not represent just the ruins of Jewish memory, for it is a convert's desperate attempt to grab and take home a past. But the memories that emerged were immediately lost in the abyss. Timescape, not landscape. That night I felt despair and internal divisions more keenly and more profoundly, because more personally, than I had felt them at any other point on the trip or in all my conversion years. Perhaps, I thought, I should leave the country earlier than planned.

Afterward, when I did return home to the United States, I tried to make sense of what had happened to me in Germany. At first, the only meaning was loss and anger. Facing the Holocaust in the country where Nazi power originated devastated me. Even approaching it as a witness distanced by time badly shook me, and not understanding the historical complexities troubled me. Dominick La Capra's writings about the Holocaust and memory finally helped me sort out my experience abroad. He explains: "The secondary witness or empathetic observer may nonetheless undergo muted trauma. Indeed the muting or mitigation of trauma that is nonetheless recognized and to some extent acted out may be a requirement of working through problems."[23] By the time I had arrived in Munich, after visiting Neuengamme, Bergen-Belsen, and Berlin's bombed Neue Synagogue, I was already in a state of melancholia, despairing and identifying strongly with what was lost: the Jews of Europe and their sacred places. I certainly did not have to seek out the places I visited. On some level, perhaps I wanted to enter despair, precisely this kind of despair. Perhaps I am of a generation so visually and emotionally shocked by interracial rioting and by war brutalities from Vietnam onwards that I can no longer be shocked. Was I in search of the real worst? I honestly don't know. I chose this despair, maybe from guilt, false guilt, desire, sentiment. Maybe to feel history in its geographical location. I did not go to honor the dead, as many travelers do, but to encounter evil and emptiness. On the day I made my house pilgrimage, however, I added my husband's life in Europe and that of generations of his family to the list of losses. And I understood why he wished never to return. There was nothing there.

The fact that the past became fully present to me in Munich, the fact that I became my husband in childhood and his parents even for moments—and then could not give it up or get any distance on it psychologically—was, for me, an identification with loss. Still, while I was in Munich, I moved unconsciously from melancholia into mourning, a quite different state of mind. Meeting my friend for dinner the night after visiting the house, I was disconsolate and eventually shared with her my anger and sadness at the giant loss represented for me by the house. Later on I talked to my husband by phone. My brief talks with both my German friend and my husband must have helped me get some critical distance from my earlier response, for something occurred in the night. I woke up with a sense that I no longer wished to identify with loss and death or my husband's past and needed to embrace the present and future. At this point I needed to accept the Holocaust but move on. I could now spend the rest of my stay as a tourist and a friend, albeit a Jewish one. I would no longer allow the past to be always present; I would realize it was uncapturable and unfathomable by me. But I also would not forget it.[24]

The Jewish sages do not offer one answer or model of how to respond to suffering. Typically, as David Hartman suggests, they encourage our use of it as a catalyst for renewal.[25] As I write this, we are in the week of Tisha B'Av, the fast day that commemorates so many tragic moments in Jewish history. Jews who observe the day, visiting the Western Wall or reading the book of Lamentations in worship groups and synagogues, reflect on the relationship in Judaism between disaster and hope, endings and beginnings, destruction and renewal.

Tisha B'Av, the ninth day in the Jewish month of Av, culminates a period of nine days of mourning. On this day, according to rabbinic tradition, many tragic events occurred, not only the destruction of the First and Second Temples. For instance, it saw the fall of Betar, the last fortress holding out against the Romans during the Bar Kochba rebellion in 135. It was a fateful day for the Jewish people. In 1492 King Ferdinand of Spain issued the expulsion decree of the Inquisition, setting Tisha B'Av as the final date by which Jews had to be off Spanish ground. World War I began on this day, inaugurating a downward spiral toward the Holocaust.

Tisha B'Av, like Yom Kippur, is a fast day. We are not allowed to wash, anoint ourselves, or wear leather shoes. Yom Kippur is a day of forgiveness and atonement that is solemn but holds seeds of joy, whereas Tisha B'Av is a day of mourning. Therefore, we are further prohibited from reading any selection of Torah or Talmud that might bring contentment or happiness to us. Only certain sections are permitted.

However, these days are not fixed forever in our calendars. At some point in the process of redemption, advises the prophet Zechariah (8:19), fast days, including Tisha B'Av, will become "days of joy and rejoicing and holidays." The Talmud takes up this issue in Rosh Hashanah 18b. According to halakhah, this change will occur "when there is peace." Major commentators such as Rashi and Maimonides debate what the phrase "when there is peace" might mean, whether it is linked to Jewish sovereignty or to the restoration of the Temple, and further, whether the Third Temple will be made by man on earth or by God. But my reading of peace means neither Jewish rule nor a return to the Temple cult, but the establishment of a just society on earth.

Tisha B'Av, by definition, does not include mourning for the Holocaust, although it is difficult to forget the Shoah and a loss of one-third of the Jewish population while reading Lamentations alongside one's Jewish brothers and sisters. And I am not sure we should forget it on the ninth of Av, considering the central meaning of this day: warfare, the deprivation of human rights, exclusion, torture. The Holocaust is memorialized, however, by its own day in the spring: Yom Hashoah. It is a day set aside specifically to remember the victims and survivors and also to remind ourselves of the evil that can inhabit the human heart.

A relatively new addition to the Jewish calendar, Yom Hashoah is still evolving in its observances. In Israel all places of entertainment close, a siren is sounded throughout the country for moments of silent reflection, and schools present special programs. It is customary in Israel and the diaspora to light memorial candles, to hear presentations from survivors, to read the names of the dead, and to listen to special readings. It is a day of introspection and learning and relearning. Yet it is also a time to think about how to strengthen the Jewish community and how to increase tolerance in our Jewish, non-Jewish, and mixed communities.

Just as the destruction of the first and second Temples forced Jews to find new avenues to sustain themselves and their identity as a people, so the Holocaust has demanded more of Jews. There is a dynamic interaction among tradition, continuity, tragedy, and change that the Jews have uniquely faced for centuries. Despite dispersion, exclusion, destruction, and genocide, Jews have endured, and their evolving traditions, cultures, liturgy, and belief system are a testimony to inventiveness and faith.

For all its inventiveness and adaptability, Judaism has not provided a way to teach us to internalize the Holocaust lesson beyond victimhood and survivorship. Lawrence Langer asks us, eloquently, "to rewrite the internal scenario of our lives to include the deaths of others—the victims of our violent time."[26] This is a simple statement but an enormous task—morally, emotionally, and intellectually. Yet I think we have an even wider and deeper responsibility at this point in history.

In my view, Jews and Judaism are conditioned to think of themselves too often in terms of victimhood or chosenness. Both paradigms, deeply rooted in our traditions, in our history, and in Torah, are inhibiting, but they don't have to be. They can challenge Judaism itself to turn (teshuvah), but to turn back to a loving, present God, as Abraham Joshua Heschel has advised, one who waits for man to do that turning. I am suggesting that Judaism, as represented by its boards and halakhic committees, its individual rabbis, its synagogues, its splinter worship groups, its women's groups and men's groups and children's groups, its critical literature, its observant people, its secular people, has not *sufficiently* responded to our violent times with its own turning. It is time to move beyond victimhood and chosenness and embrace a paradigm of equality.

Conservative Judaism, in particular, has a responsibility now to shape its future and the future of Judaism by increasing intellectual debate about pressing social issues and halakhah. Holding differing, and even sharply divisive, views on important religious and social issues,

Conservatives need to find the ways and means to talk to each other about their priorities and commitments.[27]

We have at least one model on which to build: the Commission on the Status of Women as Spiritual Leaders in the Conservative movement, which recommended the ordination of women to the chancellor of the Jewish Theological Seminary in 1979. The seminary approved women for ordination in a vote on October 24, 1983. This important commission was composed of seminary faculty, rabbis, academics, and laypersons. Chaired by Chancellor Gerson Cohen, it featured the leadership of other outstanding members as well, notably Rabbi Gordon Tucker. It met as a body in New York, but it also held public meetings in six American cities at which anyone affiliated with the Conservative movement could speak. It discussed the issues for another two years. The report, including majority and minority statements, was presented to the Rabbinical Assembly at the 1979 convention in Los Angeles and then debated. Members of the seminary faculty were invited to write statements; eleven were circulated. A market research firm surveyed representative congregational opinion. With a decision tabled, more debate followed, some of it divisive. Nevertheless, the tremendous value of this report, its aftermath, and its results lies both in its comprehensiveness and rigor and in the public meetings it encouraged. The report and the subsequent debates considered the halakhic dimensions, the ethical dimensions, and the sociological dimensions of the ordination of women.[28]

With similar analytic rigor and public debate, Conservatives need to rethink how they reach out to each other in maintaining Jewish observance and how they reach out to all others on the important social issues of our time. In the first instance, it does not matter whether that outreach is initiated or co-initiated from the federations, the rabbinical organizations and colleges, the seminary, the day schools, the universities, United Synagogue, Hillel, the worship groups, or individuals. In the end, however, it matters critically, both pragmatically and spiritually, that such leadership, debate, and transformation continue to take place.

PASSAGE 6

❧

Coming Home Again

THOUGHTS ON YOM KIPPUR

No matter how religious they are, more Jews face Judaism and themselves directly on the Day of Atonement, Yom Kippur, than on any other day in the year. For me the morning Torah readings point the way to the deep internal changes leading to action that we as Jews must continue to make if we are to survive meaningfully and help create a more just society for all people.

I gave the following dvar Torah on Yom Kippur, October 9, 2000, at the Conservative services in Richardson Auditorium at Princeton University.

When we leave this hall tonight, we depart as a people granted extraordinary gifts: forgiveness for our sins, a sense of closeness to God on this highest of holy days, the sweetness of hope, and a choice about how to live out the months lying before us. The section of Leviticus 16 we read today concerning the unimaginable loss of Aaron's two sons at the greatest moment of their lives reminds us of the inescapable presence of danger in even the holiest of places at the holiest of times. And the ritual of sending the scapegoat to Azazel in the desert and hurling it over the sheer cliffs, into the abyss, speaks to the presence of the demonic evil impulse always lurking in chaos and requiring appeasement. God's will is unfathomable, and we do not know what is in store, or when—nevertheless, Judaism offers us choice over how we live and how we can make the world better for our having lived.

The choice we are given entails which direction we will take and, although we know what to do, it is not always easy to translate knowledge into willpower or willpower into action. Will we choose lying or truthtelling? Cheating or fairness? Betrayal or fidelity? Selfishness or giving? The list could go on and on, and it does so in the liturgy for today, shaped by rabbinic tradition, where it is significant that the transgressions we enumerate are the fiercely terrible things we do to each other. Forty-four of them, double the number of letters in the Hebrew alphabet, not one of a ritual nature.[1] All about human nature.

Moreover, neither the liturgy nor Torah presents us with binaries, as I have just done, since moral choices are never contextless or easy. Instead, the Hebrew Bible presents many narratives involving dilemma, moral ignorance, and ethical failure. And Talmudic commentaries, offering majority and minority views, stress the challenges, not the simplicities, of particular cases. Torah knows the trials of choice.

Judaism is often called the religion of the Book owing to its replacement of the Temple cult with the study of Torah. However, Judaism may also be called the religion of relationship, based on the covenant at Sinai and reaffirmed, after the episode of the Golden Calf, on Yom Kippur, the tenth of Tishri, when Moses is said to have brought down the second set of Tablets and we were granted a second chance to draw near to God as His holy nation. Yom Kippur is a day for acquittal and purification. According to Rabbi Akiva, God identifies Himself on this day as the mikvah of Israel.[2] But Yom Kippur is also a day of choice-within-covenant about how we will renew relationships that sin has broken: relationships with God, with our community, with the righteous dead, with each other, and with our ethical and moral selves.

Still, what many of us, including myself, no longer possess is a close relation to the Hebrew language. The original audience for the Torah and Haftarah readings from Leviticus, Numbers, and Isaiah would have intuitively grasped the enormously rich complications of the Hebrew roots and words used to signify what is being given to us and asked of us on this day. But like the simple child at the Passover table, who asks, "What is this?" I have been driven back to basics—to the dictionary, to transliterations, and to concordances—in order to come closer to the beauty and wisdom of Yom Kippur.

Embedded in the very root of the word *kippur* (from the root *kaf/pey/resh*) are multiple meanings that complicate the nature of atonement.[3] In addition, on this day when we are asked to *afflict* ourselves and to confront wounds that must be *healed*, we find that the Hebrew words chosen for affliction (*anot*, from the root *ayin/nun/hey*) and healing (*arucha*, from the root *aleph/resh/kaf/hey*) in both the Torah and Haftarah readings bear a similar richness of meaning.

Variations of the word *kippur* (atonement) go back to the root *kpr*, and these variations, as Rashi points out in commentary on Genesis 32:21, are themselves related to words from the root *kfr*.[4] These variations, appearing in different contexts in Torah, add significantly to the meaning of this day and illuminate today's readings. *Kofer*, for example, is used as a protective pitchlike covering for Noah's ark in Genesis. Also, in Exodus and in Numbers it is used as protection money, as payment in place of punishment. *K'for* is chosen in Exodus to describe the way in which manna covered the ground like hoarfrost, supplying Israel with food for forty years in the wilderness. *Kapparah* is used in Leviticus for the ceremony with special sacrifices for purifying the sanctuary and the Kohanim, those who must be protected from the presence of God. Most important, perhaps, throughout Torah the word *kapporet* is chosen for the cover of the ark, as in Leviticus 16, verse 2, when God explains that He appears "over the ark cover in a cloud." This cover is always described in terms of its protective qualities. In Exodus 25, God commands Moses: "Make two cherubim of gold at the two ends of the cover. The cherubim shall have their wings spread out above, shielding the cover with their wings." Face to face, but with their eyes down, as watchful guardians of the tablets, these forms also serve as protectors of the space between them, a space from which God says he speaks to us.

Through such linguistic variations, the ceremony of Yom Kippur, then, may be seen as involving much more than a purification. It also provides *sustenance* (as much of a gift as manna), and it offers us *protection*, like a cover or a veil, against the punishment of God on the day when the book of life and death is sealed for another year. As the high priest must approach the ark with incense rising to veil the Shekhinah from his sight, lest he die like Aaron's sons by being too close to pure holiness, so we are commanded to perform acts of repentance in order to maintain the closeness of our precarious relationship to God.

When we look at a second cluster of words, *anot* and its forms—including *eeneenu*, meaning affliction—further complications arise. Although *anot* is usually translated in connection to the word *tzom*, or fast, the prophet Isaiah, in the Haftarah passage for this morning, harshly criticizes those of us who might think we can effect repentance or healing by ritual fasting devoid of a change of heart. In Isaiah's handling, the meaning of *anot* turns away from the self. It becomes not just the self-affliction of our own body and soul, but the afflictions we impose on others and the pains that others suffer. Isaiah reports God as crying out: "Do you call this a fast and a day of favor to Hashem? Surely this is the fast I choose: open the bonds of wickedness, dissolve the groups that pervert justice, let the oppressed go free. Surely you should divide your bread with the hungry, bring the moaning poor to your home, when you see the naked cover him, and do not ignore your kin. . . . Offer your soul to the hungry and satisfy the afflicted soul."

Isaiah reorients the word *anot*. The twin pillars of Yom Kippur must be ritual observance including the fast *and* social justice—self-affliction for self-healing *and* the healing of others' afflictions. To perform one without the other, he implies, is an act of hypocrisy. The Haftarah draws on the multiple meanings of *Kippur* and the root *kpr*: not just atonement but a material protecting, covering, and nourishing of others. This emphasis is then taken even further by the midrash Leviticus Rabbah 34, which counsels us to go beyond supplying material necessities: If you have nothing else to give, give comfort and say, "My heart goes out to you."

A word for "healing," *arucha*, hardly ever used in the Hebrew Bible, but found in Isaiah as *aruchatecha*, "your healing," also involves the idea of a covering and protection. Although other words would have served, *arucha* is a brilliant choice because it refers to the first stage of healing of a wound—new flesh growing over an injured spot, which will only later completely heal.[5] As Maimonides valuably reminds us in *The Laws of Repentance*, lasting change of any kind is a slow and incremental process. However, as Isaiah promises, our healing will speedily "sprout" if we attend to those who suffer.

The imperative to act on behalf of the other finds one of its most eloquent modern expressions in the philosophy of Emmanuel Levinas. Of the many conjunctions of philosophy and Jewish thought in the twentieth century, no work has generated as much response, after Franz Rosenzweig's and Martin Buber's, as his. Many of you know of him, but for those who do not, Levinas was born in 1906 in Lithuania, where the first language he read was Hebrew, and he died in France in 1995. He survived the Second World War as a French POW in a German internment camp and lost most of his family in the Holocaust. The indelible influence of such horror shaped all his future work. From his first book, *Totality and Infinity*, to his *Nine Talmudic Readings* to *On-Thinking-of-the-Other, Entre Nous*, Levinas studies the possibilities and limits of a life lived with decency in a post-Holocaust world.

Like Buber, Levinas expounds a philosophy of self and other, one of intersubjectivity. But whereas Buber describes the "I and Thou" relation in terms of mutuality, Levinas describes the initial relationship between the self and the other in terms of *duty*, without the expectation of any return. In his words: "The face of the other commands me." That is, the face of each other—of each unique individual—commands me.

Levinas's emphasis on ethical relationship has its roots in the Jewish concept of mitzvah as commandment and the Torah's deep concern with the welfare of the poor, the orphan, the widow, the stranger, and all others who are in distress. While much modern philosophy stresses consciousness as the basis of reality—as in Descartes' "I think, therefore I am"—Levinas argues that the relationship with the other puts the self into question. He sees subjectivity as a response to what lies outside the self and offers instead the Hebrew phrase of readiness: "Hineni," meaning not just "Here I am" but "Here I am *for the other.*" This statement is Abraham's reply to God when called from Ur and upon Mount Moriah;

it is how Moses answers God on Mount Sinai. And it is also God's response on Yom Kippur to those willing to help heal the affliction of others. As Isaiah reports: "Then you will call and God *will* respond. You will cry out, and He *will* say, 'Hineni/Here I am.'" Though such readiness can, of course, be employed to serve fundamentalism, Levinas rejects any form of institutionalized power in which individual human life and dignity are placed under threat.

In the ethical relationship to the other, where duties are as abundant as rights, we find the genesis of a just society. Thus, it is especially noteworthy that Leviticus 16 ends with three references to the inclusion of everyone in the protection and mercy of atonement. On this holy day, we read in verse 29, "you shall not do any work, neither the native-born nor the proselyte who dwells among you," and verse 33 tells us: "Upon all the people of the congregation shall He bring atonement." And again in the final verse (34): "This shall be an eternal decree to bring atonement upon the Children of Israel." This morning's Pentateuch reading ends, then, with a model of equality before the law in a just society.

We live in a brutal and unjust world, in which it often seems impossible to orient ourselves rightly, address serious social wrongs, or reach out to others. Yet the gift of Yom Kippur can inspire us all to begin again. We have the freedom—the difficult freedom—to choose to effect first healing, as, face to face, we take upon ourselves not just the burdens of our own choices but also the fate of *each* other.

To each of you a good fast, a good ending, and a good renewal.

L'shana tova.

ACKNOWLEDGMENTS

What can you give them like that which they have given you?
—THE WISDOM OF BEN SIRA

My family members generously gave me the space and time to find what I needed. I am especially grateful to my husband, Uli, and our son, Alex, for their love and support. I thank my stepchildren and their spouses for encouragement: Julie and Jay Drillings, Paul Knoepflmacher and Liddy Leitman, Daniel Knoepflmacher and Amy Veltman. During work on this book, Jared and later Hannah, then Nora and Ivan, became the first of a still growing generation in my husband's family. I thank also our wonderful extended family-by-marriage, the Leitmans, the Veltmans, and especially Raymond Drillings, of blessed memory, and Shula Drillings, who transmitted a love of liturgy when they sent me my first siddur.

My mother, Helen English Shires, modeled self-reliance and courage in ways I could only hope to emulate. She supported me in this endeavor, as in all others. My father, Philip Munroe Shires, of blessed memory, would have been deeply involved in the intellectual and religious aspects of my conversion studies.

The Conservative worship group at Princeton University welcomed me as a stranger and then as a friend. I can think of ways in which I am indebted to every person in the group, but I particularly thank, for many kindnesses, Martha Himmelfarb and Steve Weiss.

For sharing their love of Torah, I thank my teachers, especially Rabbi James S. Diamond, who guided my reading and patiently supervised my conversion. He is most responsible for helping me to become a Jew, a gift for which I am daily grateful. Rabbi David Wolf Silverman and Laurence

J. Silberstein served on my bet din. Professors Menachem Lorberbaum and Peter Schäfer gave generously of their time and their knowledge of Judaism.

I record my thanks for interventions on professional matters by Sonya Spear, Joseph Greenberg, Anne Matthews, and Professor Mark Cohen. My appreciation is also due to Professor Robert Gates, Chair of the Department of English, Syracuse University, and to Dean Robert Jensen, who arranged a research leave for me in 1999–2000.

Others stood by me and my family during these years: Steven Cohan, Bob Gates, Lee Talley, Sylvia Tumin, Melvin Tumin, of blessed memory, Tobe and Nat Fisch, Judy and Jim Diamond, Ilene Cohen and George Downs, Renee and Ted Altman, Wolfy and Pauline Jakobsberg, Monique Parsons, Bob Lebeau and Leora Batnitzky, Bill Bialek, Starry Schor, Claudia Johnson, Marcia Rosh, Bob Karp and Linda Oppenheim, and Roslyn Vanderbilt. For hospitality and for helping me confront the difficult German past, I thank Richard and Elfie Jachzel and Gabi Lieb, who hosted me in Germany during the summers of 2000 and 2002. Finally, Helène Aylon has set an unforgettable example of Jewish creativity as challenge and blessing. These friends, more than friends, have become a second family.

Any interpretive and factual errors are mine, but I have made fewer of them because of those who read and commented on all or parts of the manuscript. Here I must single out my friend Ilene Cohen for her outstanding editorial labors on my behalf. She checked the manuscript for accuracy, corrected my Hebrew, and improved my phrasing. Lastly, I thank my editor at Westview, Sarah Warner, and her colleagues, especially Erica Lawrence, for exceptional professional care.

L.M.S.

GLOSSARY

Afikoman: After-dinner entertainment; from the Greek *epikomion*. The larger part of the middle matzoh, hidden by the leader during the Passover seder and later hunted for by the children. It must be ransomed from children so it can be eaten as dessert. Symbolically, it represents the paschal sacrifice.

Aggadah: Legendary, as opposed to legal, materials in the Talmud and midrashim.

Ahavat Yisrael: "Love for the people of Israel." A commandment for all Jews to love one another.

Akedah: The binding of Isaac (Genesis 22).

Akiba (c. 50–135 C.E.): One of the greatest Jewish scholars. He laid the groundwork for the Mishnah, supported the Bar Kokhba rebellion, and was executed by the Romans.

Aliya (*pl.* Aliyot): Ascent. Going up to the bimah to perform an honor in the Torah service, to recite blessings over the Torah when it is read, to raise or cover the Torah; going up to live in the Land of Israel.

Amidah: From "stand." This is the central prayer of every service, said standing. It is sometimes called the **ha-tefillah** (the Prayer), because of its central importance, or the **Shemoneh Esri** (the Eighteen), because of the eighteen benedictions of which it was originally composed.

Amora (*pl.* Amoraim): Spokesman. Refers also to the rabbinic sages who lived in the period following the compilation of the Mishnah, from 200 to 500 C.E. in the Land of Israel or Babylonia. Their teaching forms the basis for discussions in the Talmud and later midrashim.

Bar mitzvah/bat mitzvah: "Inheritor of the commandments"; the religious status of a male Jew beyond the age of thirteen years and a female beyond the age of twelve years. The attainment of this status is recognized by calling the child to the bimah for a public reading in Hebrew of Torah in the synagogue.

Bet din: A court of at least three rabbis or learned Jews who are authorized to make legal judgments and to recognize changes in personal status (conversion, divorce, etc.)

Bimah: The platform or table from which Torah is read; the pulpit in the synagogue.

B'rit: The covenant; the contract between Israel and God.

B'rit milah: The covenant of circumcision; the circumcision of Jewish boys on the eighth day after birth as a sign of entry into the Covenant of Abraham. **Hatafah dam b'rit** is the modified circumcision for boys converting to Judaism who have had a secular circumcision a day or two after birth in the hospital.

Buber, Martin (1878–1965): Austrian-born scholar, philosopher, translator, and Zionist. He named his existential relationship between people, or between people and God, "I and Thou." He settled in Israel.

Challah: A braided loaf of white egg bread, eaten in celebration of the Sabbath and holy days. When bread was made in the days of the Temple, this was the priestly portion.

Charoset: A ritual food for the Passover seder made of fruit, nuts, wine, and spices. It is intended to look like the mortar of Egyptian bondage.

Chumash: Five. The first five books of the Bible; the Torah text.

Derash: Interpretation. One of the four methods and levels of exposition of scripture.

Diaspora: Greek for "dispersion." Refers to the Jews outside the Land of Israel.

Emunah: Faith or belief.

Gemara: Aramaic for "completion." Aramaic texts of rabbinic discussions of Mishnah that were carried on in academies in Babylonia and Jerusalem. Talmud comprises Mishnah and Gemara.

Get: A Jewish divorce decree, written in the presence of a bet din and presented by the husband to the wife, by mutual consent.

Giur: The ceremony of conversion to Judaism, traditionally consisting of milah, tevilah, and kabbalat ol hamitzvot (circumcision, immersion into the mikvah, and acceptance of the commandments).

Haftarah: Literally, "conclude." The reading from the prophets that follows the Torah reading in the synagogue on the Sabbath and holy days.

Haggadah: The book containing the liturgy for the Passover seder.

Halakhah (*pl.* Halakhot): The body of rabbinic law; the legal part of the Talmud, as opposed to the narrative and legendary part (aggadah); any individual Jewish law.

Hallel: Praise. A collection of psalms recited on special festival days as a sign of rejoicing.

Hanukkah: The eight-day festival of lights celebrating the victory of the Maccabees and the restoration of the Temple.

Havdalah: Separation. The ritual marking the end of Shabbat. The blessings recited praise God for having distinguished between the sacred time and the weekday. On the Sabbath, wine, spices, and a candle are used; on other days only wine.

High Holy Days: The period of the Days of Awe in the fall that include Rosh Hashanah and the period between Rosh Hashanah and Yom Kippur.

Hillel the Elder (first century B.C.E.–first century C.E.): The most important rabbi of the period of the Second Temple, Hillel the elder was president of the Sanhedrin (court) and an ancestor of a dynasty of presidents that lasted six centuries.

Holocaust: The murder of millions of people, including six million Jews, during World War II.

Israel: The Jewish people; the Land of Israel; the State of Israel.

Kabbalah: Received tradition. A late medieval form of Jewish mysticism that began in southern France and northern Spain in the twelfth century. *Kabbalah* can also refer to the entire body of Jewish mystical thought.

Kaddish: Aramaic for "holy." A prayer in Aramaic proclaiming the sanctity of God and praying for the speedy establishment of His kingdom. One version of this prayer is recited by mourners.

Kashrut: The dietary laws listing permitted and forbidden foods: not eating milk with meat; eating only birds and mammals ritually slaughtered; eating certain animals and certain fish and domestic birds but not others. Certain parts of permitted animals are also forbidden. Separate sets of dishes and cooking utensils must be used for milk and meat.

Kavannah: Intention. Purposeful prayer or fulfillment of God's commandments.

Kiddush: Refers to the prayer recited over wine in which the sanctity of the Sabbath or festival day is proclaimed.

Kippah (*pl.* Kippot): Yiddish for "cap," usually referring to a skullcap; also called a **yarmulke.**

Kohen: Priest in the Temple; descendants of Aaron, the first high priest.

Kosher: Ritually acceptable; especially food eaten in accordance with Jewish law.

Levinas, Emmanuel: A professor of philosophy at the Sorbonne and director of the Ecole Normale Israélite Orientale. His important works include *Totality and Infinity* and *Otherwise Than Being*. Levinas's work influenced that of thinkers such as Jacques Derrida, Luce Irigaray, and Maurice Blanchot. He also wrote a series of rich readings on Talmud.

Maimonides, Moses (The Rambam, Rabbi Moses ben Maimon) (1135–1204): Maimonides was among the greatest of Jewish scholars, rabbis, philosophers, and doctors. His works include *Mishneh Torah* and *The Guide of the Perplexed*. He formulated the thirteen principles of faith.

Maror: Bitter herbs, horseradish; eaten at the Passover seder.

Matzoh: Unleavened bread; eaten on Passover in commemoration of the Exodus from Egypt.

Menorah: A candelabrum. A seven-branched menorah stood in the Temple in Jerusalem. A nine-branched menorah, a hanukiah, is used in the celebration of Hanukkah.

Midrash: Rabbinic methods of interpreting the Bible; the nonlegal interpretation of scripture; from the same root as the word *derash*. Various collections of rabbinic materials were developed from the second to the tenth centuries B.C.E.

Mikvah: A proper ritual bath, of dimensions that allow total immersion and containing a certain percentage of fresh springwater or rainwater.

Minyan: Number. A quorum required for the recitation of certain public prayers in the worship service; traditionally a group of ten or more men. Whether women can be part of this quorum is a matter of dispute among different movements in Judaism.

Mishnah: Repetition. Books of rabbinic law, composed around 200 C.E. and organized by Judah ha-Nasi in Palestine; the core of the Talmud; the basic text of oral Torah as opposed to Torah that is written law.

Mishneh Torah: Code of Jewish Law written by Moses Maimonides in the thirteenth century.

Mitzrayim: Egypt; also limitation, boundary, narrow straits.

Mitzvah (pl. Mitzvot): A commandment of God given in the Torah; a duty or obligation or good deed. There are 613 commandments, 248 positive and 365 negative.

Mohel: A Jewish professional skilled in the ritual and medical aspects of circumcision.

Parasha (pl. Parashot): Portion. The weekly Torah portion. See **sidrah.**

Passover: The spring festival commemorating the Exodus from Egypt.

Pharisees: First-century sect of Jews; forerunners of the rabbis.

Purim: Festival in late winter celebrating events told in the biblical Book of Esther.

Rashi, Solomon ben Isaac (1040–1105): Rashi was a French rabbi and scholar and one of the greatest commentators on Scripture of all time. His commentaries are standard additions to Torah and Talmud.

Rav: Rabbi; the appointed rabbinic leader of a community.

Responsa: Legal essays written by rabbis in response to questions of practice; the total body of this literature.

Rosh Chodesh: "New Moon"; the first day of the month. Half-Hallel and additional prayers are said in synagogue.

Rosh Hashanah: The Jewish new year; the beginning of the High Holy Days.

Rosenzweig, Franz (1886–1929): A German theologian, Rosenzweig influenced Buber and Levinas. He wrote *The Star of Redemption.*

Sadducees: First-century sect of Jews; rivals of the Pharisees; upheld the ancient priestly concept of Judaism.

Sanhedrin: Group of seventy-one scholars in Palestine who served as the court to settle disputes from the time of the Romans until the early fifth century.

Seder: The liturgical meal observed at the family table on the first and second nights of Passover.

Sefer Torah: A scroll of the five books of the Torah, handwritten on parchment in the ancient manner.

Shabbat: The Sabbath; the seventh day, dedicated to rest and revitalization of the spirit. Shabbat begins at sundown on Friday and ends at sundown on Saturday when three stars can be clearly seen in the night sky.

Shacharit: The morning service; from the word meaning "dawn." It is composed of the Shema and the Amidah, among other prayers.

Shalom: Peace. It can also mean "hello" and "good-bye."

Shalosh Regalim: The three pilgrimage festivals, Passover, Shavuot, and Sukkhot, for which the Jews visited the Temple in Jerusalem.

Shavuot: The spring harvest festival of first fruits; commemorates the giving of the Torah at Mount Sinai.

Shekinah: The Indwelling; God in the feminine aspect of closeness to the world.

Shema: Literally, "hear"; the three paragraphs from the Torah that are recited at the evening and morning services every day, accompanied by blessings before and after. The first paragraph is recited at bedtime, and the first line is recited before death.

Shiva: The seven days of mourning during which mourners remain at home and receive condolence calls from visitors.

Shofar: The horn of an animal, usually a ram, blown in the synagogue on Rosh Hashanah and at the end of Yom Kippur.

Shul: Yiddish for "synagogue."

Siddur: Order. A Jewish prayer book containing the order of liturgical prayers for the weekdays, festivals, and the Sabbath, as it has evolved from ancient times to today.

Sidrah: Arrangement. The weekly Torah portion. The Torah is divided into fifty-four portions, all of which are read in a year, at the rate of one and sometimes two per week.

Sukkah: A temporary roofed harvest booth in which Jews eat during the week of the festival of Sukkot; a reminder of the booths in which the Jews lived during their forty years of wandering in the desert.

Tallit: The prayer shawl, to which fringes (tzitzit) are attached at each corner; also called a tallis. A traditional Jewish male wraps himself in a tallit for morning worship, on the afternoon of Tisha b'Av, and all day on Yom Kippur.

Talmud: Study, or learning. Basic text of the oral Torah, composed around 500 C.E.; the book of ongoing rabbinic interpretation of the Mishnah. There is a Babylonian Talmud (Bavli or Babli) and the shorter Jerusalem Talmud (Yerushalmi). Over the years discussions by other rabbis have been added. The word *Talmud* can also mean, by extension, all learning.

Tanakh: Acronym for Torah-Nevi'im-Khetuvim, the three parts of the Bible. Tanakh refers to the Bible used by the Jews.

Tanna (*pl.* Tannaim): The early sages who lived in the Land of Israel from the second century B.C.E. until the completion of the Mishnah in 200 C.E. Their teachings form the basis of that work and for early midrashim.

Teshuvah: Return; repentance.

Tevilah: Immersion in a mikvah. Required for conversion and for ritual purification.

Talmud Torah: Torah study.

Tisha B'Av: A fast day in the summer, commemorating the destruction of the First and Second Temples and other sad events in Jewish history.

Tractate: One of sixty topical sections in Mishnah or Talmud.

Tzitzit: The fringes attached to the four corners of a tallit to remind the wearer of God's commandments.

Yahrzeit: The annual observance of the death of a parent, spouse, or child through the lighting of a candle and the recitation of the Kaddish prayer.

Yizkor: Remember. Prayers in remembrance of the dead and especially the martyrs of Israel, recited on Yom Kippur and on the last day of Sukkot, Passover, and Shavuot.

Yom Ha Shoah: Holocaust Memorial Day.

Yom Kippur: The Day of Atonement, ten days after Rosh Hashanah.

Zionism: Modern national liberation movement of the Jewish people.

Zohar: A word used in the Book of Daniel, where it means "radiance"; thirteenth-century premiere text of Kabbalah or Jewish mysticism, written by Rabbi Moses ben Shemtov de Leon and attributed to Rabbi Simeon bar Yochai.

NOTES ✿

CHAPTER ONE:
FROM PASSING AS A JEW TO STANDING AT SINAI

Note on the epigraphs: The Talmud (Shevuot 39a) explains that "those not here today" refers to future converts whose souls were at Mount Sinai when God gave the Torah to the Jewish people and when they accepted the covenant.

The quotation "And strangers shall join them and shall cleave to the House of Jacob" is repeated in Talmud Kiddushin 70b. I owe thanks to Rabbi James S. Diamond for mentioning and locating this Talmudic reference and for offering different midrashic readings of it.

1. A minyan is a prayer community with a quorum of ten adult Jews. In Conservative, Reform, and Reconstructionist wings of Judaism, the quorum may include women. In the Orthodox wing of the religion, the quorum must be men.

Passage 1
Who Counts?: Thoughts on Bamidbar,
Numbers 1:1–4:20

1. The rabbinical age refers to the period 70–700 C.E. (common era, equivalent to the Christian term A.D.). The destruction of the Second Temple and the fall of Masada in the first Jewish-Roman war necessitated a reorganization of Judaism.

2. It is the custom in our worship group to discuss each week's section of Torah after it is chanted in Hebrew. We take turns leading such discussions.

3. Rabbi Moses ben Nahman, also known as Nachmanides (1194–1270), was a famous Spanish Talmudist and biblical scholar. He reestablished the Jewish community in Jerusalem.

4. Rashbam was Rabbi Samuel ben Meir (1080–1158), a member of the Tosafist school and a grandson of Rashi who was renowned for his commentary on Talmud—and also on Torah—in which he develops literal meanings.

5. Rabbi Solomon ben Isaac (1040–1105), known as Rashi, was the most respected among Jewish commentators. He flourished in Troyes, France. His

commentary on the Bible, printed in 1475, was the first Hebrew book ever published, and no edition of the Jewish Bible or the Talmud is complete without it.

6. "The rabbis," or "the rabbinic authorities," refers, unless otherwise noted, to the rabbis of the Talmud, the majority of whom argued halakhic (legal) points or transmitted aggadah (nonlegal narratives or homilies), or a generic mixture, during the period 200–750 C.E.

CHAPTER TWO
TIME, TIMELINESS, TIMELESSNESS

1. See Anita Diamant, *Saying Kaddish: How to Comfort the Dying, Bury the Dead, and Mourn as a Jew* (New York: Schocken, 1998).

2. See Ira Steingroot, *Keeping Passover* (San Francisco: Harper San Francisco, 1995), 53.

3. *Omer* means "sheaf." It is a measure of barley offered on the second day of Passover in the Temple. We count this measure for forty-nine days, the period between Passover and Shavuot.

4. Abraham Joshua Heschel, *The Sabbath* (New York: Farrar Straus & Giroux, 2001), 12.

5. Dayan I. Grunfeld, *The Sabbath: A Guide to Its Understanding and Observance* (New York: Feldheim, 1988), 31.

6. Pinchas Peli, *The Jewish Sabbath* (New York: Schocken, 1988).

7. Kiddush means sanctification and it is the blessing recited over wine or bread to consecrate Shabbat or festivals.

8. Reuven Hammer, *Entering Jewish Prayer: A Guide to Personal Devotion and the Worship Service* (New York: Schocken, 1994), 156. See also Lawrence Hoffman, ed., *The Amidah* (Woodstock, Vt.: Jewish Lights, 1998).

9. Hoffman, *The Amidah*, 15, note 8.

10. Rabbi Moshe ben Maimon, or Maimonides (1135–1204), also referred to as Rambam (formed by his initials), was born in Cordoba, Spain, and died in Fostat, Egypt. He is considered the greatest post-Talmudic authority on Judaism. He authored a classic commentary on the Mishnah and a philosophic text, *The Guide of the Perplexed*. In addition, he was a physician to the caliph, an authority on medicine, and the leader of Egyptian Jewry.

Passage 2
So God Turned Them:
Thoughts on Beshalach, Exodus 13:17–17:16

1. Abraham Ibn Ezra was born in Toledo, Spain, in 1089. He was a renowned Bible commentator, poet, and astronomer.

2. Rabbi Yisrael Isser Zvi Herczeg, ed., *The Torah with Rashi's Commentary*, Exodus 16:14 (New York: Artscroll, 1995), 189–190.

3. W. Gunther Plaut, ed., *The Torah: A Modern Commentary* (New York: Union of American Hebrew Congregations, 1981), 499, note 15.

CHAPTER THREE
GOD, WOMEN, AND GENDER

1. References to the Talmud are to the Bavli (the Babylonian Talmud, 200–750 C.E.), unless stated as Yerushalmi (the Palestinian Talmud, c. 400 C.E.).

2. My point here is that archaeological evidence and, in a larger sense, history may influence how we think about current practice but should not be solely determinative of that practice. In other words, each issue must be thought through on its own merits for today. If today we followed the historical precedent of Temple ritual, for example, we would be sacrificing animals. Events in Jewish history (or any history) are important but should not be determinative without debate and discussion.

3. Johanan ben Zakkai petitioned the Romans successfully for permission to establish an academy (Bet Midrash) in Yavneh, south of present-day Tel Aviv. He wanted to show his followers that the destruction of the second Temple did not mean the end of Judaism.

4. For an argument about the inextricability of halakhah and ethics, see Louis E. Newman, "Ethics as Law, Law as Religion: Reflections on the Problem of Law and Ethics in Judaism," in *Contemporary Jewish Ethics and Morality: A Reader,* ed. Elliot N. Dorff and Louis E. Newman (New York: Oxford University Press, 1995). For a classic statement on tradition and law versus faith and spirit, see Rabbi Jacob Agus, "Theoretical Evaluation of Jewish Law," and "Comments and Discussion," *Proceedings of the Rabbinical Assembly of America* 22 (1958): 81–117.

5. For discussion of the complexities involved in defining halakhah as a concept, applying it, and interpreting the halakhic process over time and discussion of the relationship of the Conservative Committee on Law and Standards to local rabbinic decisions, see the following papers written by rabbis promoting different points of view from within the Conservative Rabbinical Assembly over many years: Agus, "Theoretical Evaluation of Jewish Law"; Rabbi Kassel Abelson, "The Rabbinical Assembly and the Development of Halakhah," *Proceedings of the Rabbinical Assembly* 45 (1983): 77–84; Rabbi David Feldman, "The Rabbinical Assembly and the Development of Halakhah," *Proceedings of the Rabbinical Assembly* 45 (1983): 84–92; Rabbi Phillip Sigal, "Some Reflections on Rabbinical Assembly Halakhah: Past and Future," *Proceedings of the Rabbinical Assembly* 45 (1983); 93–106; and Rabbi Bradley Shavit Artson, "Halakhah in a Conservative Synagogue," *Proceedings of the Rabbinical Assembly* 55 (1993): 23–32. For a learned, incisive discussion of the status and meaning of change for Classical Judaism, see Judah Goldin, "Of Change and Adaptation in Judaism," *History of Religions* 4, no. 2 (Winter 1965): 269–294.

6. For a clear outline of some of the internal problems facing the Conservative movement in the 1990s, see Rabbi Lionel Moses, "Centralization of Halakhic Authority: In Defense of the Authority of the Committee on Jewish Law and Standards," *Proceedings of the Rabbinical Assembly* 55 (1993): 33–39.

7. As quoted in Gary A. Phillips and Regina M. Schwartz (editors for the Bible and Culture Collective), *The Post-Modern Bible* (New Haven: Yale University Press, 1995), 242.

8. Feminism, of course, does not exist. Only feminisms exist. Feminism is not a method of interpretation, though it is often taken as such. Rather it is a set of political stances and strategies. It is as contested an intellectual landscape as Judaism is a contested religious one. But the common denominator of feminisms is that women are oppressed, not by all men, but by patriarchy—an institutionalized system, an economics, and an ideology that perpetuates dominance over women. Patriarchy also encourages the dominance of some women by others, which is why it took so long for white, middle-class feminism to recognize fully women of other races, disabled women, lower-class women, and other female minorities. Gender, the cultural and historically changing construction of male and female, of masculinity and femininity, is a crucial category for analysis because it bears power relations. But it does not always affect women in the same way or to the same degree. Postmodern feminism illustrates that women live out their lives in multiple (and competing) identities: race, class, ethnicity, religious identity, sexual orientation, and others. We can see these multiple affiliations and the conflictual nature of them within feminist Jewish studies and within individual authors. The feminist stance, however, in its various permutations, features a resistance to the normative and universalist position accorded to and equated with man, who is often at the center of subjectivity, discourse, and epistemology. (This explanation of universalism is found in many sites within postmodern feminism, but see Phillips and Schwartz, *The Post-Modern Bible*, 234–235). Feminism has also come to include a critique of various forms of misogyny in cultures, including its control over ecology, psychology, and sexuality. Lastly, feminism has often been complicitous with dominant modes of thought in any one of its various versions—liberal, radical, Marxist or socialist, psychoanalytic, and others—and is therefore not always usefully resistant to the status quo.

9. Alicia Ostriker, "Out of My Sight: The Buried Woman in Biblical Narrative," in *Feminist Revision and the Bible* (New York: Blackwell, 1993), especially 39–42.

10. Bernadette Brooten, *Women Leaders in the Ancient Synagogues* (Chico, Calif.: Scholars Press, 1982); Carol Myers, *Discovering Eve: Ancient Israelite Women in Context* (New York: Oxford University Press, 1988).

11. Carole Pateman, *The Sexual Contract* (Palo Alto, Calif.: Stanford University Press, 1988). Like the word *feminism*, the word and concept *patriarchy*, in my usage, is never a monolith, just as Judaism is not, Orthodoxy is not, the rabbinate is not, and the Jewish Theological Seminary is not. All are psychological projections, cultural constructs, and heuristic devices, as well as institutions. All are in another sense ideals as well as realities. As social theorists have shown us, each of these institutions, like most others, is riven by conflicts, power politics, and struggles over what is right or true. Each is therefore also finely nuanced in its expressions and beliefs. Thus, I would not be satisfied by any view that reduces the complexity of the voices within any of these institutions or sits easily with monolithic tags. However, I am also aware that powerful factions do operate within institu-

tions, positions are codified, and principles are enacted. Clearly, I also believe that both external and internal pressures can change institutions. An ancient example of change brought about by external pressure is the replacement of a sacrificial cult of Judaism, after the destruction of the temples, by the rabbinic movement of the Yavneh period; a modern example of internal pressures to change are the social and psychological pressures on contemporary patriarchal cultures by the twentieth-century developments of feminism. From another, more religious, point of view, nothing is singular except the Hebrew God. Everything else, as I see it, including a dictated written Torah and an oral Torah, is conflicted and multiple. Moreover, to me this is one of the lasting strengths of Judaism as a religion.In Chapter 4, I explain more fully the Jewish version of the sexual contract, based in a connection of body and spirit (unlike Christianity, which is based in dualism), a formulation that has particularly far-reaching social consequences for the positioning and treatment of women and other minorities within Jewish imagination, representation, law, and practice.

12. An interesting issue is embedded in this sentence: whether or not to include male scholars as taking up this position. For example, Daniel Boyarin has worked for some years, especially through his *Carnal Israel: Reading Sex in Talmudic Culture* (Berkeley: University of California Press, 1993), to offer resistant readings to the sexual domination evidenced in rabbinic texts. Howard Eilberg-Schwartz has written about how the sexual body of a father God is troubling to Judaism, especially to its conception of masculinity. Jacob Neusner, in *Androgynous Judaism* (1993), discusses the value that rabbinic thinking puts on femininity when it portrays men as wives of God. Clearly this line of gender analysis is related to feminism, but it also addresses another set of issues that have more to do with masculinity and men's perception of women than with changing laws about women. The fact that these issues are related is very important—probably more important to me than to other feminists whom I've read. I do not believe that issues of rabbinic masculinity can be divorced easily from the status of women or the perception of women. That is to say, I don't believe that issues of men and masculinity (its construction, its versions, perpetuations of particular versions) are so easily divorced from the construction of femininity or the treatment of women. Psychology is simply not so easily separated from sociology and economics. Only a reductive or uninformed view of patriarchal ideology could make such distinctions. Nor do I think that sociology is separate from theology within a study of Judaism and women (a critical issue within Jewish feminism that I take up later in this chapter). However, at this early point in my discussion, for heuristic purposes, I follow the separatist impulses of Tal Ilan in her 1997 study *Mine and Yours Are Hers: Retrieving Women's History from Rabbinic Literature* (New York: Brill, 1997). She argues that male scholars working on sexuality, such as those mentioned, do not have exactly the same emphasis or topic as the feminists re-reading Talmud.

13. Judith Hauptman, *Re-reading the Rabbis: A Woman's Voice* (New York: Westview Press, 1998), 4.

14. Ilan has the most useful bibliography for the Beruriah materials. See *Mine and Yours Are Hers*, 28, note 107. See also David Goodblatt, "The Beruriah Traditions," *Journal of Jewish Studies* 26 (1975): 68–85; Rachel Adler, "The Virgin

in the Brothel and Other Anomalies: Character and Context in the Legend of Beruriah," *Tikkun* 3, no. 6 (1988): 28–32, 102–105; Daniel Boyarin, "The Diachronic as Against the Synchronic in the Tale of Bruria" (in Hebrew), *Jerusalem Studies in Jewish Folklore* 11–12 (1990): 7–17 (revised and published in English as part of his book *Carnal Israel*).

15. Adler, "Virgin in the Brothel," cited in Ilan, *Mine and Yours Are Hers*, 29, 69.

16. Boyarin, *Carnal Israel*, 182.

17. Ilan, *Mine and Yours Are Hers*, 69; see also 57, 63.

18. There are other areas of inquiry and sites that feminists isolate. These include the language of liturgy and the debates about whether God is a he, a she, an androgynous figure, a presexual figure, or an it. Such debates also take up the issue of whether the matriarchs should be named in services, whether we should read texts by women at services, whether we should substitute Kabbalistic texts for Torah, how the internalization of a he-God matters to all aspects of our religious lives, and the historical displacement of religions featuring women (as goddesses, vestal virgin priestesses, sibyls) by monotheism. This branch of feminism also encourages women who wish to re-center Judaism through special celebrations of Rosh Chodesh (the new moon), the daughter's naming ceremony, special all-women Passover seders with feminist Haggadot, and the discovery or uncovering of culturally "feminine" rituals. Only simultaneous work for change on both psychological and sociological fronts will help alter perceptions and realities. Other feminist interventions include those in mysticism and in the revival of midrash, from a contemporary woman's perspective. These interests and political strategies are important because they widen our Jewish experience and are, in differing ways, subversive of (or corrective to) more traditional Judaisms, but they are not paths I personally can take at this time.

19. Cynthia Ozick, "Notes Towards Finding the Right Question," in *On Being a Jewish Feminist: A Reader*, ed. Susannah Heschel (1983; reprint, New York: Schocken, 1995), 129.

20. Ibid., 149.

21. Judith Plaskow, "The Right Question Is Theological," in Heschel, *On Being a Jewish Feminist*, 222.

22. Ibid., 224. Judith Wegner notes that the conception of woman as an incomplete version of an imperfect man was widespread in Greek culture and the Hellenistic world. The Mishnaic sages classify women with other imperfect beings, such as blemished members of the priesthood, deaf mutes, imbeciles, minors, androgynes, slaves, the lame, the blind, the sick, and the aged. She asks: Is woman's subordination cultural or biological or both? See Judith R. Wegner, *Chattel or Person? The Status of Women in the Mishnah* (New York: Oxford University Press, 1988), 192–193.

23. Plaskow, "The Right Question Is Theological," 225.

24. Wegner, *Chattel or Person?*, 186.

25. W. Gunther Plaut explains that the two creation stories have been seen as coming from two different traditions. See W. Gunther Plaut, ed., *Torah: A Commentary* (New York: Union of American Hebrew Congregations, 1981), 28.

26. Thomas Tobin, *The Creation of Man: Philo and the History of Interpretation* (Washington, D.C.: Catholic Biblical Association of America, 1983), 32, as quoted in Daniel Boyarin, "Gender," in *Critical Terms for Religious Studies*, ed. Mark Poster (Chicago: University of Chicago Press, 1998), 120. On rabbinic Judaism and gender, see also 131ff.

27. Rachel Adler, *Engendering Judaism: An Inclusive Theology and Ethics* (Boston: Beacon Press, 1998), 117–125, also 242, notes 41 and 42. Adler cites Carol Myers's central point, in *Discovering Eve*, we should not take Genesis 2 as normative.

28. Phyllis Trible, "Depatriarchalizing in Biblical Interpretation," *Journal of the American Academy of Religion* 41 (1973): 30–48; and see Phyllis Trible, "Feminist Hermeneutics and Biblical Studies," *Christian Century* (February 1982): 116–118.

29. Tikva Frymer-Kensky, "The Bible and Women's Studies," *Feminist Perspectives on Jewish Studies* (New Haven: Yale University Press, 1994), 23–24.

30. Blu Greenberg, *On Women and Judaism: A View from Tradition* (1981; reprint, Philadelphia: Jewish Publication Society, 1998).

31. Ibid., 75–104.

32. Ibid., 83–85.

33. David Klinghoffer, *The Lord Will Gather Me In: My Journey to Jewish Orthodoxy* (New York: Free Press, 1999), 177.

34. See Rabbi Isaac Klein, who argues that halakhah has the central position in Jewish life, but that the human instrument through which it operates is variable and not perfect because it is part of history. "We recognize the historical process operating within Jewish law and we recognize that there are sociological factors operating in it and thus [it] is not absolute." "An Attitude to Halakha," *Proceedings of the Rabbinical Assembly* 22 (1958): 105.

35. Phillip Sigal, "Responsum on the Status of Women: With Special Attention to the Questions of *Shaliah Tzibbur, Edut,* and *Gittin,*" *Proceedings of the Committee on Jewish Law and Standards of the Conservative Movement 1980–1985* (New York: Rabbinical Assembly, 1988), 269.

36. Ibid., 288–289.

37. Greenberg, *On Women and Judaism,* 89. For the continuing relevance and power of Greenberg's ideas, note that her work is excerpted in Dorff and Newman, *Contemporary Jewish Ethics and Morality,* 315–326.

38. *Village Voice,* April 2, 1996, quoted in Robert Berlind, "Helène Aylon: Deconstructing the Torah," *Art in America* 87, no. 10 (October 1999): 142. See also Alison Gass, "The Art and Spirituality of Helène Aylon," and "The Liberation of G-d (from Patriarchal Projections): The Torah Reading in the Synagogue: To Read or Not to Read, That Is the Question: A Conversation Between Artist Helène Aylon and Rabbi Rolando Matalon," *Bridges* 8, nos. 1–2 (2000): 12–18, 19–24.

39. This letter was lent to me, with many others, by Helène Aylon, for which I thank her.

40. I don't wish to assume or imply that such lecture/discussion series don't exist. Some certainly are being held, but we should have more. Here is but one example announced in the Princeton Mercer Bucks County *New Jersey Jewish*

News, March 16, 2000, p. 36: "Open Community Discussion Series: Issues Facing the Jewish Community in the 21st Century. Sponsored by the American Jewish Committee (Central N.J. Chapter), Center for Jewish Life, Princeton University Hillel, and United Jewish Federation of Princeton Mercer Bucks." Nor do I wish to imply that federations are not responding to social crises. For instance, see the American Jewish World Service pamphlet "The Crisis of HIV/AIDS in Africa: A Jewish Response" (2001). Journals and newspapers are also filled with articles that take up contemporary issues, for instance, "The Gay Orthodox Underground," *Moment* 26, no. 2 (April 2001): 54–61, and "Conservative Rabbis Seek to Welcome Gay Clergy," *The Forward*, April 16, 1999, which records the efforts by rabbis such as Elliot Dorff and Gorden Tucker to work with the executive council of the Rabbinical Assembly to undermine the ban on gay rabbis (the 1992 decision of the Committee on Jewish Law and Standards, opinion authored by Rabbi Joel Roth).

Passage 3
The Two Tamars:
Thoughts on 2 Samuel 13 and on Vayeshev, Genesis 38

1. I am aware that the Pentateuch was written on scrolls, of course, and that sections did not begin or end as redactors have arranged them and that separate sources have been posited. While I am sensitive to the history of ancient texts and to the religious issues involved, my focus is on interpretation of the text we have before us. Religiously, my position is that this redaction was overdetermined; in this sense my position on the issue of Torah is perhaps more Orthodox in spirit than Conservative or Reform. However, the text is not fixed in the sense of mono-logical or universal and should not be read that way; it lives through its multiple interpretations over time.

2. Tikva Frymer-Kensky, "The Bible and Women's Studies," in *Feminist Perspectives on Jewish Studies*, ed. Lynn Davidman and Shelly Tenenbaum (New Haven: Yale University Press, 1994), 26.

3. Phyllis Trible, *Texts of Terror: Literary-Feminist Readings of Biblical Narratives* (Philadelphia: Fortress, 1984).

4. My work on Tamar from 2 Samuel preceded my reading of Frymer-Kensky and Trible. My study of reader response and form in midrash and Torah, howev-er, substantiates many of their insights. Their thoughts have thus helped solidify my reading of Tamar from Genesis. See also Mieke Bal, *Death and Dissymmetry: The Politics of Coherence in the Book of Judges* (Chicago: University of Chicago Press, 1988); Bal explores the relationship between sexual violence to women and politi-cal incoherence, offering a reading of "countercoherence" to the usual critical emphases on wars, historiography, and politics. While not disputing the political emphasis, she deconstructs it, arguing that the book's extreme violence is due to a social revolution concerning the institution of marriage, relations between men and women, kinship, sexuality, and procreation.

5. Moses Maimonides, *Mishneh Torah*, Issurei Bi'ah 1:9, as quoted in Rachel Biale, *Women and Jewish Law: The Essential Texts, Their History, and Their Relevance for Today* (New York: Schocken, 1984), 251.

6. Robert Alter, *The Art of Biblical Narrative* (New York: Basic Books, 1981), 73.

7. Pinchas Peli, *On Repentance: The Thought and Oral Discourses of Rabbi Joseph Dov Soloveitchik* (Northvale, N.J.: Jason Aronson, 1996), 198–199.

8. Frymer-Kensky, "The Bible and Women's Studies," 31.

CHAPTER FOUR
POLLUTION AND HOLINESS: THE BODY

1. "Reprove your neighbor" may seem to be a surprising inclusion, but it refers to intervening in situations where one can stop an action that may have dire consequences for the soul of the person. For example, if one witnesses a rape in progress or a murder, one must intervene in the name of justice to deter the sinner. One protects, in this way, not only God's name and the soul of the actor but also the reputation and moral life of the people Israel. See Mishnah Sanhedrin 5 and 8.

2. See Nehama Liebowitz, "Commentary on Kedoshim 2," in *New Studies in Vayikra* (Jerusalem: n.d.), 264–265, where she quotes Rabbi Avraham Hen, "Kedushah," in *Ma'amar ha Kedushah* (Jerusalem: Kook, 1959), 314–319.

3. I have decided not to include discussion of the body as it makes its appearance prominently in Jewish mysticism, namely, in the Ten Sefirot, charted on a model of the human body. See also David Ariel, *What Do Jews Believe* (New York: Schocken, 1995), 55, who explains that biblical Judaism is monist and rabbinic Judaism is dualist.

4. Daniel Boyarin, *Carnal Israel: Reading Sex in Talmudic Culture* (Berkeley: University of California Press, 1993), introduction, 2–10. Boyarin is very careful to historicize, as best he can, different tendencies in the first century between Hellenistic and rabbinic Jews. His main argument in this area is that the tendencies separating these groups, while not initially sharply defined, became polarized over time between the Hellenizers who became absorbed into Christian groups and the anti-Hellenizers who formed the rabbinic movement (although he notes the presence of later anti-Hellenizers within Christianity as well).

5. The books I looked at were unhelpful on the subject. A year and a half later I would buy *Total Immersion*, ed. Rivkah Slonim (Northvale, N.J.: Jacob Aronson, 1996), the anthology about the mikvah that people tend to have read if they have read anything. It too did not fit my needs. More recently I have read Aryeh Kaplan, *The Mystery of the Mikveh* (New York: Orthodox Union, 1976), which explains the mikvah's importance through the examination of texts.

6. Judith Hauptman, I believe, was referring solely to the rabbinic period, not to biblical culture, for as I later show, the biblical attitude toward blood is highly complicated. In the priestly cult the fluids connected with impurity came from

procreative organs (related to procreation or to disease of those organs). Although the priests regarded blood as a life force, they did not, for instance, consider bleeding from a flesh wound to be a defilement. On the other hand, persons having sexual relations during menstruation were to be cut off from their people (Leviticus 20:18), and menstruation could also be conceived of negatively when it was linked to intermarriage, a threat to the fertility of Israel. See David Biale, *Eros and the Jews* (Berkeley: University of California Press, 1997), 28–30.

7. Judith Hauptman, "Water Rites at the Jewish Museum," live chat with Shari Rothfarb, Jewish Theological Seminary, Learn at J.T.S. online, July 19, 1999 (transcript).

8. Ellen Umansky and Dianne Ashton, eds., *Four Centuries of Jewish Women's Spirituality: A Sourcebook* (Boston: Beacon Press, 1992).

9. Susan Weidman Schneider, *Jewish and Female: A Guide and Sourcebook for Today's Jewish Woman* (New York: Touchstone, 1985), 204, cited in Umansky and Ashton, *Four Centuries of Jewish Women's Spirituality*, 325, note 2.

10. According to David Biale, there were Jews who practiced asceticism, but they were not a dominant group, and their presence does not alter that dominant ideology of the central importance of fertility and procreation to rabbis of the Talmud. Likewise, the presence of stories in Talmud about rabbis who spent years apart from their wives as they studied Torah (Akiva, for example, or Rehumi), illustrating a conflict between the desire for marriage and the desire to study Torah, does not undo the important connection between pleasure and procreation. See Biale, *Eros and the Jews*, 55–56.

11. Ibid., 28.

12. For that matter, pollution is also part of all nature and natural processes; for instance, the fungus that grows on a house makes that house defiled. But this growth does not mean that a house is bad or good, only impure or pure in the view of an inspecting priest.

13. Ephraim Urbach, *The Sages: Their Concepts and Beliefs*, trans. Israel Abrahams (Cambridge, Mass.: Harvard University Press, 1979), 224.

14. Ibid., 225.

15. Biale, *Eros and the Jews*, 45.

16. Lionel Moses, "Centralization of Halakhic Authority: In Defense of the Authority of the Committee on Jewish Law and Standards," *Proceedings of the Rabbinical Assembly* 55 (1993): 36–37.

17. *Emet ve-Emunah: Statement of Principles of Conservative Judaism* (New York: Jewish Theological Seminary of America, Rabbinical Assembly, and United Synagogue of America, 1988), 21.

18. Bachya Ibn Pakuda, *The Duties of the Heart*, trans. Yaakov Feldman (Northvale, N.J.: Jason Aronson, 1996), xvii.

19. Note that Ibn Pakuda does not speak of celibacy.

20. Maimonides, *Mishneh Torah: The Book of Knowledge*, ed. Moses Hayamson (Jerusalem: Boys' Town Jerusalem Publishers, 1962), 50a.

Passage 4
The Akedah, the Binding of Isaac:
Thoughts on Vayera, Genesis 22:1–24

Note on the epigraph: The Kierkegaard quote can be found in Kierkegaard, *Fear and Trembling; Repetition*, ed. Howard V. Hong and Edna H. Hong (Princeton: Princeton University Press, 1983), 33, 61.

1. See Avivah Gottlieb Zornberg, *Genesis: The Beginning of Desire* (Philadelphia: Jewish Publication Society, 1995), 97–122, especially 97–98.

2. From *Pirke de-Rabbi Eliezer*, as quoted by S. Y. Agnon, *Days of Awe: A Treasury of Jewish Wisdom for Reflection, Repentance, and Renewal on the High Holy Days* (New York: Schocken, 1995), 67, and Shalom Spiegel, *The Last Trial: On the Legends and Lore of the Command of Abraham to Offer Isaac as a Sacrifice: The Akedah*, trans. Judah Goldin (Woodstock, Vt.: Jewish Lights, 1993), 39.

3. As quoted in Rabbi Nosson Scherman, ed., *The Artscroll Chumash*, Stone edition (New York: Mesorah Publications, 1993), 101, note 1.

4. As quoted in Nehama Liebowitz, *New Studies in Beresheit*, trans. Aryeh Newman (Jerusalem: Haonamim Press, n.d.), 202–203.

5. Moses Maimonides, "Laws of Repentance," in *Mishneh Torah: The Book of Knowledge*, ed. Moses Hayamson (Jerusalem: Boys' Town Jerusalem Publishers, 1962), 92b.

6. Scherman, *The Artscroll Chumash*, 103, note 3.

CHAPTER FIVE
FACE TO FACE: THE FATE OF THE OTHER

1. W. Gunther Plaut, ed., *The Torah: A Modern Commentary* (New York: Union of American Hebrew Congregations, 1981), 516.

2. Moses Maimonides, *The Guide of the Perplexed*, vol. 1, trans. and ed. Shlomo Pines (Chicago: University of Chicago Press, 1963), 85–87.

3. In one instance God orders the representation of divine beings—he requires two cherubim for the solid gold kapporet (cover) of the ark of the covenant, and they sit *face to face* (Exodus 25:17–20 and 37:7–9). Moreover, the Tabernacle itself is made of ten strips of blue, purple, and crimson twisted linen, as is the curtain, with a design of cherubim worked into them. But since God orders them made according to his specifications, this is not considered idolatry. Other parts of the Hebrew Bible (for instance, Ezekiel's vision, in Ezekiel 1:26–28, 1 Chronicles 28:18, 1 Samuel 4:4) also explain this cover as the throne of God with the kapporet, his footstool. Plaut (*The Torah*, 612) reiterates the question of how such images could ever have found a place in Judaism at all. He reminds us that they are the only images mentioned and that perhaps they belong to an old mythological tradition. In any case, adoration of them is never a problem, and they are hidden

away in a place inaccessible to the common people. With the destruction of the First Temple, these images disappeared and were not reconstructed for the Second Temple. Jewish law thereafter rejected all representations of this kind out of a heightened fear of idolatry. My own sense is that these images have nothing to do with idol worship at all and everything to do with the word of God and with the modeling of a particular kind of face-to-face relationship.

4. Mainonides, *The Guide of the Perplexed*, vol. 1, 86.

5. I am indebted heavily in this summary section to Barry Holtz's article "Midrash," in *Back to the Sources: Reading the Classic Jewish Texts*, ed. Barry Holtz (New York: Touchstone, 1984). My readings in criticism on midrash have been extensive, and I've been especially interested in how midrash is like open modernist, polysemic texts and how it is unlike postmodernist, indeterminate texts. For a project in the spring of 1999 I discovered several useful readings on midrash, including: Daniel Boyarin, *Intertextuality and the Reading of Midrash* (Bloomington: Indiana University Press, 1990); Michael Fishbane, *The Midrashic Imagination: Jewish Exegesis, Thought, and History* (Albany: State University of New York Press, 1993); Gary Porton, *Understanding Rabbinic Midrash: Text and Commentary* (Hoboken, N.J.: Ktav, 1985); and Daniel Stern, *Midrash and Theory: Ancient Jewish Exegesis and Contemporary Literary Studies* (Evanston, Ill.: Northwestern University Press, 1986).

6. Gary Porton, "Defining Midrash," in *The Academic Study of Judaism*, ed. Jacob Neusner (New York: Scholars Press, 1981), 58.

7. Steven D. Fraade, *From Tradition to Commentary: Torah and Its Interpretation in the Midrash Sifre to Deuteronomy* (Albany: State University of New York Press, 1991).

8. As I have argued elsewhere, in an unpublished paper on midrash, I do not find Fraade's whole theory convincing. It lacks a theory of ideological address, and it makes us all into second- or third-century rabbinic disciples, which we are not and can never be. His model also presumes a fairly uniform interplaying network or circulation system for meaning and a kind of uniform rabbinic assent (despite debate) that seems less historical and more universal than he may wish. The model does not stress plurality enough for me—the rabbis mentioned seem to arrive at the same conclusions at the same rate and do the same kind of sorting and sifting, so that Sifre seems a bit too dogmatic and not as multivocal as Fraade insists it is. He is not able to explain well how a text can foreground enunciation and multiple meaning making. My point is that midrash asks us to delight in the multiplicity of points of view, which illustrates the paradox of our own humanity and imperfection. It does not ask that we pick and choose among the meanings presented in order to join the consensus. In other words, in the mind of the reader, there is not always a neat resolution of contrary points of view.

9. See Rodger Kamenetz, *Stalking Elijah: Adventures with Today's Jewish Mystical Masters* (New York: HarperCollins, 1997), 261. This was my second encounter with the story. I first read a different version in David Ariel, *Spiritual Judaism* (New York: Hyperion, 1998), 87.

10. Anita Diamant, *Saying Kaddish: How to Comfort the Dying, Bury the Dead, and Mourn as a Jew* (New York: Schocken, 1998), 33–36.

11. David Ariel, *Spiritual Judaism* (New York: Hyperion Press, 1998), 85ff.

12. Pinchas H. Peli, *On Repentance: The Thought and Oral Discourses of Rabbi Joseph Dov Soloveitchik* (Northvale, N.J.: Jason Aronson, 1996), 195; see also 198.

13. "Sources dealing with suffering," personal communication (e-mail) from Aish HaTorah (Questions@aish.edu), February 21, 2000.

14. Jacques Derrida, quoted by Richard A. Cohen, introduction to Emmanuel Levinas, *Time and the Other and Additional Essays* (Pittsburgh: Duquesne University Press, 1987), 3. The relationship between Derrida and Levinas is an interesting one, particularly in terms of the ethics of deconstruction and the deconstruction of ethics. Derrida's two essays on Levinas are "Violence and Metaphysics: An Essay on the Thought of Emmanuel Levinas," in Jacques Derrida, *Writing and Difference*, trans. Alan Bass (Chicago: University of Chicago Press, 1978), 79–152, and "At This Very Moment in This Work Here I Am," in *Re-Reading Levinas*, ed. Robert Bernasconi and Simon Critchley (Bloomington: Indiana University Press, 1991), pp. 11–48, where it appears alongside Levinas's essay on Derrida, "Wholly Otherwise" (pp. 3–10). Essays by Robert Bernasconi and John Llewelyn should be consulted for discussion of the philosophical proximity of Levinas and Derrida. An important book by Simon Critchley lays out the stakes of each position carefully; see *The Ethics of Deconstruction: Derrida and Levinas* (Cambridge: Blackwell, 1992).

15. To describe the most basic elements of Levinas's phenomenological theory, I have relied on a number of texts besides his own work, including: Bernasconi and Critchley, *Re-Reading Levinas*; Critchley, *The Ethics of Deconstruction*; Robert Gibbs, *Correlations in Rosenzweig and Levinas* (Princeton: Princeton University Press, 1992; and Susan Handelman, *Fragments of Redemption: Jewish Thought and Literary Theory in Benjamin, Scholem, and Levinas* (Bloomington: Indiana University Press, 1991).

16. Emmanuel Levinas, *On Thinking-of-the-Other, Entre Nous*, trans. Michael B. Smith and Barbara Harshav (New York: Columbia University Press, 1998), 103.

17. Franz Rosenzweig, *The Star of Redemption*, trans. William W. Hallo (Notre Dame, Ind.: University of Notre Dame Press, 1985), 218.

18. Emmanuel Levinas, "On the Trail of the Other," translated by Daniel Hoy, *Philosophy Today* 10 (1966): 34–36, quoted in Handelman, *Fragments of Redemption*, 269.

19. Critchley, *The Ethics of Deconstruction*, 231–232.

20. In explaining the important transition from ethics to politics in the thought of Levinas, I have been guided by Levinas's comments in various texts, including the recent *On Thinking-of-the-Other, Entre Nous*, but also by the studies of Simon Critchley and Robert Gibbs; see also Emmanuel Levinas, *Otherwise Than Being* (The Hague: Martinus Nijhoff, 1981), 159.

21. For work in political philosophy that seems consonant from a humanitarian position (if not a deconstructive one), see Michael Walzer, *Spheres of Justice* (New York: Basic Books, 1983), especially, for this discussion, part 1, "Complex Equality," and part 13, "Tyrannies and Just Societies."

Passage 5
Their Faces Shall Be One Toward the Other:
Thoughts on Terumah, Exodus 25:1–27:19

Note on the epigraph: Malbim quoted by W. Gunther Plaut, *The Torah: A Modern Commentary* (New York: Union of American Hebrew Congregations), 614.

CHAPTER SIX
IN PIECES: FACING GERMANY

1. For extensively quoted recollections, see Lawrence Langer, *Holocaust Testimonies: The Ruins of Memory* (New Haven: Yale University Press, 1991). The book is based on evidence from the Fortunoff Video Archive for Holocaust Testimonies established at Yale in 1982. On the suffering of a highly educated upper-class North German intellectual living in Bavaria who was shot at Dachau for anti-Nazi writings, see Friedrich Reck-Malleczewen, *Diary of a Man in Despair,* trans. Paul Rubens (London: Duck Editions, 2000). For examples of literature, see Lawrence Langer, ed., *Art from the Ashes: A Holocaust Anthology* (New York: Oxford University Press, 1995).

2. In trying to make sense of what happened to me in Germany, I have been helped by Dominick La Capra, "Revisiting the Historian's Debate: Mourning and Genocide," in *History and Memory After Auschwitz* (Ithaca, N.Y.: Cornell University Press, 1988), 43–47. However, see Tim Cole, *Selling the Holocaust: From Auschwitz to Schindler, How History Is Bought, Sold, and Packaged* (New York: Routledge 1999), for a listing of the varied reasons Americans tour Holocaust sites (pp. 113–115), an issue raised by other Holocaust scholars who write about memorials and monuments, such as James Young in *The Texture of Memory: Holocaust Memorials and Meaning* (New Haven: Yale University Press, 1993). These reasons include trying to understand the past, to see material evidence, to ease guilt, to express sympathy, to view places of mass death as a voyeur, to face pain long ignored, to be sexually titillated covered by "worthy" reasons, to experience the thrill of the killer as well as the terror of the killed, and to make a moral or intellectual or emotional pilgrimage. Cole finds many of these reasons problematic, including his own "loftier" ones. In exploring what the Holocaust means to Americans and how it has come to mean what it does and to be used as it continues to be used, the historian Peter Novick substantially complicates such reasons in his dense and important book *The Holocaust in American Life* (Boston: Houghton Mifflin, 2000). To select a point or to summarize is a disservice to this book in the extreme, but I do want to second Novick in his understanding of the issue of guilt, which he discusses with reference to America in 1945 and then with reference specifically to American Jews (p. 75). Guilt comes in various kinds: the guilt of not acting, the guilt of privilege and safety, the guilt of turning the eyes away. In discussing the embeddedness of the Holocaust in "guilt talk" (p. 74), Novick makes the point that there is often a slide in accounts of 1945 that follows this course: from the guilt of the United States and the Allies (for not doing enough to rescue

the Jews), to the belief that they should have felt guilty, to the belief that they must have felt guilty, to the belief that they did feel guilty. This he calls a "tenuous progression. Some seem to confuse sympathy for the survivors, which there was in abundance, with guilt for the Holocaust, of which there is no contemporary evidence—a strange equation" (p. 74). I think the same kind of slippage happens to individuals and within individuals: that sympathy can become confused with guilt and that one belief about guilt can slide into another too easily, so that moral discriminations are, in the end, lost, not gained. The paradigm of trauma and repression, which Novick also warns us about (pp. 2–3), can also be used with extreme slipperiness and overgeneralizing falsity to account for why the Holocaust lives at the center of American consciousness so strongly after the event.

3. The theological question posed by the Holocaust—Why does God allow evil and suffering? Why did He let this happen? Where was He?—are not my questions. To ask them at all means to me to deny a God who cares deeply about the fate of the Jews and has a larger design. I view the Holocaust as a human failure of the highest proportions, not as a divine failure, and I believe in a God who offers us freedom to choose, but that includes duties and responsibilities to create a social order that is just. My position on this matter is probably closest to that of Abraham Joshua Heschel. For the variety of theological responses to the Holocaust and a reading list on the subject, see Neil Gillman, *Sacred Fragments: Recovering Theology for the Modern Jew* (Philadelphia: Jewish Publication Society, 1990).

4. W. Michael Blumenthal, "The Public and the Struggle over Memory," public lecture at Princeton University, Princeton, New Jersey, April 17, 2000.

5. Roger Cohen, "A Jewish Museum Struggles to Be Born: Berlin's Efforts to Honor Lost Millions Are Mired in Dissent," *New York Times*, August 15, 2000, E1, E3.

6. Ibid.

7. For a summary that discriminates among certain groups and political wings and remains sensitive to the Holocaust as part of a larger series of war conflicts, see Novick, *The Holocaust in American Life*. Among other issues, he takes up the question of the chances for rescue that were bypassed, the bombings that were nixed, the question of complicity (pp. 48–49), and America's belated understanding of events in Germany and skewed confrontation with the Holocaust (pp. 64ff).

8. However, there are plenty of groups, publications, individuals and academicians who are Holocaust deniers. For one version of the history of Holocaust denial, see Deborah E. Lipstadt, *Denying the Holocaust: The Growing Assault on Truth and Memory* (New York: Plumsock, 1994).

9. Joseph Brodsky, quoted in David Remnick, "Profile: The Exile Returns," *The New Yorker*, February 14, 1994, 73; and in Lawrence Langer, *Admitting the Holocaust: Collected Essays* (New York: Oxford University Press, 1995), 5.

10. I hold mixed feelings about the Anne Frank materials. I am glad they are there to document a young girl's encounter with the Holocaust, but troubled when they are used to mute horror or to stand for all other personal stories.

11. For a probing look at the Holocaust and America, see David S. Wyman, *The Abandonment of the Jews: America and the Holocaust 1941–1945* (New York: New Press, 1998).

12. La Capra, *History and Memory After Auschwitz*, 52.

13. Barbara Distel and Ruth Jakusch, *Concentration Camp Dachau 1933–1945* (Munich: Lipp GmbH/Brussels: Comité International de Dachau, 1978), 85.

14. *Voyage of the St. Louis*, "Introduction" (Washington, D.C.: U.S. Holocaust Memorial Museum, 1999), 12.

15. This story is told fully in ibid., 1–31.

16. "Jan Karski Dies at 86; Warned West About Holocaust," *New York Times*, July 15, 2000, C15.

17. Reports on the exhibition and reactions in Germany can be located in Laus Naumann, "Wenn ein Tabu bricht: Die Wehrmachtsausstellung in der Bundesrepublik," and reactions in Austria in Walter Manoschek, "Die Wehrmachtsausstellung in Österreich: Ein Bericht," both in *Mittelweg 36*, no. 5.1 (1996): 11–24, 25–32.

18. Hamburg Institute for Social Research, *The German Army and Genocide: Crimes Against War Prisoners, Jews, and Other Civilians in the East, 1939–1944*, ed. and with a foreword by Omer Bartov, trans. Scott Abbott (New York: New Press, 1999), 8.

19. See Billie Ann Lopez and Peter Hirsch, *Traveller's Guide to Jewish Germany* (Gretna, La.: Pelican Publishing, 1998), p. 191, for the history of Munich's Jews.

20. Roger Cohen, "New Attacks Raise Fears About Anti-Semitism in Germany," *New York Times*, August 8, 2000.

21. The story of Julius Hess and Max Schohl is reported by Michael Winerip in "Dear Cousin Max," *New York Times Magazine*, April 27, 1997, 36–41, 49, 65–68, 74.

22. Young, *The Texture of Memory*, 127.

23. La Capra, *History and Memory After Auschwitz*, 45.

24. Sigmund Freud, in *Mourning and Melancholia*, describes "normal mourning" as what happens when one "overcomes the loss of the object. Each single one of the memories and situations of expectancy which demonstrate the libido's attachment to the lost object is met by the verdict of reality that the object no longer exists; and the ego, confronted, as it were, with the question whether it shall share this fate, is persuaded by the sum of the narcissistic satisfactions it derives from being alive to sever its attachment to the object that has been abolished." Quoted in Adam Phillips, *Darwin's Worms* (London: Faber & Faber, 1999), 123.

25. David Hartman, "Suffering," *Contemporary Jewish Religious Thought*, ed. Arthur Cohen and Paul Mendes-Flohr (New York: Free Press, 1988), 944–946.

26. Langer, *Holocaust Testimonies*, 12.

27. That many Conservatives disagree but want to discuss their beliefs and priorities, and learn from each other, is clear from synagogue meetings, from the questioning audiences at public lectures attended by Jews with very different beliefs and backgrounds, and from listserves on the Web, whether those devoted to Judaism generally, to Jewish philosophy, to Conservative Judaism, or to specific intellectual matters—such as Jewish bioethics or rabbinic history—that turn into compelling arguments about Judaism.

28. For two discussions of this commission and its aftermath, see Neil Gillman, *Conservative Judaism: The New Century* (West Orange, N.J.: Behrman House,

1993), chapter 8 ("The Ordination of Women"), and Rabbi Samuel Fraint, "The Truth About Conservative Judaism: Where Rabbi Shafran Went Wrong," *Moment* 26, no. 4 (June 2001): 54–55, 65.

Passage 6
Coming Home Again:
Thoughts on Yom Kippur

1. Chancellor Ismar Schorch of the Jewish Theological Seminary articulated this point in an online High Holiday Shiur.

2. Talmud, Tractate Yoma. I thank Menachem Lorberbaum for discussing this tractate with me.

3. Having decided to write about *kpr*, I was delighted to find a shiur on uses of the root for Yom Kippur 1997 by Menachem Leibtag at www.vbm-torah.org/roshandyk/yk.tm. This confirmed other uses in Torah and led me to further research.

4. See Pinchas Peli, *On Repentance: The Thought and Oral Discourses of Rabbi Joseph Dov Soloveitchik* (Northvale, N.J.: Jason Aronson, 1996), 50–51.

5. I thank Nat Fisch for pointing out the precise meaning of this word to me, while guiding me on translation.

INDEX ✧

Abraham, husband of Sarah, 83–84,
    143–144, 153–160, 186, 225
Abstinence, 148–152
Adler, Rachel, 86, 88, 89, 96
Akedah, the, 153–160
Akiva, Rabbi, 97–98, 138, 222
Albo, Yosef, 156
Alter, Robert, 122
Amidah, the, 61–65
Angels on ark of the covenant, 173,
    192–194, 247n3
Anti-Semitism, 1–3, 10, 47–48,
    210–211
Areopagitica, 146–147
Ariel, David, 177
Ark of the covenant, the, 184,
    192–194, 247n3
Auerbach, Erich, 169
Austin, J. L., 171
Avdimi, Rabbi, 139
Aylon, Helène, 98, 103–108

Bal, Mieke, 84
Barthes, Roland, 19
Bartov, Omer, 206
Baruch of Medzibozh, 31
Ben Abuya, Elisha, 181
Ben Azzai, 97, 111
Ben Dosa, Hanina, 155
Beruriah, 87–92

Biale, David, 138, 139, 246n10
Biale, Rachel, 14, 86, 120
Birth family of Linda M. Shires, 3–5,
    14–17, 31–32, 41–45, 177–178,
    200
Blumenthal, W. Michael, 198, 199
Body, the
    and abstinence, 148–150
    and childbirth, 136–139
    and circumcision, 143–148
    and holiness, 126–136, 148–152
    and the mikvah, 131–136
    relationship with the soul, 125–131
    and sexual orientation, 139–143
Boyarin, Daniel, 88, 89–90, 95, 130,
    138, 139
Brooten, Bernadette, 85
Buber, Martin, 35, 65, 174–175, 185,
    225
Buffam, David H., 204
Butler, Judith, 18–19

Catholic Church, 17, 197, 202, 213
Center for Jewish Life, 9
Children
    circumcision of, 143–148
    conversion of, 144–145
    and death, 41–45, 178
    and wrongdoing, 179–180
    and Passover, 52–53

Children of the American Revolution, 5

Christianity, 4, 16, 17, 20–21, 32, 44, 125–126, 130, 169

Churchill, Winston, 204

Circumcision, covenant of, 143–148

Cohen, Gerson, 219

Cohen, Roger, 199

Cohen, Shaye J. D., 75–77

Committee on Jewish Law and Standards, 77–78, 101–102, 140

Concentration camps, 204, 206–209

Conservative Judaism, 28, 38, 76, 77–78, 101–103, 108–109, 131–133, 140–145, 148–149, 218–219, 252n27

Conversion
  of children, 144–145
  and circumcision, 144–146
  of David Klinghoffer, 100
  and Jewish identity, 8–9, 80–81
  of Julius Lester, 12–13
  and the mikvah, 131–136
  of Nan Fink, 11
  process, 9–11
  reactions of friends and family to, 10–11, 16–17, 48
  rewards of, 10
  understanding the Holocaust before, 195–196, 202–203, 215–216, 250–251n2–3
  women and, 79–80

Converts, Status of, 1, 37, 226

Critchley, Simon, 187

Dalai Lama, the, 108

David, King, 119–123

Day of Atonement. See Yom Kippur

Death, 14–16, 39–43, 119, 128–129, 159, 174–178, 181

Derrida, Jacques, 184, 249n14

Diamant, Anita, 175–176, 177

Diamond, James S., Rabbi and supervisor of conversion, 9,

14–16, 17, 31, 56, 134, 177, 202, 237

Diversity of Jews, 28–30

Donin, Hayim Halevy, 30

Douglas, Keith, 200

Duties of the Heart, The, 131, 148

Eden, Anthony, 205

Egypt, exodus from, 36, 39, 50, 52, 55, 67–74

Episcopal Church, 16, 20–21

Epstein, Lawrence J., 8

Exodus, 200

Exodus from Egypt, 36, 39, 50, 52, 55, 67–74

Feld, Edward, 20, 22–23

Feld, Merle, 20

Feminism, 6–8, 12, 18, 76, 79–97, 100, 240–241n11, 240n8, 241n12, 242n18
  and homosexuality, 141
  and patriarchy, 83–87, 107–109, 114–119, 123
  and the Torah, 75–109
  traditional rejection of, 99–100

Fink, Nan, 11

Fischer, Joschka, 210

Five Books of Miriam, The, 38

Forgiveness, 178–184

Foucault, Michel, 140

Four Centuries of Jewish Women's Spirituality, 134, 135

Fraade, Steven, 169, 170–172

Frank, Anne, 200, 203

Frankel, Ellen, 38

Freedom and Judaism, 49–51

From Tradition to Commentary, 171

Frymer-Kensky, Tikva, 97, 112, 113, 123

Fundamentals of Judaism, Sefer Ha-ikkarim, The, 156

Gamliel the Elder, 87
German Army and Genocide: Crimes Against War Prisoners, Jews, and Other Civilians in the East, 1939–1944, The, 206
Germany
  under Hitler, 203–209
  modern, 196–199, 211
  before World War II, 210
Gibbs, Bob, 184, 185–186
Goodblatt, David, 88
Gottlieb, Lynn, 106
Greek Orthodox Church, 4, 17, 44
Greek society, ancient, 44, 130–131, 150
Greenberg, Blu, 86, 92, 98–103, 108
Grunfeld, Dayan, 54–55
Guide of the Perplexed, The, 64, 164, 167, 173

Hadas, Pamela, 111–112
Halakhic Man, 14
Halevi, Judah, 137
Hammer, Reuven, 62
Hanukkah, 11, 61
Hartman, David, 216
Hartmann, Geoffrey, 169
Hauptman, Judith, 86–88, 132–133
Hebrew language, 222–226
Heidegger, Martin, 185
Hellenistic culture, 130–131, 150–152, 242n22
Heschel, Abraham Joshua, 18, 54, 55
Hess, Julius, 212–213
Hirsch, Samson Raphael, 148, 158
Hitler, Adolf, 203–209
Hoffman, Lawrence, 64
Holiness
  of the body, 125–131
  definition of, 126–128
  and sexuality, 128–129, 245–246n6
Holocaust, the, 2–3, 225
  aversion to and denial of, 199–203, 250–251n2
  concentration camps of, 206–209
  and converts, 195–197, 202–203, 215–216
  literature on, 201
  mourning those who suffered during, 216–219, 251n3
  museums and memorials, 198–199
  myths and truth about events of, 203–209
  refugees, 204–205, 212–214
Holocaust Survivors, 202
Holtz, Barry, 169
Homosexuality, 30, 108, 125, 131, 139–143
Hopkins, Stephen, 3
How to Do Things with Words, 171

Ibn Ezra, 70
Identity, Jewish, 8–9, 19, 27–31, 52–53, 80–81
  and circumcision, 143–144
  and the Holocaust, 197
  of women, 82–91, 133
Ilan, Tal, 87–88, 90
Illness, 128, 131, 175–178. *See also* Death
Isaiah, 63, 224–225
Ishmael, Rabbi, 68

Jacob, Wenzel, 199
Jesus Christ, 21, 125, 202
Joseph, son of Jacob, 113, 116–118, 122
Judah, 115–118, 123
Judaism
  abstinence in, 148–152
  and angels on ark of the covenant, 173, 192–194, 247n3
  and the ark, 184, 192–193
  concept of holiness in, 126–131
  Conservative, 21, 22, 23, 28, 30, 33, 38, 76, 77–79, 101–103, 108–109, 131–133, 140–145, 147–152, 218–219, 221, 237n1, 252n27
  converts to, 8–11, 80–81, 131–136
  counting people in, 34–38

cultural *versus* observant, 7
and death, 39–43, 119, 175–178
diversity in, 28–30
dual commitments of, 161–164
family traditions of, 20–21
and feminism, 6–8, 18, 75–77,
    91–97
forgiveness in, 178–184
freedom in, 49–51
and Germany, 197–199
and the gift of manna, 71–73, 224
and the Hebrew language, 222–226
holidays of, 22–24, 46–61, 71–73,
    158–159, 216–218
and homosexuality, 139–143
identity, 8–9, 27–31, 52–53, 82–91,
    143–144, 197
and the exodus from Egypt, 36, 39,
    50, 55, 67–74
literature of (Torah oral and
    written), 14, 29, 95–96, 168–173,
    244n1
and melakhah, 54–55
Orthodox, 28, 77, 78, 98–103,
    108–109, 131–132, 135, 140–143,
    237n1
patriarchy in, 83–87, 107–109,
    114–119, 240–241n11
and race, 28–29, 32–33
Reconstructionist, 38, 142, 237n1
Reform, 28, 38, 77, 134, 135, 142,
    144–145, 237n1
relationship between the body and
    soul in, 125–131
rituals of, 46–47, 48–65, 54–61, 73,
    105–106, 131–136, 143–148,
    153–160, 184, 216–217,
    221–226
sacrifices in, 153–160
and sexuality, 90, 93–96, 128–129,
    139–143, 150–151
and who are Jews, 27–31
women of, 18, 35–38, 82–91

Karski, Jan, 205
Kierkegaard, Søren, 153
Klinghoffer, David, 100
Kluger, Ruth, 195
Knoepflmacher, Alex, 45–46, 57–59,
    133, 136, 144–148
Knoepflmacher, Daniel, 2–3, 19–20,
    23, 46
Knoepflmacher, Julie, 2–3, 19–20, 23,
    46
Knoepflmacher, Paul, 2–3, 19–20,
    46–47
Knoepflmacher, Uli, 2–3, 19–20, 23,
    45–46, 57–59, 136, 199–201,
    211–216
Kraus, Rabbi, 34–35
Kugel, James, 169
Kushner, Harold, 181

Lacan, Jacques, 195
La Capra, Dominick, 204, 215
Lacquer, Thomas, 140
Langer, Lawrence, 199, 218
Last Days, The, 202
Laws of Repentance, The, 225
*Laws Relating to Moral Dispositions and
    to Ethical Conduct*, 151
Lester, Julius, 12–13
Levinas, Emmanuel, 161, 164, 225,
    249n20
    on panim el panim, 173, 175,
        184–188
Levitt, Laura, 135
Liberation of G-d, The, 103–105
Libeskind, Daniel, 198
Literature of Judaism, 14, 29, 95–96,
    244n1
    and panim, 168–173
Lorberbaum, Menachem, 113

Maimonides, Moses, 64, 68, 131, 148,
    150–151, 156–157, 164, 167, 217,
    225, 238n10

on panim, 167–168, 173–174,
    185
on repentance, 156, 182, 225
Manchester Guardian, 204
Manna, 70–73, 224
Meir, Rabbi, 87
Melakhah, 54–61
Men
    homosexual, 139–143
    othering of women by, 87–91
    and rape, 119–123
    rejection of feminism by, 99
Menstruation, 128–129, 132–133,
    245–246n6
Midrash, 168–173, 248n8
Mikvah, the, 9, 129, 131–136
Milton, John, 96, 146–147
Mimesis, 169
Minh-ha, Trinh T., 81
Mishnah, the, 29, 50, 88
Mishneh Torah, 131, 150, 182
Moers, Ellen, 85
Moment, 8
Moses, 115, 126, 128, 186, 222, 226
    and the exodus from Egypt, 27, 34,
        36, 39, 68–70, 73–74
    and holiness of the body, 136–138
    and panim el panim, 164–168,
        186–187
    and the Tabernacle, 33, 189–190
Moses, Lionel, 140
Musaf, 61
Myers, Carol, 85

Nachmanides, 33, 68, 129, 155–156,
    237n3
Nazis, 202
New York Times, 199
Nine Talmudic Readings, 225

Ocean Avenue, 133
On Repentance, 180
On-Thinking-of-the-Other, Entre Nous,
    225, 249n16

*On Women and Judaism: A View from
    Tradition*, 98
Orthodox Judaism, 28, 77, 78, 98–103,
    108–109, 131–132, 135, 140–143,
    237
Ostriker, Alicia, 83–84
Owen, Wilfred, 200
Ozick, Cynthia, 75–77, 89, 91–94

Pakuda, Bachya Ibn, 131, 148–150,
    151
Panim and panim el panim
    defining, 161–164
    and relationships with God,
        164–168, 247–248n3
    and relationships with literature,
        168–173
    and relationships with the
        community, 178–184
    and relationships with the other,
        173–178
Paradise Lost, 96
Passover, 46–54, 184
Pateman, Carole, 86
Patriarchy in Judaism, 83–87,
    107–109, 114–119, 240–241n11
Peli, Pinchas, 56
Pentateuch, 170, 191, 244n1
Pirkei d'Rabbi Eliezer, 158
Plaskow, Judith, 14, 91–94, 141,
    142–143
Plaut, W. Gunther, 72, 95, 165, 190
Pollution, 126, 129–131, 137–138,
    247n12
Porton, Gary, 169–170
Prince of Egypt, 68–69
Princeton University, 6, 9, 20, 23, 221

Quakers, 21–22

Rabbis
    Conservative, 75–78, 101–102, 108,
        218–219
    ordination of female, 219

Orthodox, 78, 98–99
in the rabbinical age, 129–130,
    169–170, 237n1, 245n4,
    245–246n6
Race and Judaism, 28–29, 31–33
Rape, 119–123
Rashi, 34, 68, 70, 88, 100, 129, 148,
    154, 217, 223, 237–237n4–5
Reconstructionist Judaism, 38, 142
Reform Judaism, 28, 38, 77, 134, 135,
    142, 144
Relationships
    with the community, 178–184
    dual commitments of, 161–164
    exteriority in, 162
    with God, 164–168
    with the other, 173–178, 245n1
    with sacred literature, 168–173
    and social justice, 184–188
    types of, 162–163
Repentance, 178–184
Rituals of Judaism
    Amidah, 61–65
    circumcision, 143–148
    conversion, 9
    handling of death, 40–41
    Hanukkah, 61
    mikvah, 131–136
    Passover, 48–54, 184
    and the relationship between body
        and soul, 130–131
    Rosh Hashanah, 153, 158–160
    sacrifice of animals, 153–160
    Shabbat, 54–61, 73, 105–106
    Tisha B'Av, 216–217
    Yom Hashoah, 217–218
    Yom Kippur, 24, 60, 62, 158, 173,
        179, 180, 217, 221–226
Roosevelt, Franklin, 204, 205
Rosenzweig, Franz, 18, 173, 184, 191,
    225
Rosh Hashanah, 153,
    158–160

Rothfarb, Shari, 132–133

Sabbath, The, 55
Sages, The, 138
Sarah, wife of Abraham, 83–84, 154
Sassoon, Siegfried, 200
Saying Kaddish, 175
Schäfer, Peter, 29
Schindler's List, 202
Schohl, Max, 212–213
Schroeder, Gerhard, 211
Self-control, 148–152
Sexuality, 90, 93–96
    and childbirth, 136–138
    and holiness, 128–129, 245–246n6
    and homosexuality, 139–143
    and rape, 119–123
    self-control of, 148–152
Shabbat, 54–61, 73, 105–106, 162–163
Shekhinah, 7, 173
Shires, Linda M.
    birth family of, 3–5, 6, 14–17,
        31–32, 41–45, 177–178, 200
    causes for conversion, 22–23
    child of, 23, 45–46, 57–59, 133, 136,
        144–148
    conversion study, 9–10, 12–19,
        27–29, 161–162, 195–196,
        202–203
    decision to convert, 23–25
    early friends of, 4–6
    early religious life, 20–21
    experiences in husband's Jewish
        family, 2–3
    first thoughts about conversion,
        19–20
    marriage, 2–3, 19–20
    mikvah experience, 131–136
    professional life, 17
    reactions of family, students, and
        friends to the conversion of,
        10–11

relationship with her rabbi, 9–10,
    14–16, 133–134, 202
view on who counts as Jews, 30–31
visit to Germany, 196–199, 203
Shires, Philip M. and Helen M. E.
    (parents). *See* Shires, Linda, birth
    family
Shoah, 202
Shoah, the, 204, 217
Showalter, Elaine, 85
Sigal, Phillip, 101–102
Social justice, 184–188, 226, 249n21
Soloveitchik, Joseph Dov, 11, 14, 123,
    180–181
Spielberg, Steven, 68, 202
Spiritual Judaism, 177
Standing Again at Sinai, 14, 141
Steinsaltz, Adin, 161–164, 173
Stranger in the Midst, 11
Straus, David, 27–28
Suffering, 178–184, 216–218, 250n1,
    251n3

Tabernacle, the, 189–194, 247n3
Talmud, the, 7, 14, 29, 31, 59, 69,
    75–76, 85–90, 129–130, 175–176,
    237, 246n10
Tamars, the two, 111–123, 244n4
    and patriarchy, 114–117
    rape of, 119–123
    as a text of terror, 112–113
Tarfon, Rabbi, 88
Targum, 7
Temple Har Sinai, 27
Tisha B'Av, 216–217
Tobin, Thomas, 95
Torah, the, 7, 29, 30, 31, 38, 40, 50,
    54, 59, 63, 67, 97–98, 102, 237n2
    on abstinence, 148–150
    on childbirth, 136–138
    on circumcision, 143–144
    concept of holiness in, 127–131
    on homosexuality, 140–142

interpreters of, 85–86
and midrash, 168–170
and mikvah, 136–137
on panim el panim, 164–168
on relationships and responsibilities
    to others, 164
on Shabbat, 54–56
and women, 75–80, 82–83, 92–96,
    99–101, 113–123
and Yom Kippur, 221–223
Totality and Infinity, 225
Trembling Before God, 140
Trible, Phyllis, 96, 113
Troper, Morris, 205
Tucker, Gordon, 219

Urbach, Ephraim, 138–139
Uris, Leon, 200

Von Hindenburg, Paul, 203

Wasserman, Sue Ann, 135
Wegner, Judith, 94, 97
Weiner, Kathe, 45
*When Bad Things Happen to Good
    People*, 181
Winerip, Michael, 212
Women
    and childbirth, 136–138
    and feminism, 6–8, 18, 75–77,
        82–109, 114–119, 141,
        240–241n11, 240n8, 241n12,
        242n18
    and Jewish identity, 82–91, 133
    male othering of, 87–91
    menstruation by, 128–129, 133,
        245–246n6
    and the mikvah, 132–136
    ordination of, 76, 102, 219
    and patriarchy, 83–87, 107–109,
        114–119
    rape of, 119–123

and revision of Orthodoxy,
  98–108
roles of Jewish, 75, 79–80, 99–108
and sexuality, 90, 93–96, 128–129
and the Torah, 75–80, 82–83,
  92–93, 99–101, 113–123

Yehoshua, Rabbi, 88
Yehuda, Rabbi, 158
Yerushalmi, Yosef Hayim, 107
Yom Hashoah, 217–218
Yom Kippur, 23–25, 60, 62, 158, 173,
  179, 180, 217, 221–226a